HANG THE TEACHER OUT TO DRY

Mark Whitworth

Copyright © 2021 Mark Whitworth
All rights reserved.
ISBN: 9798467742137

Dedications

To my father, Reginald Richard Whitworth, who at the age of 96 has spent the last six months in isolation, unable to see his family. These memoirs are dedicated to you, as a teacher, not only of your students but also of your four daughters and son.

For all the students who have graced my classroom over nearly thirty years. You have made teaching a joy and kept me on track when at times it seemed as if I might walk away from my profession. I always knew that retirement would mean giving you up and that is a wrench that tugs my heart; I will miss you more than anything else. Thank you, not only to those of you who have stayed in touch but to all of you for giving me such wonderful memories that will remain with me until the day I die. Please feel free to contact me, I would love to hear your stories, which will be the flowers on the stems of my memoirs.

To Andrea Noel Kidd, my wife, with whom I have spent the last twenty years, both at home and at work. It is a difficult balancing act and you have been the enabler, have kept me sane, prevented me from making more serious errors than I have and have loved me throughout. Thank you.

Acknowledgements

To my friend, Ian Self, who patiently edited my work and provided guidance that prevented my meandering into self-indulgent streams of consciousness. He demonstrated skills I had no idea he possessed and infinite patience. This book would not have existed if not for him.

To my friend, Scott Taylor, for his excellent work on the front cover. He has always been my favourite artist and will remain so for as long as I live. To Ayat Rashid, who created the cartoon of me on the back cover during one of my classes when she became a little bored! To my friend and ex-colleague, Jenny Besford, who read through the original manuscript providing feedback, most importantly lending her encouragement as to the readability of the prose. Jen, I guess we will meet again in the North-east because I am certain they will not let me back into Qatar. To Kath Wallace, Carol Spalton, Peter Gray and Franco Szczepaniak, who as strangers accepted the brief of reading through the complete draft of the manuscript and accommodated me with feedback that was both positive and negative, but most importantly constructive: you have each done me a huge favour. To Richard Mycroft, Sue Swanston and Dinah Faulds for organising those complete strangers!

Lastly, although most importantly, to my wife, Andrea Kidd, for being infinitely patient, providing me both the time and space to write and from holding herself back from saying, "You can't say that!" too often. She has been my lifeline. Squid, I owe you several big and fancy meals out with fine wines, but I guess we will have to wait until we this pandemic is over for that.

Preface

Many people have become much more appreciative of teachers over the last year. It is a profession that has always commanded the respect of the few, however, it would now appear to have grabbed the attention and affection of nearly every parent of school-age offspring. Undoubtedly, this feel-good factor will diminish, unless of course the "return to school" manages to decimate teachers, leaving them in such short supply that the kids are sent home again. As a very recently retired teacher, do not expect me to be rushing back to fill the gaps caused by Covid-19 deaths, I have done my time.

It would surprise many of those parents that the profession I feel comes closest to my view of teaching is that of a stand-up comedian. Not a nanny, a tutor or a policeman, but that guy or girl who stands up on stage to make you laugh, entertains you and in the process educates you. For myself, as a bit of an oldie, I learned far more from Jasper Carrott, Ben Elton and Billy Connolly than I ever did from the majority of my teachers.

Although a teacher may be extremely knowledgeable, they will not impart much knowledge unless they are entertaining. A teacher may be skilled in the techniques of teaching, however, the students will learn little unless their techniques are entertaining. A teacher may care greatly about developing skills, but unless the skill progression is evident and entertaining the kids do not acquire new skills very easily.

The vast majority of students learn soundly, swiftly, enthusiastically and happily if they feel they are having fun. Teaching is not rocket science.

As a secondary school teacher of almost thirty years, I have seen many incidents in the classroom, playground, staffroom, school offices and on school trips that teachers are not often encouraged to speak about openly. My experiences span ten years in England and twenty as an international teacher, including spells in Tanzania, China, Qatar, Bangladesh and Malawi. This account is an attempt to lift the lid on some of those secrets and to expose both the humour and the more serious nature of a teacher's job.

These memoirs began as a project set to document my last one hundred teaching days, having determined to retire at the end of our school year, which was due to close on Friday 19th June 2020. Measured only in school days, the account commenced in mid-January. Each day, one of my students kindly wrote in the number of days left to my retirement on a calendar in my classroom. The calendar no longer hangs in its usual place as the room has been emptied; the last number hastily scribbled on the countdown was forty-three.

Whilst the project was successful to a point, it became derailed with just over forty days remaining when the school campus closed and we commenced online teaching due to the Covid-19 pandemic. The subsequent weeks were so fraught in terms of workload that maintaining the journal became impossible and small details were forever forgotten.

I had so much longed for that last day with the kids, knowing that my send-off would be raucous, tearful and full of both joy and sorrow. For I have loved my students and many of them, to everyone's surprise, have loved me.

The original account highlighted incidents within a six-month period and then flashed back to related events over my teaching career. Finally, when my work as a teacher came to an end, some weeks later than expected, I was able to re-think the project and it morphed into something much larger.

Contents

Dedications iii

Acknowledgements v

Preface.. vii

Introduction... 1

Teaching Career.. 3

One: For a Fistful of Dollars...................(Interviews) 5

Two: For a Few Dollars More……...(New School Year) 35

Three: Lean on Me……………………….....(Pastoral)..... 65

Four: Two for the Road…………………(School Trips) 95

Five: Crime Scene Investigation….(School Inspections) .. 125

Six: Planes, Trains & Automobiles……………(Travel) ... 149

Seven: The Good, the Bad and the Ugly. (Curriculum).... 187

Eight: Wherever I Lay My Hat……….(Living Spaces).... 217

Nine: Stayin' Alive………………………….....(Health)..... 241

Ten: The Exorcist……………………….…...(Discipline).... 265

Eleven: The Big Chill…………………….…..(Playtime).... 299

Twelve: The Usual Suspects………....(Online Teaching).... 327

Thirteen: Crossroads……………….(Selling Your Soul) ... 353

Introduction

This account has a chronology that spans my final year and, fortunately for most, the chapters follow a fairly standard sequence from July 2019 to June 2020, when the year closed whilst we were engaged in distance learning. The first chapter deals with the end of the holiday before commencing my last year and the final chapter deals with the period when the kids had all gone and it just remained to sever the ties to my career.

Within the basic chronology, each chapter is themed and after the initial exploration of events in the defined period, the musings on that theme then dart back and forth over the last thirty years and occasionally more.

Although teaching and learning are central, many other aspects are additionally explored, particularly elements of my life as an expatriate teacher since 2001. Whereas some of this book is about teaching, it is about a great deal more besides, there is also a focus on my rollercoaster relationship with school managers. As an Australian teacher friend remarked, halfway through my career, *"At least someone's got the balls to tell them where to stuff it."*

A very brief outline of my teaching career may be found on the following page: in essence, it spans ten years working in UK state schools and twenty in international schools around the world. As an estimate, I would guess that I have taught many thousands of students of over one hundred nationalities, all races and most religions.

In an effort to keep non-teachers reading, I have attempted to minimise the use of acronyms. For any readers who are teachers please excuse this, I am sure you will be able to wean yourselves back onto them in time for the next staff meeting!

Teaching Career

Year	School	Location	Role
1991-1993	Westlands School, a mixed secondary modern school	Sittingbourne, Kent, England.	Trainee Geography teacher
1993-1997	""	""	Head of Geography
1997-1999	The Gleed School, a boys' secondary modern school	Spalding, Lincs, England.	Head of Geography
1999-2000		Lincs, England.	Various teaching cover work and short-term contracts
2000-2001	The Priory School, a mixed secondary special school	Spalding, Lincs, England.	Multi-subject teacher
2001-2003	International School of Moshi	Moshi, Tanzania	Multi-subject teacher
2003-2004	Clifton School, a mixed secondary school	Rotherham, South Yorks, England.	Assistant Special Needs Coordinator
2004-2007	Suzhou Singapore International School (SSIS)	Suzhou, China.	Humanities teacher
2007-2008	Utahloy International School (UIS)	Guangzhou, China.	Humanities teacher
2008-2009	Suzhou Singapore International School (return)	Suzhou, China.	Humanities teacher
2009-2010		Suzhou, China.	Spent writing & private English language tutoring
2010-2013	International School of London Qatar (ISLQ)	Doha, Qatar.	Humanities teacher
2013-2016	International School of Dhaka (ISD)	Dhaka, Bangladesh.	Humanities & Economics teacher
2016-2020	Bishop Mackenzie International Sch. (BMIS)	Lilongwe, Malawi	Humanities & Economics teacher

One: For a Fistful of Dollars

(Interviews)

There are significant moments in your working life when you make a fundamental change. For the most part as a teacher, this may involve a change of school, although in my case many of these moves also necessitated a change of country. Key to these moves are interviews with prospective employees and these trigger points to each new adventure are expanded upon below. However, the story commences with my enjoying a solo holiday amongst the rugged scenery of central Mexico just before returning to Malawi for the final year of my teaching career; I was most definitely unprepared for an interview.

La Carretera de la Muerte, Mexico: Friday 19th July 2019

There is nothing quite like the muzzle of an AK47 pointed directly at your left temple that could persuade you to cooperate more fully. I brought the Volkswagen to a halt and smiled at the older man sitting on the rock next to the vehicle. The man with the semi-automatic.

It had been one of those epic journeys, travelling from Zihuatanejo along the Carretera Nacional 134 in a north-easterly direction away from the Pacific coast. To this point, it had taken three hours to cover only one hundred kilometres and it was noon when I reached the highest elevation of the journey, just over 1900 metres above my starting point at sea level. It had proven to be one of the most breath-taking and seriously strenuous roads in the world.

La Carretera de la Muerte translates as the road of death. For much of the journey to the top I could see at most forty metres of tarmac ahead of me, at worst it was more like five. The route rises up and up and up, there are hairpins and zigzags almost without a break. When a short flatter section does appear, there are only a few moments to relax before the switchback process begins again. The driving would be quite fun if it were not for all the boulders that have fallen into the road, randomly scattered and from house brick to wheelbarrow in size. Then there are the cows, dogs, donkeys and goats that suddenly appear as you round a bend. Fortunately, there were few cars; in three hours I had seen fewer than five.

The view from the col is exceptional and ten minutes watching the Andean condors, with a wingspan of around three metres, was not enough. They had been flying with me on the journey up, sometimes level with the car, such were the precipitous cliffs. The col gave me a chance to view them more calmly. Andean condors are huge; apparently, only the wandering albatross has wider wings.

Beginning the descent, several hand-written signs advertising "Mezcal Primerio", "Mejor Mezcal" and "Mezcal Originario" appeared. Clearly, moonshine mescal was on offer. Beautiful tree-clad mountains stretched in every direction; the views were sumptuous.

Rounding a corner, the road dipped towards a dilapidated stone bridge; it was necessarily a go-slow area. Completely focussed on the rapidly deteriorating surface it took me a moment to clock the handful of men sauntering into the road. It was a few moments more before there was a realisation that they were all heavily armed. Although my momentum had slowed, I tried to keep going, but the guy sitting on the rock at the side of the road raised his AK47; it is not something that can easily be ignored and he was very evidently the boss. As I drew to a halt, another half a dozen hombres appeared from under the shade of some trees. Looking around there were about twelve men in all each toting a well-oiled semi-automatic and several with double bandoliers. The scene was reminiscent of a spaghetti western. Los Banditos!

It is at this point that I should have become somewhat agitated, which quite bizarrely did not happen. It was more like something out of Monty Python than an early Clint Eastwood classic. One of the group, presumably the lieutenant, signalled for me to get out of the car by waving his gun pointedly and directed me to open the boot. With the thought that my belongings were about to disappear I picked up and pocketed my phone on exiting, although they did not try to take anything from the interior, they just poked around a bit. Once in the boot, they prodded the suitcase, but on hearing it only had clothes inside they lost interest. After asking both my destination and departure point, they determined I could go.

The lieutenant who had directed me out of the car laughed, patted me on the shoulder and indicated I was free to leave. Strangely I shook his hand before returning to the vehicle and driving off slowly; he was all smiles. As the car pulled away the boss man, who remained perched on his rock in the shade, averted his eyes.

Apart from the initial gun pointing and instructions, they were all very polite, jovial even although it would be hard to say non-threatening because, with that amount of hardware, no one could be considered that. Unbelievably, I had stayed very calm and confident throughout; it was only after rounding a few bends and having put them out of sight that my bowels gave indications they might loosen. The hombres waved as I drove off.

The bandits took nothing from me, although there was quite a lot of equipment, cash and of course credit cards in the vehicle. It was hard to work out what their plan had been. The few ideas circulating in my increasingly confused and scrambled brain did not make a great deal of sense. Did they not want the hassle of robbing someone who was so obviously a foreigner? They would have supposed the gringo was an American, an impression that would have remained uncorrected until I noticed one of them had been wearing an anti-Trump t-shirt or something. Maybe I looked too poor? There are a whole lot of things that go through your mind when you have just been through that sort of experience. The shock did not set in until later that night after I had spoken to Andrea and had a few chatty emails with a friend.

The following day this posting on the Internet caught my eye: *"Oh, you can see what may appear to be quicker routes or more scenic routes on a map, but you don't want to take them. You may never arrive if you do. Specifically, I'm referring to what is called the Toluca Highway (Carretera Nacional 134), also known around here as "la carretera de la muerte". The major routes are as safe as any, but the less travelled secondary roads are poorly maintained and are favourites for highway bandits due to their isolation."* [1]

Other, more detailed articles about vigilante groups flicked up on the search engine. At the end of the day, it seems the reason I had not been robbed or indeed killed is that the group were vigilantes, fighting the drugs gangs, not part of a drugs cartel themselves. The vigilante groups are generally armed with AK47s, they do stop road traffic to investigate what it is carrying and they generally request donations, although they are not insistent. This may well explain everything, but it does not make for such a good story.

It transpired that the day before the hold up a couple were executed by gangs on the road just outside Zihuatanejo. My heart was still beating more quickly than normal on my return to school less than two weeks later. If the grim reaper had been avoided then it was best

---

[1] Zihua Rob. **Driving Routes**. 1997-2020

to make the most of the year ahead. My school were lucky to have me back in one piece, I had survived the oddest interview of my life.

What is Normal?

Over a year later and it occurred to me on the morning of Friday 11th September 2020, that I had never worked in what most would regard as a normal school. This was a somewhat shocking realisation and one you would have supposed might have been surmised during my teaching career, not after it was over. The thought inspired me to plan to jot down further notes about what has been an idiosyncratic journey through the teaching profession. After boiling the kettle and settling down on the veranda with a coffee another thought occurred, today was the nineteenth anniversary of the 9/11 attacks on the World Trade Center and the Pentagon.

Exactly nineteen years previously, I had been taking a short trip down to the Moshi Tennis Club in Tanzania with an American called Andrea, having no idea at the time she would later become my wife. On the way we stopped off at a friend's house to check up on her wellbeing, she was lying on the sofa recovering from an appendectomy; the TV was on and she was watching CNN. We all stared in horror as the Twin Towers collapsed.

It was an horrendous event that led to a fundamental change in global geopolitics; something changed in the world that week and it has impacted us all since that time. If I had remained in Lincolnshire, my last abode in the United Kingdom and seen out my teaching days in the rural backwaters of my country, then I guess the impact would have been much smaller. If Andrea had confined herself to a life in Redding, California, which is a far more remote concept, then she too may have been similarly less affected. However, as regular international travellers and not being constrained by either small-town America or the fenlands of England, our lives have been vastly more compromised by 9/11 than would otherwise have been the case.

Today, as Covid-19 rages around the globe, I have completed the second part of my journey bookmarked by two global tragedies. As my career ended we were more or less stranded in a small nation in South-east Africa; back then we were at the commencement of our international journey together that has seen us live in Tanzania, China, Qatar, Bangladesh and Malawi, with plans to settle into retirement in Mexico. We have additionally visited scores of other countries together and undergone adventures that we could never have expected.

Whilst this book documents my last year as a teacher. It also explores the events of the last two decades in which Andrea and I have shared both living and working space. In addition, it takes in my own teaching career before that pivot of 9/11, the path that led to my standing in front of that TV set watching the world order come tumbling down.

My account omits a significant segment. Andrea had worked in Colombia, Brazil and Spain's Canary Islands prior to our meeting in Moshi. It is not for me to tell that part of the story, her story, although maybe one day she may sit down and pen the many tales I have heard of those times. As you may imagine, living in Medellín in the early-Nineties, both before and after the death of Pablo Escobar, with the accompanying cartel violence, was not something for the fainthearted.

That pivotal period in my life, hinging around 9/11, saw extreme geographic relocation, the commencement of a new relationship and as regards my career, the focus moved from being a teacher of the disadvantaged to a teacher of the advantaged, for I have never worked in a normal school.

To appreciate the significance of this change, it is necessary to understand what is meant by the English terms, "secondary modern school" and "special school" (the two types of institution that moulded me in my first ten years as a teacher) and the term "international school", in which I have spent most of the last twenty years. They are almost the polar opposite in terms of educational establishments.

My first two schools in England were both secondary modern schools, although this term is now completely outdated and was not entirely popular at any time. They were and still are, establishments for the education of students who have failed, which is a disturbing concept. Although comprehensive, all ability education had been adopted as UK national policy in various stages from the mid-sixties to the mid-seventies and now accounts for 90% of England's students, some Local Education Authorities held out against it and maintained an eleven or thirteen plus testing system, pushing successful students into grammar schools, with the remainder entering secondary modern schools. I was unfortunate enough to work for two such reactionary local authorities, first in Kent and later in Lincolnshire.

Both were state schools, the one in Sittingbourne, Kent being quite large with about 1500 students of mixed gender. The school in Spalding, Lincolnshire was a boys' only school of about 400 pupils.

The UK school that hosted my third permanent teaching post was a special school. These schools were established to cater for students who had difficulty accessing the normal curriculum, either for behavioural reasons or due to mental or physical disabilities. There are, for example, schools for the blind, for the deaf, as well as for autism, dyslexia and emotionally disturbed students amongst others. Clearly, many students with one or more of these problems may well attend a run of the mill school, but the special schools exist to cater for those students who may not cope in such an environment.

My earlier use of the term disadvantaged is not intended as a slur on either the individual students who failed their age-related assessments or on those who have one or more of the conditions outlined above. Having worked with de-selected students for eight years it had become very clear that whilst a grammar school education could be greatly advantageous to those students passing the tests, it would not necessarily have benefitted those that did not. Sadly, very often they were regarded as second-class citizens and very often saw themselves as such. It is also obvious, that something such as dyslexia, for example, is an immediate disadvantage to the sufferer if they are trying to complete an academic education; this does not mean it cannot be overcome.

Due to the nature of the areas I taught in during those ten years in the UK, the vast majority of the students were white Europeans; in fact, this could be narrowed down further to white English. On reaching the pivot in 2001, all that was to change.

For the last twenty years, I have been asked if I teach in a local African or Asian school, teaching local kids, with basic facilities, as part of a charitable venture. Unfortunately, I have never been sufficiently wealthy to give up a properly paid job to pursue such an ideal, although it would have been lovely to have been philanthropic in my approach to my profession. We have been exposed to some of the most basic schools that exist in this world, but other than the odd lesson here and there, we have not worked in them. Both Andrea and I are (or have recently been) paid teachers who need to sustain ourselves with wages and a pension fund in our retirement. Teaching is a job, it is a career, it is a profession; only the incredibly young, very wealthy, or those with ideals that override their needs can afford to think otherwise.

In the last few years of the twentieth century, if anyone had asked me, or if it had ever crossed my mind, the idea of moving from the state sector to the private version of my industry would have been enough to have me frothing at the mouth, having been born and raised a socialist. In a confused and somewhat random moment, the idealism of my youth was thrown out for a somewhat unexpected return to the capitalist fundamental. The fact that I had no real idea of what I was doing says a great deal about my state of mind.

My friend asked the other day, what does it mean to be an international school? It is a tough question to answer because they are all so different. Fundamentally, they will run a curriculum different from the country they are hosted in, although there may be certain legal restraints on this. Often the curriculum will be based on the International Primary Curriculum, the International Baccalaureate, Cambridge International or Edexcel, although they could just make up their own. They normally have small classes, large fees and the students come from all around the world, although local students may make up a significant proportion of the school roll.

The term, fee-paying is an indication that these students are normally financially advantaged, although this hides a whole range of circumstances. As a generalisation, international schools are attended by the children of parents who find themselves living away from their home country for a sustained period, in addition to children of parents who are nationals of the country where the international school is located, who both have the means and can see an advantage to their offspring of attending such a school. Thus, a school in Aberdeen, Scotland, may have students from around the world, whose parents' work is probably focussed on the oil industry, yet also local students whose parents wish to pay for an alternative to the state provision. In developing countries, there is often greater demand from local parents as the state educational provision may be of a lower standard.

International schools may be day or boarding schools, they may admit all abilities or there may be entrance conditions or even a test, in a few cases they may be single-gender schools, although the vast majority are mixed. They may be independent establishments, part of a chain or they may have reputable "mother" schools. They may be for-profit, non-profit based subsidiaries of a profit-based entity or be owned by a religious, cooperative, or parent-based body that seeks only to cover costs.

What is normally the case, is that the teaching staff will have an international bias, although national regulations may limit this and that the non-teaching staff will have a national bias, although this is less apparent in areas such as the Middle East.

Another question asked regularly, is how you can gain employment in an international school? Andrea and I sourced all our international jobs together through the Council of International Schools, largely through the London job fair they run. In some respects, it is easier than securing a teaching job in the UK. All teaching jobs require interviews but these vary wildly in shape, form and of course success. Sometimes it feels there is a gun being held to your head and at other times it feels you are holding it yourself, but there is always a gun.

Interviews in England: 1991-2001

Interviews for teaching jobs in the UK are not exciting. Sometimes it seems they are designed to be as boring as possible, maybe to ascertain whether the applicant can cope with drudgery. To me, there was one element that sometimes seemed like a game of Russian roulette, that being that decisions were made on the spot. For many with little experience in the public sector, this seems perverse, but the potential employer is expected to make an offer immediately after interviewing and the potential employee is expected to accept or decline the post there and then. If, as is normal, there are several applicants for the post, then the interviewing panel will make the interviewees wait until their first choice has made a decision, if that decision is to turn down the job it is then offered to the second choice. It is something akin to having a gun at your head.

Although I have had several successful interviews within the English system, I can recall little of the detail. It is possible that there was so much going on, that they were so pressured or that they were so boring that my memory has chosen not to involve itself in the minutiae. I do know that I was never a second choice, which would not have been great for the ego, but it is hard to recall what competition there was anyway.

However, instead of trying to detail each successful tryst, which would probably be a little tedious, it seems more interesting to highlight three failed interviews that my memory seems to have no problem recollecting.

The first two came from the time when looking for my first teaching post. I had already been accepted onto the post-graduate day-release course at the University of Canterbury, however, a school was needed to employ and pay me for the scheme to work. After an application to a girls' grammar school in north London, they invited me to interview.

The whole process went well, it seemed certain the job would be offered. Having met much of the team, the headmistress conspiratorially pulled me into her office right at the end and asked me if I would withdraw my application. It was weird; I wanted the job, they wanted me, what was going on? She confided in me that she was leaving at the end of the term, that she would have felt unable to ask me to withdraw if she was staying on and went on to explain her reasons.

The headmistress was quite clear, she was acting in my best interests, not the school's, as they were desperate to fill the position. She felt if I started my teaching career in a girls' grammar, it would make it problematic to teach anywhere else; the position lacked sufficient difficulty. She recommended finding an all ability, mixed school with a few problems and that I should find my feet in terms of running a disciplined classroom. It was some of the best advice I ever received and it seems unlikely such advice would have been given in the private sector. My application was withdrawn. I have not spoken to the lady since and she may no longer be with us, but she has my eternal gratitude.

The second interview was at a Roman Catholic school. As a hard-line atheist, this may seem a little strange, but as I did not associate the teaching of Geography with religion back in those days, the school's broader theme was ignored. There were two of us at the interview and my opponent had also had a career in the travel industry, working for a sister company to my own, the airline Air Europe. We had quite a long chat and it became clear to both of us that I was by far the better qualified to teach Geography, although he had the significant advantage of being a Roman Catholic.

Never have I been interviewed by a panel of seven people before. They asked a question each, going clockwise around the long table with me sat at one end. At least the first three were reasonable questions. It then came to the priest's turn, he was at the other end of the table, directly facing me, in a slightly bigger chair than the others.

His question was interminable, rambling on and on, in fact, he kept on answering his own sub-questions. When he had finished, about ten minutes after he had started, he might have asked whether I believed Roman Catholicism was important in the teaching of Geography. I replied, "No" and turned my head to the fifth questioner. It was clear from that moment that the less qualified guy would get the job.

Just before determining to work overseas, I was searching around for a new job in the UK. I had returned to Westlands School, the one in which my teaching career commenced and was being interviewed for a job similar to the one held four years before. Everything seemed copacetic, especially when they asked me to fill out a couple of forms for their records. I requested they locate the same forms that had been filled out at my original interview, as it was easy to pull out the right information. It was and I worked down to the end of the questions in minutes, all the way down to the signature. There, on my old form was my signature and a date. It was exactly ten years to the day that it had been signed the first time.

I paused for thought. It became a long pause. Blood flow hammered in my ears for minutes before it was finally silenced and I ripped up the new application.

Never go back!

International School of Moshi (ISM), Moshi, Tanzania: 2001

There is little of interest in my receiving a job offer from ISM. My application for a post there came from a Times Educational Supplement advertisement; it was a late vacancy and they were rather desperate to get somebody in. The interview was at the director's UK home in Nottingham, which made a nice change and I was able to meet his family briefly. We shook hands and it was a done deal, there was only a wait of a day or two for the paperwork formalities. From application to my arrival in Tanzania was around five weeks, which proved a logistical nightmare.

The shock lasted for most of those few weeks. Having not worked outside a region bounded by the English Channel, Hadrian's Wall and Offa's Dyke, suddenly Africa beckoned. It was all rather head spinning. On one particular day, I had four inoculations, one in each arm and one in each leg. Flying over the Sahara Desert for three hours brought the realisation that England was behind me, however, it never occurred to me that I would never call it home again.

The process was quite typical in a way I only gleaned in later years. The director was an absolutely normal guy. It was not until I arrived in Moshi that I was to discover that he was the only one there with that attribute. I was to have the pleasure of working with a quite wonderful bunch of completely deranged individuals. It is unclear why ISM had managed to collect together such a strange bunch, but I felt at home amongst them immediately. I do not believe that the director could have used the unique nature of his teaching staff as a selling point.

Moving to Tanzania was a massive turning point in my life. They had hired me as a jack of all trades and that is exactly what my role was. They proved to be two wonderful years, although they could only offer me more of the same and I desperately needed to specialise more to cut my workload. Leaving meant a heavy heart, not just for Moshi and the friends that had been made, but also for Andrea who stayed on. It took me two months before it sank in just how much I loved and missed her.

Very sadly, ISM is no more, having been taken over by United World Colleges, a group that has eighteen schools and colleges on four continents with over 9,500 students. What was an exceedingly small school is set to become much bigger and probably more successful, although it certainly will not be as charming as it was. It now has the title, United World Colleges East Africa, which is one hell of a mouthful.

Suzhou Singapore International School (SSIS), Suzhou, China: 2004

Andrea and I had never interviewed together before. She had previous experience of job fairs, both in London and in the USA; I was a novice and had to be led by the hand through the complexities. It is not in my nature to do as I am told but fortunately, we were in a bit of a honeymoon period and could excuse each other's flaws more readily. This was fundamental, for the accommodation we had booked was so small it was impossible to stand up straight in half the room and in the other half was the bed. It was necessary to be getting on well!

It is a little strange to be interviewed as a couple and most schools do split you up for part of the time, although most of the process is conducted with both of you in the room. This makes some sense for the schools as there are enormous cost benefits from employing couples as well as the idea that it provides greater stability in employment. Faced with difficulties in a new country, couples have an immediate support mechanism and on the whole, they are less footloose.

Although Andrea has been to other teachers' job fairs, this was my first. We ended up doing four together, all in London. After preliminary briefings, the attendees are deluged with information from the eighty to a hundred schools advertising their job vacancies, whilst the schools receive the details of all the potential employees. It must be simpler today, but what happens next is something akin to a street market, the schools being the stallholders and the potential employees the shoppers; I believe the market was open for three hours. Each stall lists the school's name and the positions available and if one of the shoppers sees something to their liking, they can attempt to arrange an interview.

This process should be simple but one issue is that some stalls are enormously popular and some not; there is often a bit of argy-bargy in the queues. Wiser candidates have preselected their choice schools, although this tactic becomes unravelled as jobs are filled, and more experienced school representatives have approached candidates before the cattle market; these are the two most relaxed groups of people attending the fair. Nevertheless, some teachers acquire unexpected jobs and some schools acquire unexpected teachers in the free market system; it does have some benefits.

The most experienced school leaders and teaching candidates break all the rules and have interviews before the starting gun is fired. Having secured their posts within the first day they then find they are free to enjoy London for the weekend.

Neither of us can remember the details of our interview for SSIS, except that it was with the director, who later became a good friend. He told me some years later, that when he had seen the name "Clifton" on my curriculum vitae, he had assumed it was the famous Clifton College in Bristol, whilst I had been working at Clifton Community School in Rotherham, a somewhat different kettle of fish entirely. Whether his mistake contributed to us being offered the jobs we will never know, although it almost certainly guaranteed us the interview.

If the SSIS director had made an error regarding my background, he made none as regards describing the school and the vacancies. For the first two years that we were in Suzhou, the leadership team at the school were first-rate, possibly the best I have worked for. In addition to the director, the secondary and primary headteachers were also excellent; it is my view that they set the gold standard and when we assessed later management teams they often had difficulty reaching those high standards. Our fellow teachers were many, varied and a great deal of fun. The only surprise about SSIS was China!

Utahloy International School (UIS), Guangzhou, China: 2007

It was both costly and a pain in the ass to travel to the London jobs fair from Suzhou, only to be offered a job in Guangzhou; the thought that there must be simpler ways of achieving gainful employment occurred to us right then, but did not see us act on it until nine years later.

This was the year that we were interviewed for jobs in Switzerland and I found myself lying on a bed for much of the interview due to the shortage of chairs in the room. It was also when we came head to head with the concept that Andrea and I interviewed very differently. Halfway through it became clear that I was not suitable for the job they had available and that Andrea was equally unsuited for the position they were offering her. I said so and suggested we could all save time by bringing the interview to an early close. Andrea was gobsmacked and the glare aimed in my direction indicated there may be dire consequences. Andrea works on the basis that you sell yourself in an interview from start to finish. I have difficulty selling myself (perhaps the product is defective) and take much more of a mutual benefit stance into interviews. This bi-polar system can break down unless great care is taken and it is a good job you are not expected to give an immediate yea or nay to a job offer.

Guangzhou, in the south of China, proved to be quite a comfortable place to move to in terms of my work and I would be prepared to say that teaching there was probably the closest I have come to a perfect workload. We also had some great colleagues. However, my better half had a terrible start to her employment at UIS.

We had been employed at a London jobs fair in January by the school director, having been offered jobs running a unit for students who were not quite ready for mainstream classes. Unfortunately, in the intervening period, the director had been released by the school and it seems the main reason for his ejection was that he had employed the two of us. Not that we were unsuitable, but there was something of a power struggle going on within the school and we fell foul of it. Whereas I landed on my feet, albeit as a Humanities teacher, rather than running the unit we expected, Andrea was moved from pillar to post in an extraordinarily complex dance; her job specification changed completely five times, twice between primary and secondary and the last of these was after the start of the term. It was not long before we negotiated ourselves out of our two-year contract and left after one year. It remains the only international school where we have spent less than three years and the first few days there left an indelible impression on us.

In many ways, it was a shame to leave, but Andrea's position was untenable and it had created other stresses that needed to be put to bed. We were welcomed back to our previous school without an interview.

International School of London Qatar (ISLQ), Doha, Qatar: 2010

For some reason, we were unusually nervous about the London job fair in the January of 2010. Perhaps it was because of my twelve-month lay-off from teaching, perhaps a lack of certainty had crept in as we had witnessed significant issues at our two schools in China. Certainly, having felt three times that it was time to move on, and those from only two schools, our confidence may have been eroded somewhat.

It had never been our intention to work in the Middle East, basically due to our concerns over sexism. Although this did become an issue at one point, it turned out it was not as bad as the racism in Qatar. I have little memory of the interviewing process nor who was involved. ISLQ seemed to change its educational leaders on a regular basis; the only constant being the ownership of a father and son team. By the time we left there was first-rate school management in place, although I am unsure how long that lasted.

In all likelihood in the interview we were suckered by the remuneration package, which seemed to be excellent at the time; in fact, I believe it may be the most we ever earned. However, it proved to be our least profitable employment in terms of savings.

It is easy to be lulled into thinking the biggest sum on offer is the best offer. For the job fair each school has to post an information pack and included in it are the savings one could expect to make with the package on offer. This is a much more useful figure than the total amount paid although it is still open to exaggeration. In Qatar, a country that at the time had no taxation on either income or sales, it proved that prices were hugely inflated by the largely Qatari owned ventures, this price inflation acted like taxation and pushed them higher than in London for example, affecting all goods and services.

In addition, Qatar Airlines operated as a near-monopoly on entering and returning to Doha. When I investigated their prices, it became clear by just how much; it was normal to find prices for London to Johannesburg, via Qatar, much lower than the price of a ticket from London to Qatar. As the country itself is exceptionally boring, regular trips out were necessary for the preservation of sanity; the costs soon stacked up. It was not the school or any decisions by the school's management that persuaded us to leave, it was the country itself.

International School of Dhaka (ISD), Dhaka, Bangladesh: 2013

January 2013 was our very last attendance at the CIS jobs fair in London. It snowed, which was pretty wonderful as the area around St. Katherine's Dock is rather beautiful with a few inches of the white stuff, although rather changed from the scene that appears on the front of The Jam's album, Snap! One of my mates was the project engineer on parts of the area and it does seem they did a good job of re-vamping that particular part of London. Unfortunately, for one such as I, it is a bit too high end now.

It is also rather costly flying halfway around the world and paying for accommodation in one of the world's most expensive cities simply to attend job interviews. Although we tend to dart in for just a few days, it has always been possible to catch up with a few friends who generally marvel at the idea of spending three days and going back home with a new job in a completely new area of the globe. Bangladesh proved to be the biggest shock of all.

In those intense three days of interviews, it is necessary to be as close as possible to the hotel where the job fair is staged. We were pretty confident, had excellent references and expected to be able to choose our jobs. Our only concern was that our ages (or certainly mine) were becoming a double-edged sword. We were expensive to any school that made remuneration adjustments for experience and employers always want to keep a balance between youthful exuberance against experience and proven competence. To offset the fact that I was turning fifty-five later that year, I was throwing my ability to teach Economics into the mix for the first time, which proved to attract a lot of interest.

The preliminary rounds have already been explained, but suffice to say, once you have agreed on an interview, these nearly all take place in hotel bedrooms. As a couple, this is not too challenging, although it is possible to imagine a single interviewee with a single interviewer might raise a few eyebrows. However, I would suspect that sort of problem instigated by an interviewer would be an extremely unusual prospect as the consequences for the school would be awful. I am unsure how likely it might be the other way round; perhaps it is possible to utilise alternative methods in acquiring a job!

Whilst we had two interviews with ISD, meeting the headteachers of both the primary and secondary schools, it was the

CEO who sold us on the school. He was a massively eccentric man, tall, prepossessing, with wild hair, some of which stood straight up and in other parts straight out. It is a near certainty that we would not have signed up for Bangladesh if not for his immense enthusiasm. The ISD team proved to be an excellent interviewing unit and although it was the last place on earth we had expected to be going they had grabbed our attention from the start.

Some months after signing the contracts we discovered that the CEO was leaving at the same time we were to join. As this was something that had occurred once before, for the Guangzhou positions, we were immediately concerned. As it turned out, his replacement was extremely affable and proved to be a really good guy, one whom we were later proud to have worked for.

ISD was the least international of the schools we have worked at. Although I cannot speak for today's student body, whilst we were there over fifty per cent of the students were Bangladeshi. The nature of some of the students' backgrounds was such that a posse of armed body guards would wait at the gate during teaching hours, having escorted their employee's children to school, been on hand if there was an attempted kidnapping and being there at end of the day to carry their charge's bags and drive them home again. We used to pop outside for a cigarette and it is alarming to see so many men sporting bulges in their pockets just outside a school gate.

It was a wonderful school to work at and there were some lovely teachers, a large number of whom were Bangladeshi, some of the warmest, friendliest people in the world. I felt there was a high level of professionalism amongst the staff and there was certainly pride in being part of that team. My only problem with the management team was that by our third year the secondary headteacher began to make some changes that were incompatible with my teaching, although it did not stop her from being very pleasant, along with everyone else. It was an unforeseen development, but we never regretted having been press-ganged as we were.

Bishop Mackenzie International School (BMIS), Lilongwe, Malawi: 2016

Our interview for the jobs at BMIS took place in cyberspace or more specifically on a Skype video call. The school's director was in a hotel room in London and we called from our residence in Dhaka. The line was not good at our end and after a few minutes we had to shut down our video and proceeded with sound only. Our interviewer left his video running and after only a few moments it became evident that he had a bit of a problem. It has to be believed that he thought his camera was also turned off because during the interview he spent much of the time scratching himself.

It should be pointed out that this was not inappropriate scratching, confining itself largely to his torso, back and arms, but it was apparent he was suffering from many bites and it has to be suspected that these had been inflicted by mosquitoes.

It was pretty clear we were going to be successful, we had the qualifications and experience nailed, we were keen to move back to

Africa and it seemed the only doubt was as regards having the perfect fit of jobs for us both. Our biggest problem was to stop ourselves from laughing. We did consider mentioning it to the poor guy and our sympathies were definitely with him, but we could not find a way to do so without jeopardising our prospects of being offered employment.

It did cross my mind that there could be a technique involved in the interviewer's itching. Many years before, back in the late Seventies in fact, I had been interviewed for my first proper job after leaving university. On that occasion, the lady on the other side of the table leapt up in horror and exclaimed that a large spider was climbing down the side of my face. As university leavers, we had been coached to expect the unexpected in interviews and I had carried on answering her question, completely ignoring her spider antics. As it turned out, there was a spider, it was big and she was terrified. It is unclear whether my calmness in the face of her arachnophobia led me to my being selected for a second interview. However, I believe that those weird interview techniques bit the dust well before the end of the twentieth century.

Having ignored the off-putting behaviour of the school director, after a few days the offer of jobs was confirmed. We were delighted to have minimised the expenses associated with securing new international employment and only one question had remained unanswered.

To be honest, the question had not been asked, probably due to our being somewhat distracted, but it concerned the name and nature of the school. In England, any school with a name beginning with the word bishop is almost certainly a Roman Catholic school and we were determined that our new employment should be in a secular institution. We were safe. It turned out that BMIS was not a religious school unless you regard the fashion for post-modern Buddhist mantra as a religion. For some obscure reason entirely lost to us in the twenty-first century, the school is named after a missionary bishop who arrived in what is now Malawi in June 1861 and died in January 1862 of a malarial complication. Bishop Mackenzie's career could not really have been considered a success, however, his name lives on, even if the good he did may well be interred with his very bones. There are many other more suitable candidates, who certainly contributed far more to the development of the area, but the school has the name it has and for good or bad appears stuck with it.

Joining a new school, without visiting it, is the norm for international teachers. It does bring an element of excitement and surprise to the first few weeks of any new employment. The other surprise in store is the people that you will be working alongside, which is generally a very positive experience, and those who will be in control of your destiny, let us call them 'the management'.

In most cases, although not all, the offer of a contract is made by the school director or CEO and the inline management will have minimal involvement. This can prove problematic, as a perfectly affable school director may have a management team that is somewhat less attractive and it is this team that dominates your day to day existence as a teacher. Just as an interviewee will tend to gloss over any personal shortcomings the school director will gloss over issues in the ranks of the management; they generally remain undiscovered and dormant until well into your second or third month of employment, which may well be nine months after the contract had been signed.

After four years of employment, it is clear that BMIS has the potential to be an excellent school, but it is not. There are aspects of the school's operation that seem compromised and it is hard to put a finger on what that is. Certainly, the fact that many senior figures have been in place for so long is not necessarily healthy. The director and the primary headteacher have recently been changed, although my focus had been on the secondary division and that has had too much staff turnover at the bottom and not enough at the top. If anything, my opinion would be that the secondary management lacked any breadth of experience in international education, they were too parochial and disliked any change they have not fomented themselves. This was not an opinion that could be expressed whilst still employed by BMIS.

Although the reason for leaving was the fact that I was retiring, I believe in a better-managed school it would have been possible to have tacked another two years onto my working life. However, with the full effect of the pandemic yet to become apparent, I consider myself lucky that I did not even contemplate that option.

Two: For a Few Dollars More

(New School Year)

These passages deal with the commencement of my last year of teaching. Not just another start of another school year, but one in which I would be going through some of those annual processes for the last time. For teaching is often a matter of repetition; there are some lessons I have taught that have been replicated year on year for over a decade, with minimal changes. However, there is always something that means the new school year is not the same as the last, something novel, sometimes for the good and sometimes absolutely disastrous.

Looking back, I then examine some of the more interesting incidents that occurred at the start of all those previous school years, returning to the very start of my teaching career and settling into new, exotic and often exciting locations, such as Rotherham.

Bishop Mackenzie International School (BMIS), Lilongwe, Malawi: August 2019

The school year starts early in many international schools. For new staff, it was Monday 5th August, for old hands Wednesday 7th and for the students Tuesday 13th. It was time to prepare for the end.

This proved to be one of the more interesting starts to a school year. After making a risk assessment of continuing in the job for a few more years it had seemed clear that this must be my last. The chances of a cardiac arrest, stroke or nervous breakdown seemed relatively high; however, my bigger concern was the possibility I might kill somebody. This makes it sound as if one of my students might be a victim, although the reality was that the senior management team were far higher on the at-risk register.

It has to be confessed, this had been the situation for a few years and it had been harder and harder to accept instructions that were at best nonsensical and at times were probably damaging to children. Whilst most teachers feel duty-bound to love their charges, there is no such rule for their masters. I had learned to love even the most objectionable students, although found it almost impossible not to dislike many of those who purported to run the schools. As a spin-off to this condition, I had also found it more and more difficult to reconcile my relations with some staff members especially if they went out of their way to adopt fawning positions and refused to argue diabolical decisions.

By the start of the final year, everything appeared under control, both at home and at school; it seemed that nothing could go wrong.

This last year was set to be exceptional and I was geared up to go out in style. It was the way it should be, focussed on the classroom, focussed on the kids and focussed on having some fun.

Throughout my teaching career, I have fought to remain at the bottom of the pile as a classroom teacher. Early on there was pressure to take additional responsibilities (and with them additional remuneration) but I had only succumbed on one occasion. It took six years to fight my way back to the bottom again. My love of teaching is being in the classroom...teaching. It is not in educational theory, which has far too many long words for my liking, the management of other teachers, which is something akin to herding cats, or coordinating the programmes that are taught, which is probably the best route to hypertension.

It is not as if a classroom teacher does not have power and by this, I do not mean over the students. Teaching is a strange profession and is best managed consensually, which should mean the power does reside with the bulk of the teaching body and that is the classroom teachers, be they Physicists, Linguists or Historians. It is when these unwritten rules of school management break down that the problems begin. Woe betide the individual in school management that attempts to manage against the staff; it is a prerequisite to have the teachers onside.

To achieve my aim of a year of fun (and it has to be suspected that most can guess this is not necessarily where this tale is heading) I had applied a little pressure to acquire the ideal timetable. On arrival at BMIS, my teaching load was spread across six different year groups from the youngest to the oldest. In my final year this came down to three-year groups, Years 7, 9 and 11 and the latter, being taught on rotation, would only be running for the first two-thirds of the year. What made it even better was that I was the sole teacher in Year 9, running all three classes, my course in Year 11, being Economics, was virtually independent and in Year 7, I was teaching two of the three classes; the upshot being that communication on curriculum issues involved only one other teacher and I was leading all the courses I had to deliver.

To a layman, this means little. Any secondary teacher will immediately see the upside, only three preps (courses to prepare) and the only downside was potential boredom (marking the same piece of work forty-five times). A bit of boredom was quite acceptable if it meant going out in style. It did not seem to occur to the management that there was a major flaw in the set-up, this being that when I left, there would be no teachers with experience in teaching my curriculum. And it was my curriculum, everything I was to teach in this closing year had been written by myself.

Whilst I regard myself as an extremely competent classroom teacher, I think of myself as even better at writing curriculum. This might sound like an ego waiting to explode, however for the most part it is true and has objectivity to it that has come from outside assessment. Whilst I have only rarely been assessed as "excellent" as a teacher, in inspection or accreditation visits from outside teams, I have never been assessed as anything less than "very good". My work references go further with the praise. Any external assessment of the courses I have written has only ever focussed on minor flaws or technicalities, not on the bigger picture and much of my written curriculum has been assessed as excellent. Yes, there is an ego and it is huge, although it comes with a stamp of approval. It has been rare for me to be criticised for how I do my job, particularly in the classroom and it was quite a shock when this began to change in this final year. It became clear that someone was moving the goalposts.

In determining to retire I wanted to make it clear that the reason was not that my performance was declining, more that it would begin to decline if the considerable pressures continued much longer. Teaching is a tough job, tougher than most imagine and teaching well is an exceptionally tough job. It can be made easier or harder by those who manage the teachers. With well-considered management, I felt that my career could possibly have continued for another two years, in my opinion it was unfortunate that was not the case at BMIS.

My decision came as a surprise to some, many of my colleagues seem to feel you should continue until you have either squeezed the last cent out of the system or narrowed the final artery. However, a particularly good friend of mine, a teacher, had died recently and there has been more than one colleague who was taken well before they had the chance to see the benefits of life after teaching. To be honest, I did not feel it was my duty to die on the job, which in any case would have seriously disturbed and inconvenienced the kids.

And there we have it. The students. If I was rated as a very good classroom teacher by professional assessors, my ratings from the students were and continued to be until the end, exceptional. Who would you rather trust to make a judgement of the quality of your work, a couple of hundred students who see you teach day in and day out, or a manager who doesn't teach anymore, has little idea of the complexities of the job and has never observed you teach in four years? It is obvious, is it not?

There are some clear organisational requirements at the start of a school year the first being to tell teachers what they are teaching and when. It is called the timetable which tells you what, when, where and who you will be teaching. Secondly, yet married to this, is the school calendar, which provides an extension of the "when" aspects and for example, allows you to work out how many lessons you will teach over the year. These two documents are absolutely crucial to the classroom teacher and it is even more important that they are both correct; most school managers understand this. Unfortunately, there were some at BMIS who disagreed with this logic and, as had been the case four years running, the calendar was once again incomplete and inaccurate.

This may be regarded as petty by some; however, we are expected to have planned the entire year in terms of delivering the curriculum. Without a complete calendar, the only way to attempt to structure the curriculum and associated assessments is to make assumptions. For example, of one hundred timetabled lessons, perhaps ten per cent will be lost to items that are not yet calendared. The most irritating aspect of this is that it is perfectly possible to have a calendar that is virtually complete, although everyone would accept that there is the odd event that the school has no influence on, which cannot be incorporated early on.

This broader approach also causes problems on a microscale. During the school year, there are events to which the curriculum has to be tied, such as exams and reporting cycles, making assumptions may well cause difficulties in meeting these pre-ordained deadlines. For example, whilst all teaching groups in a certain year level would have an equal number of classes per week, the calendar could cause more days to be missed for one class than another, in an extreme example this could amount to a ten per cent difference.

This had been argued at the end of the previous year, laying out how we could achieve a much better calendar. One of the examples I gave were the house competition days, which only takes the P.E. department to grind a couple of brain cells together and say they will be doing exactly the same thing as the previous year. Another was Eid-al-Fitr, which was due to fall on a weekend in May 2020, towards the end of the school year, on a crucial date as regards final assessments and reports. It was obvious, twelve months ahead, that the Malawian government would nominate the Monday following Eid-al-Fitr as a holiday, although it is also the case that the government always leaves this decision to the last minute. I suggested avoiding the hassle of a last-minute day off and instead calendaring it in advance. The response was that it was too risky. Well yes, I suppose it was, the moon could well have been knocked out of its orbit during the coming twelve months, but if that were to be the case schooling would be playing second fiddle to the survival of life on Earth. The announcement of our day off for Eid on Monday 25th May was made on the preceding Friday, putting many teachers into something of a dither. For myself, I had it covered. This is called planning and it is a shame it is not more common.

Other aspects need to be covered in those teacher days before the arrival of the students. For the new staff, many in the country for the first time, they are shown how to survive. In the past, international teachers used to term jobs in countries such as Malawi as hardship positions. Whilst there are reasons for this most can be worked around. Some new teachers are shown how to do this very well and others are not, because it depends largely on which of the old hands have been allocated to assist them. In the case of new teachers, the first few days may leave an indelible impression on them and there appears to be a clear correlation between this and those of them who leave either before their contracts are complete or as soon as they have been completed.

Then there are the all-teacher meetings, some dealing with practical matters, such as the students who have special needs and some dealing with the more esoteric aspects of education. It is the latter that bore me stupid. There is one thing worse and that is those meetings where everyone ends up sticking up pieces of paper onto posters. This is done so that all teachers feel they are inputting into the process. It matters little what the process is because all those comments are taken away by the management who then edit them, selecting any that fit what they want, allowing a few to flutter away as the glue releases its hold and putting some ideas into a bin (apologies I mean file) for future use. Strangely, I have only once seen those bins reappear.

And then there are the bun fights. I have no idea who thought of this game but have previously seen it played out at more than one school. Teachers are generally, although not always, seen as being giving and caring. If this was the case, the bun fight might work. However, unless the teacher has been clever in arranging their timetabled workload, often the only influence they can have on their schedule for the next ten months is concerning activities outside the timetable. At BMIS this meant both an after-school activity and two break duties. It is at this time those kindly teachers become rabid animals.

It has to be said, that placing a blank timetable on the wall for duties, things like break time playground, library, cafeteria supervision, means those in the know fight for the nearest pen, whilst the new teachers, especially those new to teaching, watch as a scrummage descends on the by now tatty scrap of paper. Of course, the old hands pick the prime slots. I am as bad as the rest; my favoured duty being the cafeteria. By the time the more experienced staff have selected their options only the worst jobs remain for the new staff. At BMIS a similar system applied to the after-school activities although this was done digitally, allowing the old hands even greater leeway to get in first, as many new staff have not always mastered the ICT systems. Invariably almost all of the newbies had some ability in the use of a pen and many could even remember their initials.

I believe that the after-school activities were what caused the first wheel to loosen on my final year chariot. Having rushed to secure the cushy Humanities Homework Club, which could be undertaken in the comfort of my own room and which attracted only a few kids, I was persuaded by an older student to supervise softball instead. Softball is a sport I have never played, do not enjoy watching and certainly could only coach to a minimal extent; the things you do for your charges!

If you are not a teacher, it is hard to imagine what teachers do when there are no kids in school. This state of affairs exists in many schools for between five and ten days a year. Although teachers are generally quite good at teaching and it must be said this does not hold true in all cases, they are often pretty poor about organising themselves. Thus, a typical couple of days before the start of the school year tends to achieve what most businesses could achieve in an hour or two. In August 2019 this was confused further by the absence of a head of the department in my speciality, this was a structural policy decision by the management, to which many staff objected.

My problems were a little bit more mundane. At the close of the previous term, I had been asked to pack away the contents of my room for a planned move. Of course, school organisation being what it is, the planned move did not happen and everything had to be unpacked again. As luck would have it, there was assistance from one of the cleaners, which was much more interesting than hanging around with the other teachers. We got the job done remarkably quickly whilst engaging in entertaining conversations that steered well clear of education.

I love a clean, tidy classroom. On arrival at BMIS, back in 2016, my room had been a complete mess; it took twelve months to get rid of all the crap, some of it dating back to the previous century. No one had helped me then and that is the sort of thing you do not forget.

Notwithstanding the irritants, for a couple of weeks at the start of the final year, I was on good terms with the management, my fellow teachers, my students, ninety percent of whom were new to me and my little world seemed a good place to be, softball or not! The countdown to retirement had commenced.

Westlands School, Sittingbourne, Kent, England: 1991

The fact is my entry into teaching was relatively late, when I was in my early thirties, I had previously had a successful career in the travel business. My teaching qualification came about through a newly established government scheme to encourage the likes of me to enter the profession. What I had not realised is that a number of the staff at Westlands did not like the scheme and as a result, they would hardly speak to me. It took me several years to find out why I was seen by some as a pariah and this, in turn, generated my intolerance for some teachers from almost my first day. Admittedly, two of the worst offenders eventually apologised to me, although they did leave it for three and four years respectively. Another, who was my inline boss, eventually left the school having not exchanged a civil word with me in over two years.

Whilst most of the management were rock solid and supportive of my position, one stood out like a sore thumb; he gave me a hard time for my entire six years at Westlands. It is hard to work out the impact of these experiences and I repeatedly mention first impressions. If I were to be analysed in the same way we might assess a student, I suspect it would be discovered that the traumas of my first month in the profession may well explain my negativity particularly regarding those managers and managements that I find sub-standard. Of course, any analysis of a student would conclude that it was not their fault. May I have the same excuse slip, sir?

Westlands School, Sittingbourne, Kent, England: 1993

Everyone imagines that Kent is full of beautiful villages and pretty towns; this is not entirely the case in North Kent. Sittingbourne is a linear settlement lying along the Roman road of Watling Street. It generally has a higher rate of unemployment than the rest of the country and a lower level of educational attainment. Whilst the number of foreign immigrants in the area is low, it has a very high number of traveller communities and an even higher number of settled travellers; this group comprised a significant minority on the school roll and also caused a significant number of discipline issues at the school.

I did not spend much time outside working hours in Sittingbourne, as my home was in South London. The journey was forty-five minutes each way and I commuted for six years. It did enable me to keep my home and work life entirely separate and the commute became incorporated into my planning time.

When they made me the head of Geography at Westlands, it allowed me to clean out a huge walk-in cupboard. In it were sets of textbooks dating back to the early 1950s, posters of the Apollo 8 lunar flyby and set after set of completely unused textbooks. Half of the stuff we managed to offload on to a charity serving African schools, however, the other half was simply too decrepit or in some instances wholly inappropriate. I recall opening one book and finding a derogatory reference to black Africans in Ghana as second-class citizens; it really was that bad.

However, it was a piece of equipment that occupied much desk space that I most wanted rid of, an incredibly old weather station computer. To be blunt, it was unusable, although it was a massive struggle finding out why it had been kept. Eventually, it turned out that one of the members of my department had included on her list of evaluation objectives that she would get the weather station going again. As her head of department, I should have been aware of this, however as she had insisted that her evaluation should be done by someone other than myself, the information was never shared. It turned out to be a two-year uninformed struggle.

There are times when the management structure of schools has to be questioned…as an entirety. Most teachers have two or three different line managers, although only one of those is their inline manager. Strengthening the management structure and ensuring teachers have a clear understanding of their position would not only ease the inherent stresses in the job it would also lead to clearer expectations, evaluations and workload distribution. However, it seems the profession is going in the opposite direction and one enormous reason for this is a lack of trust between those at the top and those in the classroom. Teaching needs its lower middle-managers; however, it seems to lose more of them every day.

The Gleed School, Spalding, Lincolnshire, England: 1997

Having lived and worked in locations 50 kilometres apart for six years, in moving to Spalding my commute shrank to 500 metres. I discovered there were major disadvantages to living so close to the school, had my property attacked by kids on more than one occasion and received random pizza deliveries on a regular basis. Still, it was a pleasant walk to work and effectively saved me an hour and a half a day over my previous job.

Spalding, on the surface, is a pretty Fenland town of 25,000 people with an annual flower festival. However, you soon find out that it is not worth going into town on a Friday or Saturday night due to the regular drunken fights, often involving students from the school you might work at. I had several discussions with the police in Spalding and they put the violence and thefts in the town down to a handful of families. It seemed when they were banged up the crime rate fell substantially. That is a small town for you.

That area of the Fens is primarily agricultural, although in Spalding itself there were two large food processing factories. Whilst I made friends outside the teaching community, being a small town, it was difficult to avoid co-workers outside work. However, they were largely a friendly bunch and it was always nice to share a Friday afternoon beer in Ye Olde White Horse, the oldest thatched pub in the country.

The biggest danger was bumping into students when they were behaving inappropriately. On one such occasion, walking back from a few early evening pints at another local, we bumped into one of the pupils who had just been in a fight. His nose was broken. I know this because when I held the bridge it moved a significant distance in my hand as he screamed. I was perhaps not in the best condition to administer first aid. Having got hold of the police and an ambulance it seemed the matter was closed, although a home visit from the local constabulary the next day indicated it had not. I suspected there might be trouble, although it was not clear what for. However, the cops were just after backup information on yet another kiddie's boozy bust-up, not for the accidental tweak of the boy's nose.

International School of Moshi (ISM), Moshi, Tanzania: 2001

Arriving in Africa, back in 2001, the greetings and the induction were exceptional. Moshi, Tanzania was a cool place to be. Nestled under Mount Kilimanjaro, it was a wonderful introduction to the continent. The school made the welcome even better by taking us off within the first few days to Arusha National Park, where we had a somewhat different type of introduction to our fellow staff members. It was there that I met my future wife, Andrea.

Everything seemed very organised and relaxed, although little did we know that when it came to the curriculum, it was not quite as tidy. I was teaching English, Comparative Religion, History, Geography, Life Skills and something else, that does not come back to me right now, to students from ages eleven to eighteen. To the best of my recollection, only the Geography course for the 17-18-year olds was mapped out. When I asked the head of English about the curriculum content, he showed me a cupboard full of sets of novels and plays. Quite how I got through it, I am unsure, but there was an awful lot made up on the spot.

In Moshi, I was lauded by the headteacher for bringing my laptop. The fact that it was almost destroyed by the road surface from the airport to the school appeared to pass him by. When we eventually had the time to get online, it proved that the Internet connection ran in bytes/second most of the time, forget kilobytes, megabytes, gigabytes or whatever 5G will bring us…bytes per second! Today, this would be regarded as an exceptionally serious hardship.

As an induction to Africa, Moshi was ideal. It was a town of 150,000 spread out on the southern slopes of Kili, pretty much above the malarial prone areas, although these were gradually creeping up the slope. Life in Spalding had prepared me to some extent, in that the community we mixed in, tended to be quite small and focussed on

ISM and the Kilimanjaro Christian Medical Centre; there were also a few NGOs in town.

Unsurprisingly, the local flora and fauna were somewhat dissimilar to the Fens. Andrea and I developed our penchant for safaris while we were in Moshi and had soon bought a tiny Suzuki Vitara to get us around. Day to day, week to week and term to term life was fun, although something was missing.

Recently I spent some time going through my diaries for the few weeks at the start of employment in Moshi and the single biggest beef concerned the difficulty in communicating with the UK; it seems I somehow coped with the problems of preparing lessons and African wildlife. When you move you move away from friends and this can hurt. What you do learn, although it takes a long time, is that those who are true friends will remain so, wherever you are in the world.

Suzhou Singapore International School (SSIS), Suzhou, China: August 2005

Without any doubt, the two biggest 'start of the year' challenges were in China. The first actually occurred at the commencement of our second year in the job, when we had to move to a new campus. Building work had only commenced the previous January and the school site was not ready on time; we finally opened three weeks late. Even after we had started teaching there were still builders sleeping in the flooded sport's hall.

In what I suspect was an attempt to reduce costs, the teachers ended up playing the role of removers, which was probably one of the biggest levers behind my now obsessive desire to rid myself of unnecessary physical rubbish. Moving box after box, with no air conditioning and no lifts, in high humidity and temperatures in the mid-thirties, is no one's idea of fun. Even when we settled into our classrooms, we found there were massive teething issues and for half the year we scavenged for equipment, soundproofing and an escape from the manic clocks.

Clocks are essential in secondary schools, simply because you have a timetable which puts kids, teachers, subjects and rooms into a regular state of change. Hold back one class, in one room, with one teacher and on one subject and you could impact the students going to their next lesson, the room being used by a different group, the teacher missing their next lesson and the resources not being available for other students. That is potentially four different classes being impacted by one teacher over-running. It does not matter how many times you explain this to teachers, some, even though they have been in the profession for years and years, simply do not get it or chose not to.

In their wisdom, the management at our new school building in Suzhou had installed a clock in every room. In addition, these clocks were centrally controlled, so they all ran at the same time. Wonderful! The problem was that someone had set the clocks up to have an audio output as well as a visual display. Not only had they turned up the volume they had also set the audio to read the time, in Chinese, every single second. We were working in the Tower of Babel!

Various solutions were proposed; however, it was all rather dependent upon having an engineer open a locked door and change the settings on the mainframe. We were in Suzhou for six years and it is unclear if the central clock system was ever perfected; at least they turned the volume off.

Suzhou was a place of great change over the period we lived there. In 2004 you were able to cross a road without looking, only occasional bicycles might pass. Three years later it was likely you would be taken out by an electric scooter and in 2010 it was impossible to cross the roads because of the number of cars. We were located on the eastern side of the old city, in Suzhou Industrial Park, which was being developed by a Singaporean consortium in conjunction with the Chinese government. In Chinese terms it had low pollution levels, was pretty easy to get around and in the old town, there were some significant points of historic interest.

Very quickly I located a watering hole, the Black Mirage, which was run by an adorable black American from Charlottesville, who had a good taste in music and had a great pool table. There were a large number of ex-pats residing in the area, involved in all sorts of industries, although by far the largest group were the Koreans.

One of the interesting features of South Korea's operations overseas is that they seem to export their middle-managers with a business, rather than use local hire for those jobs as most European companies did. As a result, there were many more parents with school-age kids from Korea than elsewhere. At one point the school roll was almost fifty-per cent Korean. It also became clear that the Korean workers were given school places even if they had no kids and thus they entered into deals with their relatives back home who could have their children receive an international education. It was hoped they would learn English and Chinese, whilst being looked after by uncles and aunts in China. It was all slightly odd.

Two of the saddest events of my career occurred in Suzhou. One of my students, a fourteen-year-old Korean boy, had locked himself out of his family apartment and instead of waiting he thought he would try to edge around the side of the building and through an open window. It had been raining and the ledge proved slippery. He died after falling twelve storeys. The police did investigate possible suicide but this was ruled out. It is one of those rare cases where there is no one to blame, yet a school-aged kid cannot generally be held responsible for their actions. I still think of him regularly and consider what I might have been like as a kid living in a high-rise world.

Right at the start of the year, the first day we admitted students to the new school campus, a fellow teacher died of a cardiac arrest. He had collapsed in the corridor and it was fortunate that the kids were in lessons at the time. He was a nice guy, popular with both staff and students. I have often considered whether the hiatus of our delayed start and the additional pressures it put on us were contributory factors. He had not been well during the previous week but the doctors had not discovered the cause. When it had not been apparent what the cause of his pain was, I suggested he could be suffering from a hiatus hernia, a condition I am afflicted with and felt terrible later when it turned out it was his heart.

Utahloy International School (UIS), Guangzhou, China: August 2007

Thinking back on the start in Guangzhou, apart from the fiasco surrounding our jobs, one thing stands out more than any other. The owner thanked all the staff for making her so much money. Teachers might like making money, although they certainly do not like talking about it and talking about an educational establishment making a profit is something akin to the red-hot poker treatment. As we only lasted a year in Guangzhou we never found out if it was an annual announcement on the owner's part.

Guangzhou is big and grimy. Certainly, thirteen million live there today, when we arrived it would have been more than ten. It is an export powerhouse and therefore attracts buyers and manufacturers from around the world. There is plenty of nightlife and restaurants offering global fayre, some of the Indian establishments even screening international cricket.

At the time we arrived there was quite a lot of petty street crime, often involving motorbikes as getaway vehicles. Standing at a pedestrian crossing, I watched as a pickpocket standing to the right of a guy used a long metal rod with closing pincers to extract a phone from the man's left side trouser pocket. What he managed looked physically impossible, although unnoticed by the owner, he removed the mobile phone. As we crossed the road, I informed the phone's owner of the situation, the thief was quickly surrounded and he handed back the device. There was so much gratitude poured down on me I felt as if I had achieved superhero status at last.

To make the place even more surreal, Guangzhou also had an Ikea. We looked at an apartment that would have been directly above it. People have very odd expectations of what they will find in China, but an Ikea? One year, I was sat next to a lady from New York as our plane dropped into Beijing, she told me she was expecting to see rickshaw after rickshaw; instead, there were the six motorway ring roads around the capital. She would have been surprised to find a Walmart in China, but perhaps perturbed at some of the items on display. It seems unlikely that the main ingredients for three penis soup would have been on sale in Walmart in New York.

I developed a high level of respect for the Chinese people in our time there and also for their government. There is a need to entirely suspend the Western idea of human rights to appreciate Chinese governance; individual human rights are simply incompatible with their Communist government. Anyone would be hard pushed not to admit that the Chinese leadership has benefitted the greatest number to a greater extent than any other nation in the period since Mao's death. Whether you can accept that societal human rights can be more significant than those of the individual is a moot point in the present, with issues such as facemask wearing in the USA.

Suzhou Singapore International School (SSIS), Suzhou, China: August 2008

Returning to an old stomping ground can be exhilarating, it can also leave you with an empty pit in your stomach when you contemplate how much better things had been before you left. Shortly into the school year, it began to feel as if we had entered a negative feedback loop. When we had left in 2007 things had been awful. For Andrea, the year in Guangzhou had proved even worse, but in August 2008 at SSIS basic educational management was unravelling before our very eyes.

At the start of this chapter, I mention the importance of a timetable. I was quite unaware of any problems when I began my first day back with a Year 8 Geography lesson. The students did appear a little more nervous than usual and perhaps a tad young. After five minutes or so a gaggle of teachers had begun to form at the back of my room, which is a little distracting when you are trying to do a big start-up. The teachers' heads were bowed in furious discussion and demonstrated more than a little concern. It turned out that the students all had different timetables to the teachers and the students' timetables were correct; ours were not! My Year 8 geographers turned out to be Year 7 historians which went some way to explaining their nervousness.

At the end of the first week, the timetable was changed again and the first four weeks of teaching time were tumultuous, descending into chaos when the majority of the teaching staff were unable to meet their first reporting deadlines. Only I and one other teacher managed to meet the requirements. When it had become obvious the situation was spiralling out of control, I had begged that they extend the period allocated only to be rebuffed. Sometimes it is astonishing that inexperienced management will not listen to experienced teachers. I was accused of being obstructive in asking for something that all the teachers needed and took; my request had been for a two-day extension, all the other teachers ended up being two days late with their reports. Amazing is it not.

My own life had been further thrown off balance when I had to return to the UK for the funeral of my youngest sister. It was not a good time. Holding my job together and maintaining my standards was hard enough, trying to help myopic management perform their roles proved impossible.

International School of London Qatar (ISLQ), Doha, Qatar: August 2010

There is nothing like a bit of hostility on behalf of immigration to start you off on the wrong foot in a country, although you learn to cope. As by now I had become a regular visitor to the USA, to see my wife's family, we were completely used to obnoxious gits dressed up as officials greeting you at the airport. I later found out that in Doha these were the jobs that were reserved for Qataris who had been dropped on their heads repeatedly as babies. In August 2010 they did have an additional reason to be grumpy; it was Ramadan and everyone was fasting during daylight hours.

This is a little bit of an aside, but we were stopped on one occasion at Doha customs, where they X-ray luggage as a matter of course and having done so they asked to search our bags. It turned out that Andrea's binoculars, an old pair that had belonged to her Dad, had shown up as a suspicious item. When we asked them why binoculars should be regarded as suspicious, they admitted they were looking for the type that could see through women's clothing. Well done, lads!

Apart from the fact that the first few weeks were entirely free of alcohol, most of the settling in at our new school was excellent. There was one problem area, that being the accommodation we were allocated. I will deal with teachers' accommodation later in this book, although this was, without doubt, a settling-in issue.

Whereas the teaching management at ISLQ knew that we were both teachers, the administration department believed I was a teacher and Andrea was a non-teaching partner. Not only did this result in us being allocated accommodation that was simply not big enough, but it also led to errors with our visas, eventually issues with leaving the country, as well as my wife developing pneumonia. It was all extremely stressful and they never really corrected the visa situation. The whole debacle was a great shame because most things about the school were so well run. The first few days did leave an indelible impression, however, on this occasion, we tried to ignore it and get on with our jobs and lives.

I do not particularly like thinking about my time in Doha when I was not working. Everyone has heard the stories of the construction workers, the poor conditions in which they live and the way they are treated. However, there is another group who survive with terrible conditions of employment and those are the domestic workers. It is unfortunate that the walls of a Qatari's house are an outer perimeter behind which all manner of atrocities may be perpetrated. Laws were introduced in 2017, long after our stay there, and they were only really put in place because of concerns over the hosting of the World Cup.

This is an issue that I could become bogged down in as we heard so many stories while we were there and they remain unconfirmed, although a Guardian[2] article mentions a few issues such as being forced to work for 100 hours a week, maid's passports taken away, wages withheld and experience of physical and sexual abuse, the last two being what we heard most about. Several countries restricted migrant workers from going to Qatar and I would love to see the 2022 World Cup taken off them. There is far more abuse of human rights in Qatar than in China and it affects over half the people who live in the nation.

International School of Dhaka (ISD), Dhaka, Bangladesh: 2013

Dhaka is a huge city, although there is little of it that is regularly accessible for ex-pats. By this, I do not mean that there were no-go

---

[2] The Guardian. *"Qatar Passes Law..."*. 23/8/2017

areas, although at times there were, however, there were many more parts of the city that you simply would not wish to visit. The readily accessible sections of the city are actually quite small.

In addition, Dhaka is crowded, with 44,000 people per square kilometre in the metropolitan area, it is the most densely populated city on the planet. To put that into perspective, it is the equivalent of having twelve people on each tennis court when there are two million tennis courts laid out in a grid.

When these levels of population density are reached any open space is treasured. Any public open space is invariably full, or filled very quickly, which leaves only private open space that no one on a teacher's salary can afford to buy or rent. Everyone we knew lived in an apartment with virtually no outdoor space.

In addition to being a capital city and thus attracting embassies from around the world, Dhaka is also the biggest clothes manufacturing centre globally. It is the capital of a poor country beset with all sorts of geographic, environmental, political and social problems. Where there are embassies, there are embassy staff, where there are garment factories, there are countless buyers, where there are problems and poverty there are NGOs. Throw in the elite mega-rich locals, who are to be found in all the less developed nations and you have a whole raft of parents with offspring who fill the international schools.

As an international teacher, when you hit a new town, there is usually some assistance in settling in and one of those ventures was to visit the "diplomatic" clubs that have been commonplace in Dhaka for many years. During our time in the city, until close to the end, there were reciprocal arrangements between these clubs, which meant you were able to use some of their facilities on the presentation of your home club card. All in all, the welcome arrangements in Dhaka were some of the best we experienced and the staff at the school enormously warm and friendly.

At the top of the pile of international clubs was the American Club, which was huge and easily had the best facilities, in second place came the British High Commission and after that, it was a toss-up between the Dutch Club, the International Club and several others. As my wife is American, we considered the American Club, however, it was just a little bit too…American? The British High Commission had a one-year waiting list and later closed membership to all but commission staff, although they were so snooty that received pronunciation was almost obligatory, which certainly did not suit a Brummie from the arsehole of England. Which left us with the BAGHA Club, standing for British Aid Guest House Association.

Originally the BAGHA, established in 1979, was a wing of the British High Commission and one suspects it was the wing that they sent people to who they did not want in the commission club itself. However, it was a small, friendly club with lovely staff and few pretensions. Membership restrictions were a little loose, it seemed anyone could join who was a member of the European Union or Commonwealth, as long as they did not have a national club of their own in the city. We joined and had three years of fun on their tennis court, a story that can be picked up in chapter eleven.

Bishop Mackenzie International School (BMIS), Lilongwe, Malawi: August 2016

Arriving in Lilongwe, Malawi, a return to Africa after a break of thirteen years, was only a little different from our alighting in Tanzania. Whilst there was a little more in the way of curriculum, there was less in the way of easing you into a new town; it took us months to find out where to buy drinking water in re-useable containers, something so basic it should have been on a need-to-know list.

You know you are back in Africa when you hit a speed bump driving from the airport and your bag spins off the back of the trailer. Andrea's luggage held up reasonably well from its airborne adventure, but had quite a hard landing, directly at the feet of an unsmiling policeman. I would love to have witnessed this little cameo but unfortunately arrived somewhat later, without any luggage, after a three-day journey via Dubai. This delay was following an aircraft fire that brought Emirates Airlines to its knees for a few days. Sitting shivering in the school hall on one of the early teacher days my dilapidated state became the focus of some attention, not only because I was two days late, but also because my clothing consisted only of a crumpled T-shirt, manky jeans and a dirty scarf. At least I missed the most boring bits.

The City of Lilongwe is hardly a city. Depending on the source information there could be between 600,000 and 1.1 million people living here, although it feels more like a town of 100,000 or so. Notwithstanding the plethora of international residents, the facilities are limited. There is an eighteen-hole golf course, with an accompanying tennis club, a series of relatively mediocre restaurants and less than a handful of decent hotels.

The warmth of the staff in Malawi was on a par with most of the international schools we had joined. There was perhaps more of a Commonwealth bias to the teaching staff and certainly more South Africans than we were accustomed to, although what was most interesting was that the feel of the ex-pat community was so much more "southern African" than in Tanzania, this reflected in not only the accents but also the dress, customs and attitudes. It struck me as being very conservative.

As we were to find out over time, our students in Malawi were far more liberal than their parents.

Three: Lean on Me

(Pastoral)

Let us take a look at the relationships between teachers and their students and the students and their teachers, which are not necessarily the same thing at all. Much of the focus is on the pastoral system and the extent to which subject teachers should be involved in this. Over the course of thirty years, some of the expectations of teachers have changed and remarkably their involvement in the pastoral care of their students has been eroded by the growing body of school counsellors. Information about students that was once more freely available has become constrained by confidentiality clauses and in many cases, this appears to be to the detriment of holistic education.

Bishop Mackenzie International School (BMIS), Lilongwe, Malawi: August/September 2019

The start of any new school year always brings the same old things, although in each year, there is always something different, something that throws, surprises, or even delights you. It has to be confessed that the start of my final year initially threw up more delights than anything else. Once again, a little work behind the scenes had resulted in my being allowed to have my way as regards my tutor group.

Upon scanning through the names of the students in the class that I was to care for and register it was impossible to restrain a whoop of joy. Not only had my group garnered a collection of some of the most pleasant kids in the school, but it was also a tight group, only fourteen kids, with a great balance of nationalities and races. It is worth pointing out here that the students themselves often do not differentiate in any formal way, only the Asian groups tending to form cliques within BMIS, but there was a balance of Africans, Europeans, North Americans and Asians, representing some eight countries, which is not bad for a class of fourteen.

In addition, four of them were new to the school and, as it later turned out, were all exceptional students. It was a tutor group to die for, which is something of a bonus when you have to look at their faces every morning, then three times a week in Humanities classes and once a week in a specially allocated lesson for looking after their pastoral needs and administration. If you throw in a few assemblies, I could look forward to seeing this cherubic bunch for almost five hours a week.

One of the prime functions of a tutor is to register the students in the morning. At BMIS there was an allocation of ten minutes, commencing at 7.15 pm. This is an early start and not one that can be recommended as one becomes older. The reason for school beginning at such an unearthly hour has two purposes. Firstly it ensures the students finish their day before the heavy heat of mid-afternoon addles their minds to the point where crucial parts begin to fail and secondly that the Muslim students can make it in time for Madrassa, their religious schooling. I will confess that it sometimes crosses my mind that the teachers in the Quranic school must have their work cut out to keep their charges awake, let alone learning.

In the morning, it is clear that the students do not all arrive at the same time and, in a foretaste of a subject we will come on to, it is almost always the case that some groups will be later than others. On average, boys are later than girls. Is it sexist to say this? On average, southern Asians are later than most of the other races. Is it racist to say this? These are my observations. If I were to undertake an objective survey it would support my observations, but some might say that conducting a survey of this type would be both racist and sexist. Throughout the year, on nearly every day, the first students to come through the door were European or African and female, the last students through the door were Asian and male.

My reputation is of being a tough teacher. The students respect this far more than you might think, but at heart, I am a big softy and take enormous care of my charges. This will be dealt with further and in more depth in chapter ten, although one of my little rules concerns punctuality and concerning this issue, I am a stickler.

There are two reasons for this, the first being entirely personal and the other being some advice proffered upon my entry to the teaching profession. My father was late for everything, the world's worst. He was always very polite about it and always apologised, although it has to be suspected those apologies would have been uttered on most of the days of his life. A kid brought up like that either follows in his father's footsteps or takes my route, which was to become obsessive about punctuality. Interestingly, amongst my living siblings, two of us are always early and two always late, I am told that one of my sisters earned the nickname, "Lastminute.com".

The second was that early professional advice regarding keeping class discipline was to be strict about timing, the reason being that if you kept a tight ship on little things the big things would often take care of themselves. This presents itself as slightly weird advice, however, it does seem to have worked well for me over the years.

It is always useful to have a reputation that proceeds you, I did and my tutor group must have held some sort of record by the end of the year for the least number of "lates" they compiled. They were happy and I was happy, talk about a win-win situation. In fact, come to think of it, they were the happiest tutor group I have ever had the pleasure of supervising.

Around the World

At this point, it is important to mention that tutor groups are also called home rooms. At BMIS, the head of secondary used to take enormous exception to the use of the latter term, even though there is little or no difference between the two. In Japan, a home room teacher will follow their class from when the kids join to their graduation and becomes an especially important focal point to the students in their care. My first overseas school tried to adopt the same principle, unfortunately, this did not work very well due to the higher turnover of international staff. The end-results as regards my participation is that I had a Year 13 home room in my first year and a Year 7 home room in my second, which was quite unsettling and took little account of the needs of either the students or the teachers.

Other countries have systems based on variations on the theme but in all, it seems that the teachers who occupy these posts are almost uniformly treated most abjectly by their management and are generally beloved by their students. In BMIS, tutors were granted an extra "free" period a week in return for them taking on tasks that occupied two periods a week, plus the pleasure of having to attend four-day field trips, write an additional set of reports twice a year, attend to the pastoral concerns of the students in their own time, attend to the academic concerns regarding their students that are fired in from other teachers, etc. I am not keen on the term etcetera; however, the post comes laden with so many additional jobs that workload is significantly impacted, especially if you have a tough group. Etcetera is appropriate but should probably be combined with ad infinitum.

Just to make sure it is thoroughly understood, having a single free lesson allocated in a school has little impact on the teaching load you end up with. Therefore, if teacher A has six teaching classes and no tutor group, their total number of lessons may come to eighteen. In an ideal world, if the recommended limit is twenty lessons, they are not given a seventh class. Teacher B, on the other hand, has a teaching load of sixteen lessons, but has a tutor group and thus a lesson allowance, taking them to seventeen. Teacher B will be given an extra class, taking them up to twenty lessons. Thus, teacher B, the tutor, ends up with more lessons than teacher A, with a significantly higher non-teaching workload. You can pass this under the eyes of any constructor of timetables and they would agree with me. It is a crazily unfair system that hammers tutors around the world, a group of people who deserve far more respect than they ever receive.

The German name for a tutor, klassenlehrer, appeals to me, it lends the post an air of Teutonic efficiency. The Romanian term, diriginte, is awful, it makes the postholder sound like a bottle of floral detergent. For me, "home room teacher" is the most suitable term and it is beyond me why it cannot be universally accepted, admittedly translated into the relevant language. This is why, giáo viên chủ nhiệm, works just fine for both me and the Vietnamese. I make these points solely to identify that the role of the home room teacher exists around the world, albeit with minor variations in the job specification and appellation.

The job I would not do as a tutor, which is expected in over half the states in the USA, is the pledge of allegiance. Whilst I have mumbled my way through several different national anthems as a sign of respect and believe me, Bangladesh's anthem is horrendously difficult, it would not be possible for me to keep a straight face through the American pledge of allegiance, which I understand perfectly.

"I pledge allegiance to the flag of the United States of America, and to the republic for which it stands, one nation under God, indivisible, with liberty and justice for all."

The original, written by Francis Bellamy, in 1892, excluded the words "United States of America" and "one nation under God". It read, *"I pledge allegiance to my Flag and the Republic for which it stands, one nation, indivisible, with liberty and justice for all."* It has to be said that the original version is a lot more appealing and I would probably be able to cope with it, although, in an American context, "indivisible, with liberty and justice for all." remains a dream that appears to engage fewer than thirty per cent of any Americans at any one given point in time.

On the other hand, the US national anthem is really, really cool, until you get down to a line near the end of the fourth verse about God. I particularly like the fact that the music was composed by a Brit. It is an inspiring song of war, the lyrics were written by an American during a conflict with the British and it is a very handy anthem if you are always involved in wars, which the USA invariably is.

It is equally beyond me why some countries and particularly my homeland, retain the year-based system rather than the more internationally recognised grade levels. These are important numbers because in nearly all education systems students are divided into age groups. Whether this should be the case is a different matter. Of course, to switch between the two systems it is simply a matter of adding or deducting a year, but it is an embarrassing anachronism and one that causes parents, students and occasionally teachers, considerable confusion.

If I am not careful here I could go into a long rant about quite a few examples of nomenclature and systems that could be standardised, but how about this for confusion: In my final four years of teaching we had three terms, although the year was divided into two semesters, whilst running a parallel activities programme that had three trimesters, which did not match up to the terms or the semesters and had triple rotation systems in my subject area and yet another different one in the Sciences, neither of which matched up to any of the above.

Teachers are of course expected to take all this in their stride. Students are too; however, they are allowed a few weeks before anyone starts to get annoyed with them for not doing so. This is particularly difficult for kids with learning difficulties, some of whom have difficulty coping with six lessons a day, all in different classrooms and then another different set of six for each day of the week. What often goes unrealised is that perhaps as many as half of the students never really understand these interrelated, rolling timetables and rely, for the whole year, on their more organised peers to ease them through each day. This became particularly evident when we shifted to online learning, a period when many teachers found out some harsh realities concerning their student's actual individual capabilities.

If the students become confused it can be guaranteed that their parents will also. I can only go so far but here is a helpful table to identify kids' groups in secondary school.

Age range	U.K. System	U.K. AKA	IBO	USA & Global System	U.S.A. AKA	China
11-12	Year 7	First Year	MYP 1	Grade 6	Middle Sch: Grade 6	
12-13	Year 8	Second Year	MYP 2	Grade 7	Middle Sch: Grade 7	初一
13-14	Year 9	Third Year	MYP 3	Grade 8	Middle Sch: Grade 8	初二
14-15	Year 10	Fourth Year	MYP 4	Grade 9	High Sch: Freshman	初三
15-16	Year 11	Fifth Year	MYP 5	Grade 10	High Sch: Sophomore	一
16-17	Year 12	Lower Sixth	DP 1	Grade 11	High Sch: Junior	二
17-18	Year 13	Upper Sixth	DP 2	Grade 12	High Sch: Senior	三

In the table above I threw in China just for a bit of fun and clearly, there are other systems. In China, those students who would be in Year 7 of the British system, the 11-12-year-olds, are still in primary school. In Australia, and I suspect this has a significant impact throughout their entire lives, it seems primary school can run up to Year 8, but to confuse things further they call this Year 7. As far as I can see the Australians use the numbers from the international system although call them "Years" like the Brits. I find it highly likely that the person who devised the Australian system was also educated in that country.

During my teaching career, there have only been two years when I did not have a home room. When I did, they were predominantly based around students between the ages of fourteen and sixteen years of age. For some, this is the "difficult" age and many teachers work hard to avoid these kids. For myself they are perfect, adolescents in every shape and form! Normally I would prefer to take on a tutor group of Year 9s and stay with them until the end of Year 11. In 2018/19, I had taken a Year 9 group and, as convention has it is in most schools, should have taken the same group in Year 10 for my final year. However, there was an issue with an individual student that caused a breakdown in respect, on both sides, leading to my requesting a change of group.

In thirty years, I can recall only having a handful of cases where there is a loss of trust with a student. This has been almost absent from my time in international schools. However, it can happen and it does not do either party any favours to try to keep it going. There are cases where the issue has to be forced, where there are no options and individuals cannot be separated. This happens mostly among students, although occasionally between a teacher and a student.

Any teacher would confess it does not make them happy when this happens, but when you can feel the tension before a lesson and know it is centred on one individual, it is going to adversely affect performance and detract from the learning experiences of the whole group. A great deal of attention is paid to the mental health of students and far too little is paid to the mental health of teachers. A distracted, unbalanced, or fearful teacher is normally going to have a much bigger effect on a class of students than if one of those students is distracted, unbalanced or fearful; this is the nature of the job. Whilst many would argue that the teacher is not only an adult but also a professional, it does not stop the teacher from being human. Humans have frailties and teachers bring those frailties to the classroom albeit shrouded in a professional cloak of adulthood; student's frailties are more in the open.

Year 9 students are nearly always the most likely year group to rile a teacher, although they are also some of the most rewarding students to work with. In my final year of teaching I had been presented with an almost perfect tutor group, including three of four extremely high achievers, however, taken all together, they were an academically mixed bag. They were all exceptionally polite, kind, sharing and positive in their outlook and were my dream class. However, it should be pointed out that this is their home room tutor's view. It became clear during the course of the year that some of their parents and several other teachers did not all share my high opinion of them.

It is a guess, for to check would take far too long, that I have taken eight to ten Year 9 home rooms in my life. In this regard, I could be considered a specialist. Several of these groups have continued with me through into Years 10 or 11, which can be quite satisfying, but to be honest, I am more than happy seeing the progress they make in Year 9 alone. For the majority, they come into the year as children and leave as proto-adults.

The job of a home room tutor is to guide the kids through the balancing act of academics, after school activities and their social lives. We are usually assisted in this by their parents, their older siblings and their friends, alongside a pastoral team at the school that normally incudes a school counsellor.

This last position has grown more common over the last twenty years to the point where an international school, even a small one, cannot be seen to be without a counsellor. This has had the unfortunate effect that the home room tutor's role has been diminished in some regards, particularly in those cases of students with the greatest difficulties or sometimes simply the loudest parents. To my mind, this is a great shame. Although I understand that specialists are necessary in some cases, it seems that more and more counsellors and those members of management most directly linked to them are trying to turn normal childhood problems into specific personality disorders; they have to, otherwise, they would be out of a job.

Do we have greater numbers of students needing counsellors every year? There are two answers to this question. No, we do not based on the definitions remaining constant. And, yes, we do because the scope of student special needs is always being widened. Counsellors believe that counselling is a good thing, so good that they actually promote it. Having taught in schools when counsellors were a rarity or non-existent, I would suggest that most students' problems are dealt with quite well in their absence. If the advertising of tobacco and alcohol can be banned then surely it should be possible to prohibit school counsellors from marketing their services?

I admire those headteachers who keep a cattle prod in the corner of their rooms for the specific purpose of keeping the school counsellors at a distance. However, the world is changing and whilst I have little sympathy for the concept of counsellors, there is an awareness that they are not going away and we can expect more input from this direction and less from an educational standpoint. It sometimes seems as if many organisations are leaning too far away from their prime functions and if a school's prime role is to be a counselling centre, rather than an educational centre, it seems I have left the profession at the perfect time.

Clearly, there is an important role for some formal school counselling for some students. However, the trend indicates that very soon all school students will be regarded as needing specialist counselling; this is simply not the case. What the vast majority of students need is open and meaningful dialogue with their teachers. Note the use of the term "open". Whereas a student's discussions with a school counsellor are often regarded as 100% confidential and will not be shared with the teaching staff, many discussions between students and teachers are shared with other teachers. It is the sharing of information that often makes a fundamental difference to the well-being of students.

I do have enormous respect for one school counsellor. At the end of the day, she would go home and kick the shit out of a punchbag for thirty minutes. She was the only counsellor I have known who seemed to understand the difference between right and wrong, as well as the importance of the role of the teacher.

Another school counsellor I have worked with came out with an instruction to the teachers that they should not refer to their wives, husbands, boy or girlfriends as anything but partners. The reasoning behind this rule was to make it absolutely clear that we could be homosexual, or not, as the case may be. As an atheist, I do not pray but this particular diktat made me want to.

A Year 9 student is a personality disorder by definition. They do not require further labelling. There are rare cases that require specialised help, although these are not as common as they would seem. One interesting fact that I picked up early in my career, teaching in Kent, was that the children of teachers are far more likely to have tags attached to them, such as "special needs" or "statemented" and require far more visits to school counsellors than the children of normal parents. As a non-parent myself I found this information rather fascinating and set out to try to find out why. It turned out that in the UK several perks came with a kid being labelled. These range from extra funding for the student to extra time in examinations and avoiding certain lessons. What became noticeable is that teachers as parents were far better able to access the systems, to have their children defined as "special" than were most parents; it was not that their kids had more issues.

This appears to have extended almost by default into the international arena. As parents bring their kids with them to their overseas postings the labels attached to the kids and their supposed needs travel with them. The international schools are then left to cope with very clearly defined disorders, most of which are simply a symptom of normality or as close to normality as any teenager can achieve.

Westlands School, Sittingbourne, Kent, England: 1991-1996

Early in my career, I worked at a couple of schools that were the home to "de-selected" students. These students had failed national testing at 11 or 13-years of age, an assessment designed to separate academic achievers from, well, the "rest". Back in 1969 when I took the test myself, it was a pressured environment, one that I was expected to do well in, however, I do not believe there was any such thing as re-takes or re-marking if a student screwed up. In my case, it boiled down to going to a grammar school, supposedly one of the best schools in the area or attending the local technical college, which was a few hundred metres from where I lived. Passing meant that I missed out on much more woodwork and metalwork, at which I was and am incompetent, but it did mean I had to study both French and Latin, languages in which I proved to be completely useless.

One of the unhealthiest systems I observed was in northern Kent where kids all went to the same secondary school from the ages of eleven to thirteen and then took a thirteen plus examination. This separated them, allowing perhaps thirty per cent to move to the local grammar school and leaving the remainder where they were, torn away from their friends and often from the peers who had given them the most assistance. It is a great credit to Westlands School that they fought this system and won, eventually establishing a school within a school for these more academically able students and retaining at least a semblance of integration. I believe the credit for this belongs to the headteacher who not only had the balls to hire me as a non-qualified teacher, saw me through the two years to my qualification, appointed me the head of a department as soon as I was qualified and then, a couple of years later, asked how come I was one of their best-paid members of staff? A great lady!

For students, moving into Year 9 and losing some of their most able peers was something of a catastrophe. Their self-confidence already typically shaky, was ripped to shreds in many cases. The grammar schools would take a fixed number each year regardless of how much they had to raise or lower their "ability" cut off point, which meant that the schools taking the non-selected students were subject to the vagaries of fluctuating student numbers year by year. I'm not sure if this system still operates, but the school's receipt of government funding was always based on the previous year's cohort thus, whilst the grammar schools maintained a constant income, the other schools' incomes would vary wildly, making long-term planning a very difficult proposition.

I had left the school before it managed to achieve take-off, although I believe today it is a very well-regarded institution. Sadly, in Kent, the grammar school system still exists although I believe they have abandoned the 13-plus system for one selecting at 11-years of age instead. It is hard to believe that this type of education still exists, but Kent still has the highest number of grammar school places in the UK. I suppose the only good thing that could be said of the situation is that they have scrapped part of a bad system.

Having been educated myself within a grammar school and having taught in both "de-selected" and all-ability schools, it is hard to give a completely balanced view. The quality of teaching and learning in some of the de-selected schools runs from poor to magnificent, however, I do not believe that either of those extremes could be applied to the grammar schools, in which I have only taught a handful of cover lessons. As a student, I did not think a great deal of the quality of teaching at the grammar school I attended. As a teacher, for the last twenty years in all ability international schools, I have come across a wide range of standards, but none that were absolutely awful. Teaching, especially in terms of discipline, has been much easier on the international circuit and it would be almost impossible now for me to try to return to my earlier stamping grounds; I simply don't have those skill sets anymore.

Year 9 students are the most complex of any year group and most, probably by definition, should be assessed as insane. They are wonderfully erratic, emotional, have seemingly random on/off switches when it comes to caring; they frustrate and enthral in equal measures.

Bishop Mackenzie International School (BMIS), Lilongwe, Malawi: 2016-19

Quite recently, I have had arguments about the difference between male and female students. It seemed to be the accepted view at BMIS that it was somehow reactionary to identify these differences, let alone use them to assist in learning. As a hard-line feminist, something that evolved during my twenties and was provoked to some extent by female partners, I have absolutely no doubt about different sexes being afforded equal opportunities, although I also do not doubt that males and females are not the same, they never will be and never should be.

I was castigated for suggesting that male students were better, on average, at mapping and particularly the spatial understanding required when faced with the questions of horizontal and vertical scales. The fact that this is scientifically proven was irrelevant; it was not supposed to be said. Likewise, female students on average have much better communication skills than their male counterparts, particularly when it comes to a written or visual presentation. This is also proven but is not quite as politically incorrect because here it is the male that is being seen as deficient in some way, which would seem to be more acceptable to some.

Male students, particularly in Year 9, have an extremely hard time. Recent research suggests that if they are focused on a particular career or academic path that in the long run, they may be more successful than their female counterparts and arguments are linking this to the faster advancement of males in the workplace. However, this is not apparent at the age of fourteen when the boys come off second best to the girls in nearly every aspect of school life.

As educators we have developed progressive systems up to the age of 16, that have tilted in favour of learning methods preferred by females and this more than anything else has caused females to outperform males in many countries' standard testing. The situation is less clear in testing at 18, where more traditional teaching and testing methods predominate and final examinations become paramount. Perhaps in western education, we have found the right balance, but as I tell all my students, the battle has only just started in the workplace.

I would suggest that on average the difference between males and females is at its most extreme, both in terms of academic performance and social skills, during the period the students are in Year 9. Males are more likely to bring with them the infantile baggage of the previous two years whilst the girls are looking towards the following years. This does result in some remarkably interesting behaviours.

Some may say that males are less well behaved than females. Observation suggests this does not stack up. Remember the comment about girls' communication skills? Well, the girls may be up to all sorts of wildly unacceptable activities, but they certainly use their communication skills to ensure they are caught far less often and, if they are caught, they often manage to minimise the consequences by talking their way out of it. The boys often seem resigned to their fate, seeming to accept they do not have the skills to argue their own defence. Clearly, these are generalisations and there are certainly some excellent male and poor female communicators.

I have used the term average repeatedly in the last few paragraphs and, of course, average is not a real state. Every single Year 9 student who has passed through my tutor groups has been an individual, however, certain characteristics do tend to predominate in one gender more than the other.

As a Year 9 schoolboy in a boys' school, I found I was seriously attracted to a female member of the teaching staff. This was purely sexual and with only a limited number of female bodies to fantasise about outside of the covers of magazines, I became obsessed with trying to look up her very short skirts or identifying whether she had a bra on or not under her very tight sweaters (it was the seventies). I imagine that some male Year 9 students still do the same thing, although being in a mixed-gender environment with access to unlimited pornography, it is likely less obsessive than in my own teens.

I am aware that sometimes things get out of hand in this regard, but it would take a very naïve teacher to become involved with a Year 9 boy. Of course, the other way round is more common and I have two female friends who became involved with male teachers while they were still at school. How on earth does this happen?

Westlands School, Sittingbourne, Kent, England: 1991-1996

At the start of my teaching career, I took on supervision of a swimming class. It was a stupid idea because I was used to teaching kids whilst I was in the water and by the Nineties there was an extremely strict rule that teachers should only enter the water with students if there was a life-threatening situation. Needless to say, I only lasted one term in the role. However, in the class was a sixteen-year-old girl with what anyone would describe as the perfect body, so perfect it was almost impossible not to stare. I mentioned this to my mentor and he was rather taken aback, not because I had difficulty in not looking at her, but that I might have mentioned it in the first place! His advice was that it was OK to look; just make sure you do not touch.

Over time I concluded that he was wrong; it is not OK to look. I am not sure how it comes about; somehow you displace that natural impulse completely in your role as a teacher. I have since coached several girls' sports teams and have never had any temptations. This does not mean that the next day you might find yourself looking at another body of a female who may be exactly the same age, but is modelling underwear and who just happens not to be in your place of work. The whole thing is slightly strange.

Teachers who become involved, to a lesser or greater degree, with one of their students are in the wrong, although it does happen and probably more often than we would like to think. By definition, it is the teacher's fault, the students are innocent, regardless of how provocative they may have become.

At about the same time as the swimming class fiasco, I became aware of two Year 9 girls who would constantly ask about the whereabouts of another male member of staff. This particular teacher was not particularly attractive, however, the two of them had become completely obsessed with him through absolutely no fault of his own. With another year under my belt, I found the same thing happening to myself and it has continued to occur throughout my career. It nearly always involves a Year 9 female and sometimes more than one. Quite what they see in ageing teachers is anyone's guess, but it does happen and has to be handled very carefully. Well to be more explicit, it has not to be handled.

Determining to Google this particular issue and having searched for "girls fancy teachers", watching the list produced, I stopped myself. This is a throwback. Even though no longer a teacher, it still felt as if someone finding out that I had used those search terms might condemn me and the result would be the loss of my job. That is conditioning.

My guess is that it is a combination of issues that brings this on with a few female students. One aspect must be the father figure image, another could well be the idea of a successful male being a mate, yet another could be the more subliminal idea of a provenly fertile male; although as someone who has never felt successful, has been unable to produce children and is about as far from a father figure as it is possible to be, I cannot comprehend why these kids develop these feelings. It is truly fortunate, that female student attraction to male teachers appears, on average, to start and end with Year 9. When it does not, that is when bigger problems can set in.

When considering the first incident of this type, I calculate that the female involved must now be in her mid-forties and would probably react with horror at the memory. At the age of fourteen, she did give me a silk tie, emblazoned with tractors, pigs and farming produce; I still have the tie and think of her warmly whenever I see it in the closet.

I realise that much of this chapter has been written from a binary standpoint as regards gender. With the greatest respect to the LGBTQ+ communities, I cannot write from any other standpoint as I have no experience of anything else; it seems no boys have been attracted to me or if they have it has been thoroughly disguised.

International Students

With some possible exceptions in Qatar, where a significant minority of student attitudes were somewhat compromised by the country's inherent apartheid system, the students I have taught in the international arena have almost all been wonderful. The same cannot be said of teaching in the UK, as outlined below, and probably other Western countries, although I have no personal experience of the latter.

It seems to come down to rights and responsibilities. In my home country, the rights of the student are paramount and they seem to accept few responsibilities in many, although not all, schools. Much of this cannot be ascribed to the rules and regulations, as in different countries they are often similar, but it almost certainly comes down to parents' expectations as much as those of the teachers or school. The vast majority of international students seem to accept and thrive on their responsibilities rather than seeing them as a hindrance.

Counting up the number of times I have been freely offered assistance by an English student in the UK without them being asked, would probably not wear out all my fingers and toes, which is not much over a ten-year career. Doing the same thing for the twenty years I spent in international schools it would be impossible to count as it is a daily occurrence. Some might point to the fact that I spent my time in the UK in problem schools and with this I would have to agree, although the fact is that there are plenty of kids in international schools with problems, most significantly with language issues, but also with other difficulties.

The key must be in the students' desire to learn. This is often expanded by their parents' decisions to live overseas, opening up new vistas and experiences. The teachers are not seen as obstacles, they are seen as springboards to even more exposure to new experiences. Once a teacher is seen as an absolute benefit, it is very natural for many students to place a proverbial apple on the teacher's desk.

What is clear is that the students in international schools who are native to the country the school is in are not as immediately enthusiastic as those from outside the country. However, the effect remains, it just takes longer and works on a trickle-down basis starting with the ex-pat students.

I would firmly advocate a new order in UK schools, that being that you have no rights unless you take responsibilities. Unfortunately, I believe this runs counter to the United Nation's Conventions on the Rights of the Child.

Working with international students exposes teachers to all sorts of weird and wonderful stuff they would never have access to in their home countries. Working with expatriats, the students' circumstances are such that they are more likely to share some of the idiosyncrasies from their homelands. This is how you learn that the Korean version of searching for a needle in a haystack is, "trying to find Mister Kim in Seoul" or that the Taiwanese version of shutting the stable door is, "repair cowhouse after lost cow".

Over time, it also becomes apparent that the students from those countries where school counselling is not promoted, appear to have less need of counselling than those from where it is. This seems to indicate that they find perfectly adequate protection and support from their teachers and seem more likely to form close bonds with them.

Eau Claire, School District, Wisconsin, USA: 2018

Any contact between students and teachers is a dangerous area. This is one of the few passages in this book that is focused on an event outside my direct experience and is included because of its importance. Originally, for these few paragraphs, I had completely obscured the identities and location. Following a lengthy discussion with the subject, it has been agreed that I should use real names and the actual location.

Chuck Pollard is a great friend and ex-colleague of mine from our time working in China. We worked together for four years and in one of those years shared the same classroom. Although that was several years ago, we have kept in regular contact.

Chuck had determined he would spend a year back in Wisconsin to be with his ageing parents. He decided that he would apply for cover work in the local school and after being vetted found himself on his first day of supply teaching. As to what happened next, I feel it appropriate to use Chuck's words.

"As you may know, it was only one child that was moving around and it was somewhat normal in a classroom - I asked the child to sit down and he did baulk at it, that was when I touched his shoulder as I gently pointed to his seat across the room. The class was divided by lunch, so in the second half of the class he was up again and I reached out to him, but never touched him. Again, I asked him to sit. I still felt this was a normal classroom day."

The result was for Chuck entirely unexpected. It turned out that the school had just provided students with guidance on the dangers of adults and inappropriate touching, a programme encouraging kids to report incidents. This had been primarily been prompted by the scandals surrounding sexual assault by priests in the Roman Catholic Church, which had been in the news for the previous five months.

The kid alerted his parents, who contacted the school principal, who passed it to the police, who had the child interviewed by Child Advocacy and the police. At this point, the police interrogated Chuck and passed the matter to the District Attorney.

It is a salutary tale for all of us who have when needs must, hugged a child in need, leapt to the defence of a kid who was being attacked, simply tapped a student on the shoulder, lifted a girl over a hedge, pulled a boy up a slope, dressed a bleeding shin, held back a youngster when she was going to hurt herself, or simply wrapped an arm around the head of a lad who needed some solace. I have done all these things and would do them again. In all those years of teaching, not once have I been accused of inappropriate behaviour, but there again, I have not worked in Wisconsin and never will.

Chuck is one of the best guys I have ever met. We have worked as closely as it is possible to work. We have been friends for as long as most of our students have been alive. Chuck is not going to feel up some student. Full stop. Period.

Chuck believes that everyone involved in the chain was attempting to protect themselves, having little interest in the validity of a case or not. However, he believes that the District Attorney had a bias, in that he could make political capital from winning such a case.

In the bizarre and twisted ways that some of our legal systems seem to work, Chuck was put on hold for over nine months. During this period he was not permitted to leave the country or even cross the county border. For two months he was not allowed to see his son. Chuck was pilloried in the local papers, his face clearly displayed, a man who had not even been allowed his time in court to give a defence. He even went to see the editor of the local paper to point out what they were saying was wrong.

When he had seen through all this crap, almost a year of hell, Chuck was offered a solution. Go to court; if you are found guilty it will be a prison sentence or, if not guilty, your name will still be put on the potential sex offender's register. There was a caveat, accept a county non-criminal disorderly conduct charge (similar to a traffic ticket) and, whilst you will be fined, your name will not appear on a sex offenders register. After a lengthy period, for Chuck wanted to clear his name, he determined to accept the disorderly conduct charge. The other charges were dismissed and can now never be brought again. Clearly, the DA did not believe they would manage to bring a case to court or, if they did, that they stood little chance of winning it.

Chuck's take on this is that they destroyed his career. He has welcomed a further investigation into the case by the Department of Instruction, who had the temerity to ask if he wished to surrender his teaching licence. He is fully supportive of measures to protect children but is equally concerned about miscarriages of justice. He also has concerns about the motivation of the DA's office, the costs that would have been involved in a jury trial and the fact that a jury would have been exposed to the unsubstantiated press reports before a trial.

I had no idea that if a teacher were found <u>innocent</u> on a charge of inappropriate behaviour with a student that their name would be registered on a list that would prevent them from ever getting a job teaching again. I suppose that if he had been a permanent employee of the school they would have been forced to offer him his job back, but who the hell would go back to an employer who had treated you like that?

There is something very wrong with the system.

Chuck had two hundred letters of support lodged with his solicitor, from colleagues such as I, who knew the guy intimately and from headteachers, from school CEOs, from kids, from just about everyone who knew him. Chuck was desperate. He had been through ten months of hell by that stage and nobody ever, not ever in this world, wants to end up on a sex offender's register, particularly when they have been found innocent. I know why Chuck made the choice he did and respect him enormously for his decision. He accepted the minor misdemeanour being faced with permanent and damning labelling even if he were found not guilty.

His words, "*I know first-hand how false accusations can be made and how damaging they are.*" Is a massive understatement and he still finds himself having to defend his innocence.

As someone with no offspring, I would have determined to fight it and take all those bastards to court. I will always protect my right to prevent those kids in my care from hurting themselves. It is my job. My job is not to not touch kids; it is to protect them.

Four: Two for the Road

(School Trips)

Below I explore the idea of school trips, some of the benefits and the problems they can cause. They range from local Geography field trips in sub-zero conditions to lounging on beaches in sub-tropical paradises an international flight away from the school. From sport's team trips with ten kids to mega-outward bound weeks with two-hundred, several involved hospital visits, many saw anxious parents and most result in severely stressed and exhausted teachers, although it is all worthwhile because by a massive majority the students love them!

Bishop Mackenzie International School (BMIS), Lilongwe, Malawi: September 2019

In many international schools, there is an attempt made to take students on a trip in their year group, to improve bonding between them and to cement the relationship with their tutors. This is an excellent idea.

In ten years teaching in the UK, I only came across a couple of similar schemes, but neither was as comprehensive as those operated internationally. This is almost entirely due to budgetary constraints. However, it has to be said that the willingness of teachers in Britain to supervise school trips has declined substantially since I entered teaching.

In my final year, I was due to lead the week without walls trip for Year 9. It sounds idyllic, three nights on the shores of Lake Malawi, in a very pleasant resort at the northern end of Cape Maclear, a beautiful sandy beach and a patch of the lake that was relatively clear of pollution. Sleeping in tents suited me as well, although not all the students were as keen.

There were initially four teachers scheduled to attend, the three Year 9 tutors and a male Maths teacher, along to ensure the staff was gender-balanced, together with forty-two students: the nominal safety ratio being one to ten. These trips were to all intents and purposes compulsory, enormous pressure was placed on parents who wanted their children to avoid them. This did present some parents with difficult dilemmas, particularly in the Muslim community where some of the more traditional were not at all keen to have their daughters (there was never an issue with their sons) frolicking on a beach with few clothes on. However, everything was set fair and I believe the only student who did not attend was withdrawn because she was suffering from malaria.

For myself, the visit was to be my third year in a row to the same location and although the lodge had been changed, we had more or less the same activities; I was as enthused as the students. The previous year we had significant difficulties with transport, water, a lack of suitable field activities, a very dirty beachfront and issues with service activities that the students are expected to undertake. To minimise these problems I booked a private visit, with Andrea, a couple of weeks before the school trip itself.

Like many teachers, the costs of this private visit were paid by me, there was never any thought that the school might refund the expenses. It did prove to be extremely useful if only that it identified that the buses that had been booked would be unable to access the accommodation area, the result being the students would have to walk seven-hundred metres with their bags. This sort of distance is not an issue, even in the blazing heat of the afternoon, although when we also had to transport enough water to satisfy forty-five individuals for four days, it did become a point of some concern.

There were to be three main service activities, the first was training local teenagers in the use of computer software, the second was teaching lessons to classes of nursery age students and the third an environmental exercise that I never really got my head around, as in the three years undertaking this trip my involvement with it had been zero. The preparatory visit enabled me to spend time arranging how we would deliver the ICT element, which, to my mind was the only one of three activities that was worthwhile.

These service activities are supposed to work two ways; they are not entirely one-way charity. Students from our school and indeed students across the globe who are involved in International Baccalaureate programmes, must be involved in service activities, but with the service comes the proviso that the kids themselves must come away with some benefit; a learning experience of some sort.

Having observed the nursery activities at close hand there appeared to be no discernible benefit to our students, to the local toddlers, nor to the pre-kindergarten teachers, who to be honest were only interested in the teaching materials we brought with us and left for them to use. It is not for me to comment on the environmental activities, although reports from our teachers and students were that they were not particularly beneficial, which left the ICT training as paramount.

I had developed a good relationship with the African teacher, who had set up the computer training. He had pulled in a few charities, had received donations of laptops and the hardware to be able to network and was desperately trying to improve the prospects of local teenagers by giving them some marketable skills when looking for jobs. His biggest problems were the servicing of the equipment and the electricity supply.

Electricity! At the time of writing, ESCOM, Malawi's electricity supplier, is under investigation by the new government for rampant corruption. ESCOM is a parastatal, a state-owned enterprise that is run along the lines of a private company albeit as a total monopoly. The electricity supply in Malawi is erratic, although it has improved somewhat over the years. In early September 2019, we were experiencing about seven hours of blackout a day, which rotated, morning, afternoon, evening, on a three-day schedule. Normally domestic electricity could be guaranteed between nine at night and six in the morning, but that is not especially useful if you are trying to run daytime ICT lessons, particularly as many of the laptops had extremely old batteries with minimal life.

If they managed to sort out the corruption at ESCOM then it would be clear that electricity prices need to rise; the government desperately wishes to avoid this scenario, which would not be popular. However, they are not thinking outside the box or, to be more succinct, they have not removed their heads from the box. Electricity supply only services 11% of homes in Malawi. The poor who are connected to the grid use little electricity. The solution is to introduce a two-step scheme, such as is run in Zambia, which has an extremely low price for the first 200 kilowatt-hours, then increases by a multiple of at least four for the remainder. To my way of thinking it would be a win-win for the new government.

In the meantime, what they need in the Cape Maclear ICT centre is a bank of solar panels, batteries and an inverter. I had intended to try to set up a scheme to ensure this would be funded, along with a long-term training involvement from some of our Year 11 students.

As it proved, this plan was completely derailed by events back at our school.

In an attempt to give some better justification for the service elements of the visit, Year 11 students, who were on a separate trip, but located nearby, were supposed to supervise the Year 9 students in their service activities. Whilst this may have had some benefits for the Year 11 students, it did little for the Year 9s. I focussed on the ICT and tried to ensure I had a group of our kids who knew what they were doing with software.

The second wheel came off on a Wednesday about a week and a half before the trip was due to take place. Having just returned from lunch duty, I bumped into the teacher organising the Year 11 trip. He is a nice lad, very hardworking and well-liked by the students. In an interchange that must have lasted less than fifteen seconds, he told me he had sorted the groups out for the service activities. I reminded him of the ICT activities and we agreed that we and all the kids would meet ninety minutes later. This is not the way to plan for dealing with ninety kids and eight teachers and both he and I knew it.

Unfortunately, the lad leading the Year 11 trip had no idea what was going to be facing the kids in Cape Maclear. None. He did not realise that they would be teaching nursery age kids, he did not realise that the ICT had to be handled separately and he had little idea of the logistics of moving our students between venues.

To make matters worse, when we did get the year groups together, he made all of the kids stand out in the sun, a completely unnecessary arrangement, before calling out groups and trying to get the students to arrange themselves. At this point, I advised him that he had missed out the ICT groups and everything had to be halted again. I had a cohort of Year 9s ready to join me for the computer venture and was extremely surprised when none of the Year 11s showed any inclination to join us. Quite clearly, they had been primed for something else. It was time to talk to the group and explain, which I did; soon we had twenty-odd students wishing to join my task force.

In all my time teaching, I have only come across this a couple of times, a teacher with arms outspread trying to prevent students from crossing a line and ending up pushing them in the direction he wanted. I have done it myself, although only when a situation was so out of control I was forced to act. In addition, I have never seen a teacher push past other teachers, completely ignoring their suggestions, in an attempt to achieve a goal that had never been explained properly to anyone. At that point, I felt that any action I took would only belittle the other member of staff and felt I should not do that in front of the kids. In my opinion, my colleague had lost it.

There were several repercussions. What I should have done, was to iron out the problem face to face, another option would have been to make a complaint about the teacher concerned. I did neither. Instead, I fired off an email to him and the service supervisor, saying I did not accept being kept out of the loop; it seems this did not go down too well. It was a polite email, but included those precise words, "I will not accept being kept out of the loop". I chatted to the service supervisor about it the next day and apologised if I had come over a bit sharp, we had a pleasant chat and moved on. Unbeknownst to me, there were machinations afoot and a complaint was made about my email to the school director. About a week later I received an email asking me to apologise to the service coordinator, which I had already done. In protest at the tone of the email, I stepped down as trip leader.

Having spent my own money on a reconnaissance, sorted out many of the problems that would have arisen, having watched a teacher make a fool of himself and act in what I regarded as an abusive manner towards students, it was time to stand back and let them dig their graves. Unfortunately, this would also impact the kids and that is exactly what happened. I managed to salvage the ICT side of things, although not entirely to my liking. However, to have our students arriving to teach lessons to nursery age kids when they had prepared materials for 10-year olds, was only to be expected. If there was a learning experience it was focussed on our kid's adaptability rather than the teacher's planning.

Fortunately, the teacher who was put in to take my place supervising the Year 9 trip was a nice guy and, other than the poor planning of the service activities, we managed to have a great four days away. However, the incident soured my relations with the head of secondary and they never really recovered. This proved to be the second step on the downwards spiral.

All Around the World

Early on in my career as a Geography teacher in Kent, we had more days away from school than many other subject teachers. I had a good friend, who taught just along the corridor from me, she was the head of Foreign Languages and France was on our doorstep. We competed to see which of us could spend more days out of school. In our record year, we were both in the mid-thirties, perhaps as many as seven working weeks away on trips.

In those days, most of mine tended to be day trips. The most common destinations were the Isle of Sheppey and Canterbury. Trying to rack up a lot of days out of school is fair enough, however, it made little sense in terms of the stresses involved and leading school trips is enormously stressful.

My first experience of this was as a teenager when offering to help a mate's mother, who also happened to be a headteacher, in accompanying a primary school group to the Welsh coast. I had six kids to look after. Virtually nothing about this day has stuck in my memory, other than being on a train and a beach, because I was counting from one to six constantly. My mate reminds me that we temporarily lost a student on that trip, a little Sikh girl and that his mother had to resort to the gin as soon as she returned home. Not once did I think that one day I would be counting from one to two hundred with almost the same intensity.

The banal act of counting heads is one of the most important aspects of any school visit. In some schools, they insist on students wearing identical hats, bandanas, or t-shirts, to make them more identifiable. In my first school, some of the students would undoubtedly have sold the hats, in my second they would most likely have eaten them and in the third, they would have lost them before we got on the road. Still, it is a great idea...in principle.

At the start of this chapter, it was mentioned that teachers in England are now less inclined to supervise school trips, there are several reasons for this. Many would point to funding constraints. I was certainly unhappy taking trips that only catered for those students whose parents could afford to pay. Subsidising kids from poorer backgrounds when they comprise 75% of the student body, is extremely expensive. Another element is that parents, and remember the school has to take on the role of *loco parentis*, have become much more risk-averse. The school and the teachers involved have often to apply the level of supervision expected from the most risk-averse parent. This can mean that if one parent believes it is too risky for their offspring to build a raft and float out onto a lake, there is a possibility that none of the children will be allowed to do so, even though the vast majority of parents may feel it is a perfectly safe activity for their kids. A third, which is intimately tied to the last point, is that litigation is quite a likely conclusion of a student returning from a trip injured or, at worst, not returning at all.

The upshot of this is that the amount of time to plan effective trips has shot up. Hours and hours of planning have to be executed, including risk assessments for every possible scenario, in which every element has to be questioned. "Is it safe for twelve-year-olds to sleep in bunk beds? What advice should they be given?" This is not in the same realm as questions we ask ourselves in Africa, where risk assessments may include the prospects of elephants, hippos or lions around student tents and crocodiles in watercourses where the kids might be tempted to cool off.

Just think about some of the things that have been banned in some English schools. Conkers, British bulldogs, snowball fights and leapfrog banished from the playground and some schools will not allow students outside if there is snow for fear they will slip and hurt themselves. Cricket and rugby have been removed from some schools' P.E. rosters. And just who is responsible?

In my first school, towards the end of my time there, the lead teacher of a trip had to sign a document before departing that made it clear that they, not the school, were responsible for the students' safety. I was never sure about the legality of this for sometimes the trip leader was not the same individual who had completed the risk assessment.

We are talking about kids here, young teenagers, who get themselves into awful messes outside school and often in their own homes. There are almost certainly more injuries to school-age students outside school than there are in school or on school trips.

Give teachers a break. Accidents will happen. We do our best to avoid them, but they still do.

Suzhou Singapore International School (SSIS), Suzhou, China: September 2006

At SSIS I supervised back to back mega-trips. There were around a couple of hundred kids from Monday to Wednesday and another group of the same size from Wednesday to Friday. When it gets to this sort of size it is essential to have other teachers counting sub-sets, which I did. Teachers had about ten students each and were pursuing rotations of outward-bound activities. One of the teachers was the deputy head of the school.

It is quite odd that in schools someone junior to another teacher in the school can become their boss in another circumstance. For example, if the head of school is a Maths teacher and actually teaches some lessons, which many do not, they report through the head of Maths as a teacher and the head of Maths reports, more often than not, to the head of School. It is a system that does not work very well.

On this particular field trip, I was the leader; the deputy head of school was one of my team and reported to me. As he was a good mate, a very competent guy, enthusiastic and very focussed on advancing his career; he was the last teacher that I needed to worry about. Until that is, he arrived back at base minus one student. Any missing student is of concern, they are all equally concerning really. Only a kid with some particular special needs might have worried me more than another. However, this missing student was the daughter of the school's CEO, who was not inclined to accept errant behaviour from staff.

The deputy head was shitting himself and must have circumnavigated the whole area twice in an attempt to find the boss's kid. He did not. She, eventually, found him. She had felt that the group she was in was too boring and had chosen to filter into another group, probably led by a teacher who either could not count or did not do so often enough; there are a few of them. It was my job to give her a bollocking, it is not certain that the deputy head could have handled it.

Andrea and I performed a mapping exercise in advance of that trip. In most countries, it is easy enough to acquire maps on which to base your planning and develop activities, such as orienteering. In 2006 this was not the case in China. Using a hand-held GPS, we fully mapped an area of six hectares of the Daqing Valley area near Hangzhou. The rangers were delighted, they had never had a map of their own patch before. At the time our behaviour was almost certainly entirely illegal. We handed the completed map to the park authorities and to the outward-bound company the school used, although I was careful to copyright it. It is with as much certainty as to the illegality of our actions, that I can guarantee our illegal activity's copyright would have been completely ignored in China.

On many of the visits in China we stayed in hotels, however, these trips were still called "camps". On one such trip, we realised that the hotel, which had a disco in the basement, was also operating as a brothel. At the time this was quite a common thing in China, however, it was not an ideal place for twelve and thirteen-year-olds to spend the night. Several of us patrolled the corridors not only checking on the kids but also ensuring that none of the prostitutes' customers would barge into their rooms.

Unfortunately, one slipped past our defences. We found him, sitting on the end of a boy's bed, drunkenly attempting to hold a conversation with a fairly terrified Taiwanese student. It took nearly an hour to get him out of the room, even though he was as nice as pie. I doubt he ever had any evil intent; he was simply interested in the situation having never spoken to someone from Taiwan before.

When teaching overseas there is a high likelihood that a significant proportion of your students will have English as a second, third or even fourth language. Our misuse of terminology could end up with interesting consequences. Andrea told me that one of her students came into school on a Monday and told her she had been camping in Shanghai for the weekend. Somewhat surprised by this concept, she asked the student where the campsite was. The kid reeled off the name of a famous five-star hotel in the megapolis. It took a while to sink in, but our use of the term "camps" had led one little girl to believe that any stay in any hotel should be described as camping. And we call ourselves teachers!

Priory Special School, Spalding, Lincolnshire, England: 2000

Another notable trip was the one when I was teaching in Lincolnshire. This was a reverse trip, in that the students stayed at the school for a week; it had accommodation in place as it had previously been a residential school. It was a great week and the kids loved it. We did do some away days and I took them up to the Peak District for a day accompanied by a lovely guy who had taught for much longer than myself but had suffered from some sort of breakdown. It is difficult to drive and keep discipline amongst a group of kids when your fellow teacher, supposedly navigating, is so weighed down by his angst, that he could not even decide about where to make a turning. It proved a frustrating day.

I chatted with the headteacher on our return about the difficulties we had and he advised me that my colleague had been an excellent teacher until he had been put through a court case regarding child abuse. The head said it had been obvious from the start that it was a trumped-up charge and the teacher was found not guilty. It was too late; the kid's lies had destroyed him causing his breakdown.

On the same trip, I also directed a performance, or more precisely an animated reading, of The Witches by Roald Dahl. It was wonderful fun and the kids just lapped it up. At the Priory, the staff were almost entirely female, so there was no shortage of volunteers to make costumes, props and to dress up. If that sounds sexist, then so be it; I challenge anyone to question the fact that female teachers, on average, like dressing up more than male teachers do, although I do know a few male teachers who will don fancy dress at the drop of a hat.

The Witches pushed me back in the direction of involving myself in dramatic productions, something that exploded when I first went overseas. However, in more recent excursions I have gone back to the storytelling that began with The Witches and took to writing a story specifically for each trip; normally commencing the writing once we had settled in for a couple of days. It has generally taken me three to four hours and I need some downtime away from the kids to be able to complete them. However, they are brought to life by involving actual children, the real setting and with a whole lot of fantastical nonsense thrown in. My final tale involved Year 9 and their teachers being entirely wiped out by a tsunami on Lake Malawi, a highly unlikely, although not impossible occurrence. There was one survivor in the tale and it just happened to be me.

Clifton School, Rotherham, South Yorkshire, England: 2004

There is one trip that stands out above all others and it is somewhat surprising that there were any survivors. After two years in Africa, I had returned to the UK for a year to sort a few things out before resuming my international career. After a couple of weeks on supply, I applied for a maternity vacancy in Rotherham as an assistant Special Needs Co-ordinator. Some pages back it was explained that today I would no longer be able to go and teach in a rough English school and, after only two years in Tanzania, I was very ill-prepared for what Rotherham threw at me. It took two months for me to come anywhere near being able to control the classes and after eight months I still was not satisfied with my progress.

Each year a local philanthropist paid for a group of our most needy students to go away, a Monday to Friday activity trip to the seaside. This actually turned out to be in the sea, as we were staying on a boat in the middle of the Salcombe Estuary. With approximately thirty students and six staff, it would not sound like a great deal could go wrong. Think again.

The majority of the students were classified as having attention deficit disorder and all were extremely excited about being away. Half were girls and half boys, there was only one set of showers. Neither the teachers nor the students had any way of leaving the vessel, it acted to all intents and purposes as a prison ship and with the tidal currents a swim to the shore of around 500 metres in any direction, would result in death by drowning for all but the strongest swimmer. I, as probably the strongest swimmer on board, would not have attempted it and my role was as a gaoler, not an inmate. It was something akin to a floating Alcatraz.

During the daytime, the activities were sufficiently engaging to keep most of the students involved; I also found them entertaining. They were city kids, unused to fresh air and wide-open spaces, in many ways it was an idyllic trip. However, that was during the day; once we were back on board and after being fed, we simply did not have enough to keep them occupied on a relatively small boat.

Each night from around 8 pm onwards, the rioting started. There were some tough teachers on that trip, great disciplinarians, still we could not control it. At one point, and there are shades here of my earlier comments about a teacher physically controlling kids, I had to stand at the top of a metre wide stairwell holding back fifteen boys who were determined to get into the showers while the girls were still in there. It took all my strength, but I should never have been in that situation. During the stand-off various boys complained I had hurt them, when they had actually hurt themselves trying to push past my braced body; I could hardly move. The impasse ended when one or two of them finally found an alternative route through a cupboard and with me still blocking the stairwell, I watched as first three, then five and then the remainder of the boys ran past my head and into the shower room. There was one job I had been asked to do; it was just the wrong job. The whole sequence ended when the entire staff and some of the ship's crew piled in to rescue the girls; I was knackered.

We had three nights of this. They managed to punch holes in the walls of the cabins, one smaller boy, a non-swimmer, actually moved from cabin to cabin through the portholes, risking an untimely death each time; the noise was incredible and inescapable.

On the last day we went out on an amazingly fast speedboat, there were about ten of the students with me. The pilot, who had witnessed some of the kid's nocturnal activities, asked if I would like to take the wheel and with a knowing grin suggested it might be a good idea to demonstrate what the boat could do. Boy, it was fun! Fifteen minutes of high-speed twists and turns, unexpected deceleration followed by lightning acceleration, which left ten young bodies sodden, most suffering from seasickness and all with an almost pitiful desire to return to dry land. That night we managed to get them to shut up by midnight, which seemed a major triumph at the time.

Towards the rear of the boat were the boys' quarters and to the front the girls' bedroom. I cannot remember where the staff tried to sleep, but to be honest, in three nights I had only managed two or three hours myself. In the centre of the vessel, quite cut off from the rest of the boat was a bar. On the last night, we hit the drinks.

This is indefensible behaviour by teachers supervising students; I will not even try to pretend there was any justification. At the very least we should have had half the staff avoiding any alcohol and the other half confining themselves to a maximum of a couple of shandies; we did not. With the kids asleep, and they were, we let down our hair for the first time and kept at it until around 4 am.

No one knows quite how it happened, but it is definitely a good reason not to play with other people's phones. Someone and we all had our suspicions, managed to press the trip leader's phone in the wrong place and it put through a call to the headteacher, who was at home in bed. We were to learn later that the line was open for possibly as much as thirty minutes and during that time he was exposed to drunken, lewd, crude and loud stories, mostly of an obscene nature, from one after the other of us. Quite what his wife thought about it we never found out.

The headteacher was not impressed. I do not know if he ended the call himself, although about an hour later we received an incoming call from him and he, rightly, let rip on the trip leader. The early morning was spent trying to cover tracks, make excuses, provide alibis, anything we could think of. As I was not permanently employed at the school I offered to take as much of the responsibility as I could, but it is absolutely clear, ultimately the trip leader had to take the responsibility.

I was extremely attached to the trip leader, a great teacher, a lovely human being and a strong personality. Stronger, it proved, than the headteacher. Although she gave me a quick run-down of their face to face meeting, it was not detailed enough. She told me she decided to go in with all guns blazing, about what a fantastic job we had all done and just how difficult it had been and, incidentally, the kids were all fast asleep in bed and didn't he know just how much stress we had been under. I guess it was that Yorkshire spirit that saw her through; not one of us ever received as much as one word of criticism from the Head.

If that rated as one of the most difficult trips, then there have been others right at the other end of the scale. My first field trips as a teacher had involved wading into the Thames estuary in winter, dirty, cold and pretty miserable. The last field trip I had led in the UK involved wading into The Wash in freezing conditions, which was dirtier, even colder and more miserable. After only a couple of months in Africa, I found myself on a Geography field trip, paddling in the Indian Ocean, which was clean, warm and wonderful! And the kids' behaviour? There is no need to ask really…they were perfect.

To what extent should a teacher put his, or her, life on the line, both at school and on trips? I've heard some teachers say they would not confront a gunman to save the life of their students, because they prioritise the parenting of their own children's future, over that of a child they are paid to educate; I understand that. Being childless that excuse does not apply and whilst I would not do so happily, if the situation arose, I would put myself between a gunman and my charges. It is a slightly different matter when the student is the one holding the gun. Both in the UK and China, I have turned towards a student and found a fully extended, loaded bow pointed directly at my head, at near point-blank range. On an early outward-bound trip to Wales, I had the same experience with a rifle. These incidents are scary. Whilst some random nutter might enter a school to try to kill you or your students, the chance of one of your own students doing so, entirely accidentally, is possibly higher, unless you happen to live in the United States of America.

International School of London Qatar, Doha, Qatar: 2010-2013

For a couple of years, I taught a Business Studies course for sixteen-year-olds. One of the student's parents offered to host a field trip at their car showroom. Not perhaps what one would regard as the most inspiring of visits, but when we realised it was an Aston Martin and Lotus dealership, things were looking up.

We were greeted with drinks, roses and Aston Martin chocolates, treated with amazing hospitality and given the chance to get into and out of all of the nine or so models on display. The owner gave the students a ten-minute speech and then it was left to the two sales managers to field the students' pre-prepared questions. It proved a very worthwhile session for them and introduced them to the pointed end of a business.

Of course, there were other minor perks. Initially, they offered me the chance to drive an Aston Martin DB9 and the prospects was enormously appealing. I demurred and suggested a ride in the passenger seat may be more appropriate, as the thought of the consequences if there had been an accident, were simply awful. I will confess that I was a little overawed by the Aston Martins. The leather on the seats and dashboard would probably have cost as much as my 4X4, which sat patiently outside and made the area look more downmarket than it was. It was somewhat amusing when the Aston broke down going over one of Doha's many speed bumps, it would not have been quite as funny if I had been in the driving seat.

International School Dhaka (ISD), Dhaka, Bangladesh: 2013-2016

Tioman Island, off Malaysia, is a pain to reach from Bangladesh, involving two flights and a layover in Kuala Lumpur; however, it made for an incredible week without walls. A coral-fringed island in the South China Sea, most of it is idyllic. We stayed at an eco-resort, two years running, with Year 11 students. There were always interesting incidents, as there are when you take a bunch of city dwellers into a tropical rainforest, but few stand out more than the student with the brand new, state of the art, waterproof iPhone. It turned out that this lad was scared of depths. Not scared of water, but scared of the space between himself and the bottom; possibly the weirdest phobia I have come across, although it has to be said, he was a somewhat weird kid.

This fear meant that whilst he would go into the water, he would not open his eyes, even with goggles, because he was scared of the drop he might see. He was one of those students who were bright half the time and incredibly dense the rest of it. Because he was keen to see what was underwater, although under no circumstances would open his eyes, he determined to take his iPhone with him on a snorkelling trip and to video what he was missing so that he could watch it later. It has to be said, he had a plan. Unfortunately, that was where the brains ran out. For whatever reason, and we are still considering what they could possibly have been, the lad determined the right time to take out his SD card was whilst he was still in the water with his eyes shut. That was the end of both the iPhone and the record of his underwater experience.

Coming back from these trips you always have a few scrapes and minor injuries, sometimes a little more. My worst was a pair of slipped disks. This occurred off Tioman Island during one of the activities in the ocean when the students were snorkelling. The school had insisted that they wear life preservers, which was unpopular with the kids and the teaching staff, however, the guys running the courses followed the school rules to the letter. They tried to make the staff wear them as well until I pointed out that having a big yellow inflatable around my chest and back would make it nigh on impossible to rescue a kid if required; it was fortuitous that they listened.

We had enjoyed a good day and the final activity was snorkelling over a shallow reef. There was plenty of sea life and colour on display and the students were enjoying themselves, ogling octopi and flirting with the fishes. Amongst them was a group of four non-swimmers to whom I was paying particular attention. They lay in line abeam, supported by both their life jackets and a long float that they held stretched across in front of the four of them.

We had not been advised how fast the tide might be going out, but it soon became apparent that the reef from being in a metre and a half of depth was quickly becoming more exposed. At this point, the four students were fairly oblivious and not being regular ocean goers had little concern for the fate that was awaiting them, for positioned directly below and across the route they needed to travel to the boat, lay hundreds of sea urchins.

If you have never been stung by a sea urchin it will be hard to imagine the level of pain they can deliver. My own experience came from Cornwall when I was ten or eleven years old and the purple marks on my sole remained for well over a year. Realising the situation they were in, I determined it was time to tow them away from the danger. In places, the depth was now down to half a metre and it was becoming increasingly likely that one or all of them would be stung.

Fortunately, there was a rope attached to their float and even more fortunately, I was wearing fins, otherwise, the task would have been impossible. Towing four excitable kids, two of whom were adult-sized, although the two females were much smaller, in slightly choppy conditions and with a narrowing clearance to the beds of urchins was hard work; it was something of a relief to reach deeper water. However, the relief was only temporary because we had entered a strong current flowing in the opposite direction from the boat.

It was at this point I began to holler for assistance. There was another teacher on board, but incredibly he was asleep, sunbathing. It took some while before a crew member heard me and by then the disks had slipped out of place. I felt them go, although was a little unsure about the nature of the damage and certainly did not have time to stop and assess the situation. Five exhausting minutes later, pushing myself as hard as possible against the current, I managed to bring the kids into the protected boarding area of the boat. The newly awoken teacher was there to assist the four of them on board, where they sat chattering excitedly about what for them had been quite an interesting journey; they had little idea of the twin dangers they had faced, being stung or swept away, nor what impact that might have had on both them and their parents.

Exhaustion hit me and it was impossible to get out of the water unaided. The following day, I was unable to carry my bag when we left for the return journey. In the long run, what proved interesting is that my back did not hurt. I had discomfort, although not pain. Because of this I did not book in for an X-ray and lived with the condition for about a month. It was during a hospital visit for another problem that they checked out my back with an MRI scan and gave me a beautiful photo of the two disks hanging out of my spine. The reason there was no pain, although it did cause somewhat restricted movement, was that the disks were not pressing on the nerve. I have gone into more detail about the consequences in a later chapter dealing with illnesses overseas.

The most annoying thing about this incident was the series of errors that led up to it, all of which were avoidable. You read, more rarely now, about horrendous accidents on school trips and this could easily have been one of them. If I had been leading the trip, I would have insisted on far more information about the water conditions and would certainly not have had a member of the teaching staff sunbathing, oblivious to students who were in the water.

Westlands School, Sittingbourne, Kent, England: 1991-1997

This brings me neatly to two injuries that occurred in Kent in my early days. It has been pointed out that the anecdotes in this chapter follow one after the other, but to get it down to length it is has required the removal of several other alarming and entertaining incidents, including the involvement of an air-sea rescue helicopter; the two below stand out the most.

The first was a Year 11 Geography field trip to Canterbury. By this stage, we had an eighty-page manual on how to run trips, the contents of which were supposed to be memorised by the trip leader. Of course, students will find ways through any level of protection and this one surely comes under the heading of self-harm.

The toughest lad in the school was in a group that was not ideal as it mostly comprised his cronies. These groups of sixteen-year-olds were allowed to roam Canterbury within the city walls, more or less unsupervised and supposedly conducting surveys of tourists. It is hard to think of any single act that would discourage tourists more than being surveyed by our students. There are plenty of cobblestones in the town and it happened that the lad, having burst into a run for no known reason, slipped and fell.

We are pretty certain that at this point he had broken his wrist, but this is a conclusion reached through later investigation, rather than direct observation. From the stories of his little team, following the accident it turned out that he had stood up, looked at his limp wrist and announced that he had dislocated it. Although our own opinion, reinforced by that of the doctors, was that the initial injury was probably a fracture of one of the carpals. However, the lad was determined to show off to his mates and insisted he should show them how you should "fix" a dislocated wrist.

If you have ever seen the walls of Canterbury, they are solid. Perhaps five metres thick, much repaired and renovated, but Roman in origin, they have been there for nearly two millennia and they will be there a great deal longer. Primarily their function was defensive, although they were also built to create an impression, the Romans were pointing out that they were here to stay. It is unlikely that the Roman civil engineer responsible had ever considered they may have a medical application, however that was the thought that entered the mind of the lad with the broken wrist.

His little team of teenagers told us that he had said he would show them how it was possible to "sort out" a dislocated wrist and watched as he stood facing the structure and rammed his fist as hard as he could into the walls of Canterbury. We were told he did this not once, but several times.

Later, as we arrived back at school, we were told that the medical staff at the Kent and Canterbury Hospital, had X-rayed his wrist and identified several severe fractures, all but one almost certainly resulting from his attempt to correct the original injury. We were told that he did not cry, or cry out, once. Yep, possibly the toughest kid I have taught, although certainly not the brightest.

As a follow up to this tale, my colleague who had accompanied the boy to the hospital was forced to leave and the school sent down a replacement teacher, a very pleasant ex-nun. When she arrived at the hospital the medical staff mistook her for the boy's mother and waving a pair of filthy underpants aloft, castigated her for the unsanitary conditions existing below the lad's top layer of clothes. They reckoned his underpants had not been changed in two weeks. It would have been lovely to have witnessed the expression on the teacher's face.

I think it is important to round off with a tale that should serve as a warning to any teacher about how to conduct a school trip. This time it was to Broadstairs, also in Kent. Broadstairs is a cute little seaside town, popular with tourists and having small winding streets. We had only just dismounted from the bus and our string of forty-odd kids was making its way down a narrow pavement, alongside a busy lane. One of the students was huge, a fifteen-year-old, well over six-foot and built like a mountain; he was also extremely polite.

Today, some twenty-five years later, I still have to pause for a moment when I think about what happened next. The boy, seeing an old lady coming in the other direction, stepped into the road to allow her to pass. He was struck by a pick-up truck from behind. Most of what happened next is a blur, although the line I remember best, from the paramedic who arrived at the scene, was, *"If he had been half a foot smaller, he'd be dead"*.

I know the driver and his mate were devasted; they were also extremely helpful. We had an ambulance there in minutes, which was remarkable in the crowded little town. The lad was conscious and clearly in considerable pain; it turned out he had broken his femur. As the teacher in charge of the trip, it was my job to speak to both the police and the ambulance service, however, it was another teacher I allocated to go to the hospital. Quite oddly, we then continued with the activities as planned, although I had to make a phone call to the school, who then had to phone the boy's parents.

It would have been a difficult phone call at any time, but I had a secret. One of the most important rules in that eighty-page guide to school trips was that every student should have signed a permission slip. I had always been keen to get all the students on trips and when the lad's slip failed to materialise, I had phoned his parents and received verbal permission, which was definitely not what the school required.

The deputy headteacher who was the recipient of my call was unbelievable. The man was renowned as something of a stickler and I had expected the whole book to be thrown at me and possibly the prospect of dismissal. He was wonderfully supportive, the boy's parents proved to be also and the matter eventually faded away. I visited the boy, at home, as he was recuperating and his parents proved to be as pleasant as he was.

That deputy headteacher is placed on a pedestal, where he will remain while I still breathe. Since then I have never taken another student on a trip without a permission slip except with the express permission of a member of the management.

Five: Crime Scene Investigation

(School Inspections)

Here we look at methods by which schools market themselves to the public as being ideal institutions for parents to send their children. In the UK it is a legal obligation for state schools to undergo inspections by the Office for Standards in Education (OFSTED). The inspection covers the governance of the school as well as the delivery of the curriculum. The schools are given a descriptive grade of outstanding, good, requires improvement or inadequate. Schools that are described as outstanding ensure this is emblazoned on their websites and other literature.

In the international sphere, there are six main accreditation bodies and schools may choose to belong to one or more of these bodies. An international school may also choose to operate without accreditation if the national law in their physical location permits this. Additionally, schools that are following the International

Baccalaureate (IBO) programmes must have their curriculum documentation and delivery assessed by an IBO team.

It is rare for an international school to lose accreditation, except when they opt out of the deal. The inspecting organisations' reports make recommendations for improvements at the school and there is normally a timeframe proposed to implement these, usually before the next accreditation visit. As in the UK, schools with good reports will utilise them as marketing tools, however, unlike the UK, schools with poor reports ensure they bury them as deeply as they are able.

Bishop Mackenzie International School (BMIS), Lilongwe, Malawi: October 2019

In October BMIS went through a multi-accreditation process, involving the International Baccalaureate Organisation (IBO) for the curriculum and two other bodies, one European and the other American to assess the management of the school and student care. Andrea and I had been through similar multiple accreditation visits in the past.

The school had chosen to have the accreditation visits (and it is regarded as a sin punishable by death to call them inspections) take place all at the same time. This does have its conveniences but does mean that everyone is a little stretched, particularly as all the inspecting bodies are looking at somewhat different aspects of the school. For those of you who are not involved in education, this is a bit like an audit being performed at the same time as a tax inspection, a health and safety visit and simultaneously with an investigation into employment rights and conditions; it is quite a broad and major investigation. However, in true academic fashion, most of the work is conducted as a digital exercise, before the accreditation teams visiting and during their time at the school they simply seek confirmation the standards that the school have outlined in the paperwork are being followed.

Our CEO had previously been the leader of a combined accreditation team, we knew this well because he had led a visit to our school in Bangladesh (see below). Therefore, he must have had a particularly good idea of what he was letting himself in for or so you would have thought. In the aftermath of the visit to Malawi, he went on record as saying that if he had the time again he would not have chosen a combined visit as it proved to be too much pressure for all concerned.

I believe the compilation of the paperwork commenced almost two years before the visit and it was always clear that our leader wanted it to be a perfect accreditation assessment. All the teachers were allowed to choose to sit on various committees, although as these changed at the end of the first year, it meant continuity was something of an issue. To confuse things further, there were two sets of committees and we had to be on one committee within each set; I believe this was to satisfy the different requirements of accreditation teams, although cannot be entirely sure. Over two years most teachers ended up being on four committees and completely confused.

I came across a quote from Charlton Ogburn's article on Merrill's Marauders[3] that neatly summarised the situation, *"We trained hard, but it seemed that every time we were beginning to form up into teams we would be reorganized...and a wonderful method it can be for creating the illusion of progress while producing confusion, inefficiency, and demoralization."*

What was clear, was that the committees had virtually no impact on the running of the school, unless one of the members of senior management happened to be on that committee. All the new ideas that came and went, mostly went if they did not fulfil the existing ideas and ambitions of the chosen few.

For myself, I was lucky in one, ignored in another, bored in the third and desperately irritated by the fourth. In the first, I had introduced the idea of targets at the end of our student's academic reports, something which most schools did but we did not. This was latched onto by the secondary curriculum leader and we put the principles into practice within a few months. All well and good, and a step forward for the school, although it did cause quite a few moans and groans amongst the teaching staff, who were concerned about new methods increasing their workload. There was anger in some quarters, specifically within my department and when it was found out that I had been one of the instigators of change the evil eye was focussed in my direction by certain teachers.

---

[3] Charlton Ogburn Jr. **'Merrill's Marauders'**. Harper's Magazine. January 1957

It is strange, teachers generally abhor change. When they argue for change, they are normally arguing for something they have been used to in a previous school. Every year, when new teachers come in, you hear the refrain, "We used to do it this way in XYZ" followed by, "All schools should have 67½ minute lessons, it's the only way forward." This is, of course, absolute crap, everyone knows that the best lesson length is 59½ minutes with students being given a 225-second break after the first 17½.

What is even weirder is that teachers, including myself, when faced with a massive change and particularly changes to the curriculum, will fight tooth and claw to preserve elements they have previously taught and try to mould these into the new structure. In doing so, they often create more work for themselves, rather than less. However, if you then move on a few years those same teachers will go through the same process to protect and maintain the version that they had to adopt on the previous revision. Because of the repetitive nature of a school's curriculum, it takes a couple of years for everything to bed in, it then becomes the norm and the rioting in the staffroom is predictable when the next change comes along.

However, I digress. One of the committees on which I sat was particularly salient to present times because it focussed on the approach to online teaching. The thought was that an infectious disease (Ebola was the one proposed as the most likely) could sweep through Malawi and leave us having to teach online. How prophetic! I was the only member of the committee to have previous experience of online teaching, from my time in Bangladesh (see chapter 12) and felt there was much I could bring to this discussion. The CEO joined the meetings, which were led by the head of ICT and we failed to progress anything. We even failed to draw up a basic plan of how to operate in a distance learning environment, nor for a hybrid situation. In the end, I never read the vague documentation that resulted from the meetings of this committee but know for a fact, that when we did commence online learning, in March 2020, absolutely nothing was in place. What a waste of time.

Fundamentally, BMIS overdid itself on this accreditation, there was far too much paperwork and not enough mention of work in progress. It was as if we were trying to present a fully formed functional school with no shortcomings. That is not only a pipe dream, it is also destructive because an assumption can set in that further improvement is impossible.

There were highly entertaining moments. On the first morning of the visit, we were promised by the management that they had strangled the accreditation teams so much that they would not be able to conduct many classroom visits. As a classroom teacher who prides himself on his standards, I found this somewhat disappointing. I actually want my teaching and the kids' learning to be assessed, not just the paperwork. However, it was a weakness of the school that the management very, very rarely came into the classroom and basically had little idea what was going on in the lessons they were meant to be over-seeing. Individual teachers knew far more about what was going on in each other's classrooms than the school management did, which is an appalling indictment of the system at BMIS.

You have to give a huge hand to the visiting accreditation team; they saw through the barricades that had been put in place and within an hour had descended on many classrooms; it was wonderful. Of course, what was going on, in ninety per cent of the lessons, would have been of a high standard and this was down to the highly competent teaching staff, not to the documentation or management.

I had first become aware of the management's low opinion of their teachers in my first year at the school. The morning following a parent-teacher session we gathered for a pre-registration meeting in the staffroom. The secondary head announced how surprised he was that the meeting with the parents had been so successful. Surprised! When teachers meet parents, in the vast majority of cases, everything goes exceedingly well; why on earth would he be surprised? This defensive attitude only grew over my time at the school and in the last year teachers were not even supposed to email parents without having had their email approved by the management first; an absolutely farcical situation that meant teacher-parent contacts were eroded further.

My only formal meeting with one of the accreditation teams was focused on the curriculum for my subject area for 11-16-year olds, which falls under the bizarre banner of "Individuals and Societies".

For anyone who does not follow IBO doctrines, this is the subject name for what normal people might call Humanities or Social Studies. In BMIS, the banner encompassed geography, history, comparative religion, economics with some anthropology and sociology thrown in for good measure. Humanities is an excellent name for the subject area, even Social Studies, which is the more Americanised nomenclature, is reasonably acceptable. Individuals and Societies is a patently ridiculous and meaningless name.

I am told that the subject name, which has been abbreviated by everyone to I & S, or by some, including my wife, to INS, was chosen because the IBO subject of Psychology was to be included in the grouping and as this did not fall under the umbrella of Humanities or Social Studies, the subject name needed to be changed. As mentioned above, teachers do not like change and, being a teacher, I objected furiously to this particular decision and have attempted, right up until, as well as after, my retirement to use the term Humanities whenever humanly possible. It still makes my skin crawl, every time parents ask, "INS? What's that?"

In our departmental meeting with the accreditation team, we had of course to use the correct terminology. We came out of it pretty well, however, we made it abundantly clear that we wanted a head of department, a post that had disappeared some fifteen months before. The thrust of our argument was that we wanted better communication between the teaching staff and the management and the visiting team agreed wholeheartedly with us. It is disappointing, that when groups of professionals make a reasonably argued request, from a position of need and are supported by fellow professionals from outside the school, that the school's management should see fit to completely ignore that request. It is not as if they even argued it, they just ignored it. When the relationships between the management and the teachers reach such a low point it is clear something has to give. One result was that the Modern Languages department, another without a head, ended up resigning en masse, all leaving in June 2020. Of the four people in our meeting with the accreditation team, three left at the end of the year, albeit one was me and I had already made it clear I was retiring.

In a well-managed school, I reckon I could have done another year or perhaps two would have been perfectly feasible. It was interesting to note that the CEO, although he said this was also a decision made earlier, advised us on the last day of the accreditation that he would also be leaving at the end of the year. We waited a long time for the accreditation reports to come out and it was only after Xmas that most parts were officially made available to the staff. To ease the burden on us the management decided we would only be given a summary of the reports that had been edited by themselves. It is not difficult to work out why.

It is hard to find copies of the final accreditation reports. However, I did come across a little detail from the American team's report. There is a telling line, "Lack of communication between stakeholders is also a concern." and from a survey of parents, "a significant percentage disagreed that home/school communication was effective. Many parents believed that they were not included in decisions about their children's education. There was also a perception that communications were not honest and/or transparent."

Little did we know, that behind the scenes, a significant amount of shit was already hitting the fan.

International School of Dhaka, Dhaka (ISD), Bangladesh: 2013

ISD in Bangladesh had a completely different approach to their staff. The CEO was a wonderful guy, who had a consensual approach to management, was open to new ideas but was also quite prepared to put his foot down when required.

Although this approach was put under some pressure in our final year, basically by a rogue secondary headteacher, he ran a very tight ship. They had also elected to have combined accreditation visits, with the same players, although perhaps the systems of the accreditation teams were a bit more in synch back then. As previously mentioned, the leader of that team was the CEO of BMIS; the international teaching circuit is a small world.

The school had just introduced IBO programmes and this put quite a burden on my shoulders as within my department I was the only one with any experience of this system for the 11-16-year olds. Notwithstanding this small difficulty, we sailed through the accreditation both as a school and a department. It did prove a little embarrassing that I, as a newcomer to the school, was having to answer questions that more longstanding teachers should have fielded.

The big difference was that in Bangladesh the school did not try too hard. Sure, it put pressure on teachers to come up with the required curriculum and systems, but it did not overdo that pressure and was prepared to turn round to the inspectors and say, "This is our plan..." rather than try to pretend that everything is perfect.

There was one particular incident that linked the schools in Malawi and Bangladesh with a delicious level of irony. During the

Bangladesh accreditation, there was a fire drill. It is expected that at some time during these visits the school would undertake a drill of some sort, be it for an earthquake, terrorist-related or whatever.

When the alarm did go off it indicated fire and all the required procedures sprang into action. Before we had arrived in the country ISD had a real fire, in which, sadly, three members of the maintenance staff had died, since then the school had been slick when it came to drills. However, they had introduced a new element to the procedure, this being that once the fire alarm sounded the school gates would be locked and no one would be allowed access, except the fire service, obviously.

My good mate was outside the gate smoking when the fire alarm sounded. It was not a great place to smoke because just outside the gate you were surrounded by the armed guards of some of the students, many toting disclosed revolvers and the fact that any visitor to the school, be they parents, students, other teachers or even more honoured guests, would observe errant teachers displaying their tobacco habits.

When the alarm sounded, he tried to enter and was barred by security. Knowing that there was an expectation that he should take a register of his tutor group on the school field within a few minutes of the alarm he determined on a course of action. This involved scaling a wall that was more than three metres in height and jumping down the other side. It is a great demonstration of a teacher's desire not to get in trouble that he both attempted and succeeded in this task, registering his class as expected.

However, there is a downside to the tale. In his descent from the top of the wall, my friend managed to land right in front of a shocked and somewhat disorientated member of the accreditation team. I have never found out if this incident made its way into their final reports but would hope it did not.

And how does this link to Malawi? It seems, that at the start of the 2013-14 school year, the CEO in Malawi had implemented a no smoking policy on the campus. This had been met with some resistance from a band of hardened smokers, largely because the campus was so big you had to walk a kilometre if you needed a fag off-site. On the CEOs return from his accreditation visit to Bangladesh, without fanfare the ban was overturned; this remained the case until 2019 when it was reapplied just before the BMIS accreditation visit. Quelle surprise!

International School of London Qatar (ISLQ), Doha, Qatar: 2012 & 2013

Towards the end of my time in Qatar, we also underwent an IBO accreditation visit although I hardly remember it. In my final year there, the school had some very competent management and they eased us through it without too much fuss.

The previous year I had been in the unusual situation of having to prepare syllabi for both Economics and Business & Management (Business), as Diploma (17-18-year-olds) subjects. This was an interesting proposition as I had taught neither subject at the Diploma level, although it did give me the exposure needed to move to my next school as an Economics teacher.

The whole thing was a bit mystifying at the time, wading through textbooks, almost as a student would and trying to establish not only what was to be taught, but also how, and then present it in an acceptable manner for the accreditors. In the end, the school chose only to offer Business, so my work on Economics was wasted as far as they were concerned, although it did make me realise, having studied Economics as a subsidiary at university, that I was more than capable of teaching Economics to this level.

As someone who spent the best part of twelve years in business before teaching and having experience of most areas of a company's operations, having additionally run a company and spent a period in self-employment, I have quite a practical background. All in all, I feel that I have the experience to advise the schools where I have worked on how they should best tackle the two subjects of Business and Economics. For the former it would be "do not" and for the latter "think hard", as fundamentally I believe both subjects are best left to universities.

Accepting that my view of the greater scheme has been ignored, most international schools seem to think it makes sense to offer one, or both, of Economics and Business. Quite clearly, Economics is better suited to developing countries and Business to developed countries. Still, it is tougher than that. A lot of parents, particularly those who run businesses, believe that the Business course is ideal for their kids; it is not. I believe that Business should only be taught at a university level and then only after the students have spent some time, preferably years, employed in an industry and definitely not in one run by their parents. From personal preference and for suitability for the students I would choose Economics as a school subject over Business every time.

At BMIS they dropped Economics in favour of Business due to parental pressure. It is an unwise and uninformed decision, particularly when the Economics course offers a better understanding of the relationship between government and the economy, something that is desperately needed in countries such as Malawi and Bangladesh. If our students were to try to apply many of the skills taught at school level Business in their parents' businesses in Malawi, they would soon find those businesses falling apart. It is a classic case of western, liberal teaching banging up against the on the ground realities of third world exploitation. Now…if they were to come up with a Business & Exploitation course…

I have found that experience in the business sector has proved hugely beneficial to my teaching. As indicated in chapter two, this is a view that is not necessarily shared by some life-long teachers. One of the most interesting discussions I had on the subject was with someone who had moved the other way, from teaching into the same industry in which I had worked: travel. As the CEO of a medium-sized outgoing tour operator, he was able to see the crossover benefits quite clearly.

Many of the crossover benefits are focused on skills. We live in a world where the ability to adapt and adopt new skills is paramount;

if you fail to do this in industry you will end up without a job. How does this apply to schools? Many parents and indeed their children, see school as a device for imparting knowledge to the students. What many teachers want to ensure is that the students are gaining transferable skills. This is a particular focus within the IBO's system. Unfortunately, there is something of a breakdown in continuity, as their programme for the last two years of secondary education is far more knowledge-based and is focussed on final examinations.

Having been in a position where I employed school leavers at sixteen and eighteen years of age, as well as college graduates, on entering teaching I felt that my knowledge of the requirements for people entering the workforce would be useful, but this was only ever spotted by one of my headteachers and even then was not acted upon. A particular example of this has been my longstanding knowledge and skills in using spreadsheets; something so basic, yet one that is transferrable across every organisation in the world. In most of my schools, I have tried to incorporate spreadsheet use into as many courses as possible, however, the interest from other teachers and teaching management has been lukewarm.

Westlands School, Sittingbourne, Kent, England: 1992 & 1996

OFSTED. An acronym that for many years struck fear into the hearts of any teacher in the UK. I went through four OFSTED inspections in ten years, which must be something of a record. Moving overseas to teach meant my last was in March 2000 at a special school in Lincolnshire. For many teachers, the acronym OFSTED was often followed by the words, OH SHIT!

My first experience, in 1992 in Kent at the Westlands School, was relatively benign in that it was one of the first OFSTED inspections (note the terminology here; inspection not accreditation) when this august monitoring organisation was first being set up. My teacher training was still running at this time, but I was inspected and passed well, although they probably did not have high expectations of me. By the second, in 1996, the organisation had got into its swing and it was during this period, for the next five or six years, that they became so feared.

Every class observed was marked and this mark reflected directly on the teacher. My scores were always "very good", never "good" or "excellent", the two categories on either side of the one I made my own. My good friend, who was the head of Modern Languages, was nearly always rated as "excellent", which she was, although I suspected that one of the reasons for this was that the inspectors did not speak French particularly well. I also had responsibility for the Geography department by 1996 and that also did extremely well in the eyes of the assessors. Some teachers and departments did not fare so well, however, the school itself, which had some exceedingly difficult circumstances, cleared most of the hurdles by some margin.

The Gleed School, Sittingbourne, Kent, England: 1998

In the move up to Lincolnshire, one of the reasons for my appointment was because of my experience with OFSTED; my new school, the Gleed Boy's School, was to face an inspection towards the end of the school year in which I joined them. It was clear from the start that the school would fail, it was a torturous eight months before they had to face their executioners, however, the school's management was completely incapable of managing the changes needed for the school to pass.

The verdict of OFSTED, "Inadequate!" An inadequate school has significant weaknesses and is failing to prepare its students effectively for the next stages of their lives. This category is the lowest in the range, above which are: outstanding, good and requires improvement. Inadequate is further divided into two categories, "Serious Weaknesses" and, right at the bottom, "Requiring Special Measures". The school managed to fall into the latter and in my assessment, OFSTED were correct in their judgement.

In many ways, it was a great shame. There were some exceptionally good, caring teachers, some putting in incredible efforts, in what was a boys' secondary modern school, basically, an institution established to cater for males who had failed the 11-plus exam. Just as in Kent, the grammar schools in the area always maintained their school roll, their numbers were constant and to achieve this they would lower the entrance bar to suit each year's cohort. In Spalding, there were two grammar schools in the town and two secondary modern schools, all single-sex.

It was the only single-sex school I ever worked in, other than odd days as a cover teacher. The only bright kids in the school were those that were deemed as too much trouble by the grammar schools and the odd boy who had accidentally fallen through the "intelligence" test that was the 11-plus examination system. A school with an almost total absence of bright kids is one thing, a school with a complete absence of females, in addition, was quite another; I never felt the urge to work in such an institution again.

I note that some ten years ago the school was renamed and merged with the girls' school, which was handily next-door, but the grammar school system persists in Lincolnshire and the grammar schools are still single-sex, bar their sixth forms.

Upon my arrival at the Gleed, I witnessed an incident that set the tone for the year ahead. A member of staff had a student by the neck and had him pinned up to a wall in the foyer, the lad's feet dangling some half a metre from the floor, whilst the teacher berated the boy. This took place in front of several members of staff and fifty or so students, although caused little consternation. Whilst corporal punishment had been banned in state schools in England since 1986, a form of physical discipline persisted at the Gleed. The good teachers coped by teaching well, thus avoiding the need for much in the way of punishment, but of course, some of the lads became institutionalised by the persistent physical threat from other teachers and became a handful for everyone. I struggled for a few months.

By the time the OFSTED team arrived some teachers were prepared. Once again, my teaching standards were classified as very good, my department was fine and I had achieved what had been asked of me.

Others prepared differently. On the first Monday of the inspection, one of the English rooms was strangely vacant. Boys milled at the locked door awaiting their classes. There was consternation all around when it was found that the teacher was not only missing so were the entire contents of his room. It seems the stress had got to him, even so, he had been careful to remove all evidence of students' work. I never saw him again, although some of my colleagues did and have no idea if he tried to remain in teaching. He certainly set the tone for the week.

It must have been the Gleed's first OFSTED and it certainly took place at the height of the organisation's power, but there was no doubting the validity of their verdict. The shame is, as I look at a photograph of the school's staff, there were so many good teachers. Good teachers who had been hung out to dry by their bosses.

There was more than one that went missing that week. The last time the Gleed's headteacher was spotted was on the final day of the inspection; they must have airlifted him out. Some months later I heard he was working as a manager of some sort of health clinic, although as far as I know he never returned to the school. To be fair to OFSTED, they could see exactly what the problems were, these commenced with Lincolnshire's education system, were worsened by appalling management and resulted in some significant issues at the teacher/student interface. Sure, some teachers were caught up in the fallout, but they were not held individually responsible. Although it

143

has to be said, I am not sure if the same would have applied to the missing English teacher.

The fallout was significant. Lincolnshire, to its credit, parachuted in one of their most able headteachers to temporarily run the school, which he did for a year. As we had passed the date for resignation, I agreed to stay on for another year, making it clear I would leave at the end of that second year. Two of the older teachers, one being the deputy-head, were made redundant and I am sure other dismissals perhaps came under another name. However, the two redundancies made for an interesting comparison.

The one guy, who taught History and Art and had a real Gatling gun in his classroom, was a few months over the age of fifty, the other was the deputy-head and he was a few months shy of the same figure. Both were made identically redundant, except that the History teacher was deemed to have taken forced early retirement and was given a massive payout plus an enhanced pension. The poor lad who had been deputy-head received nothing and ended up as a classroom teacher in Peterborough. I will not comment on their relative merits as teachers; however, it must have been galling for one of them when the other rolled up in his newly purchased Morgan sports car.

Kicking around at the Gleed for another year was quite interesting, as significant revisions were made, but I could not continue to work in an all-boys secondary modern school, it was dispiriting and it was time for a change of direction. After my leaving, for a few months, I picked up cover work, which again was an eye-opener, from the undisciplined scrums occurring in some classrooms, most of which were secondary modern schools, to some top-notch institutions, some of which were all ability, some grammar and others secondary modern schools. In the end, it was clear; the biggest determinant of the quality of teaching and learning came down to the management and had little to do with the kids. You could be a fantastic teacher, but if the school were run badly you did not stand a chance.

Priory Special School, Spalding, Lincolnshire, England: 2000

After a few exploratory months weighing up the options, I came across a job in a special school, situated almost next door to the Gleed. As it happened, they also had an OFSTED inspection coming up. The school was exceptionally well run. There were fewer than a hundred students and all of them had varying levels of quite severe special needs, ranging from fully autistic kids, through those with Downes syndrome and Aspergers, to pupils with high levels of emotional and behavioural disorders and those with physical disabilities.

Not only was it well run, but the teachers and support staff were superb and enormously caring. When the OFSTED report was published, in the introduction it said something like *"...the school makes an excellent job of preparing its students for adult life"*. It is, therefore, a little perturbing that they should also fail the inspection. Again, it was in the lowest category, inadequate, although in the higher tier, that of "serious weaknesses".

The whole thing requires some explanation. OFSTED inspectors were given a series of checks that had to be made.

Regardless of their understanding of the quality of the school, if the tick boxes were not checked the school would fail. The tick box that had been left unchecked was the quality of the written curriculum. Having been through three of these inspections in nine years, I had pointed out the problem to the headteacher before the inspection, however, he chose to try to bluff his way through; sadly, it did not work.

One of the conditions for a school falling into the category of serious weaknesses is that you have to have mini-inspections regularly, it turned out to be about once every two months. These were called HMIs, standing for Her Majesty's Inspectorate. To be honest, everyone was sympathetic to the plight of the school, including the original inspection teams and those that followed, except for one pair.

We were given a couple of days' notice that two women from Wales would be visiting the school the following Monday and Tuesday and would be observing every teacher. One of the staff determined that this would be a good couple of days to be absent. I have some sympathy, everyone was overwrought, everyone was tired, it probably seemed a good idea to her at the time.

The missing teacher had a two-hour session on a Tuesday afternoon with the Year 10s, a time when I was supposed to be taking PE in the local council's sports hall. The headteacher asked if he could parachute me in to take the lessons, an hour of Comparative Religion followed by an hour of Current Affairs; nothing had been prepared. At least he gave me a weekend's notice.

Any teacher will understand that with the type of kids we had and with them being fifteen years old, it being an afternoon session and the subjects involved, it was going to be a tall order for a cover teacher to not only keep the lid on things but also deliver a quality lesson whilst having the students demonstrate significant learning. It helped that there were three classroom assistants, in fact, four for the second hour and that the class had only fifteen kids in it, but I delivered a fantastic pair of linked lessons and had every student fully on task over the two hours. One of the inspectors popped in for fifteen minutes in the middle of the second lesson.

I was ecstatic. I had been set an onerous task and had come through it with enormous credit. The support staff all congratulated me at the end of the lesson as I was thanking them. I felt it was a shame that in the HMI inspections, individual teachers were not assessed, for I felt I would finally achieve that holy grail of "excellent".

What they did assess was the lesson...and it failed. I believe they observed twelve lessons in total, the nine that passed were taught by female teachers, the three that failed were taught by male teachers. There were only three male teachers in the school; we had all failed. Gobsmacked is the only word that adequately describes my condition. The Design teacher felt they had made a fair assessment in that proper safety with the tools had been impossible, although that still left two of us confused and desperate for an explanation, one which was eventually forwarded by the headteacher.

It seems the inspectors took exception to a coffee mug on my desk. The coffee had been brought to me, an hour into the lesson, by the fourth member of the support staff, who joined us for the last hour. I had not given the mug a thought and had consumed the coffee before the inspector arrived; the empty mug remained on the desk. Apparently, it was not the mug itself that was objected to, it was the design on the mug, which was the shape of the Playboy bunny head. It did not say "Playboy" and not one of the kids would have had a clue where the image originated, although clearly, the inspector did.

Neither before nor after the incident did I use that mug. I would not have chosen it myself, but it was innocuous enough. To this day I cannot believe that I would fail a lesson on this basis and even more so, I cannot believe that such a magnificent lesson could be failed at all. As you might imagine, there were a few choice expletives that followed those ladies on their path back to Wales.

I resigned from the school when the headteacher said he would not support my complaint about the assessment of the lesson. It was a fundamental turning point and brought to a head many issues that had been causing some anxiety. Most of the remainder of my career was spent overseas, commencing only ten weeks after this incident. It still pains me enormously.

I quote here from the website of a teachers' trade union[4], *"In light of the serious limitations of grading individual lessons, Ofsted discontinued the use of lesson grades in school inspections in 2014"*.

---

[4] NASUWT. '**Grading of Lesson Observations**'. 2020

Six: Planes, Trains & Automobiles

(Travel)

Now is the opportunity to discuss time off school. There are some benefits to being a teacher and much of this is tied up with the fact that our students need holidays. This means that teachers receive holiday entitlements that are far more than that of non-teachers. It is not my intention to explore the holidays themselves, this would take far too long and there are only so many times you are permitted to use the word idyllic. Instead, I have focussed on barriers to and difficulties in travelling, from minor incidents and accidents to a flat refusal at a border.

Malawi: October 2019

Friday 11th October saw both the last of the accreditation team disappear into the sunset and the school break up for the half-term holidays. It was already clear that our leadership were picking up on some criticisms levelled at them and, like most partially sentient beings, had started to lash out at anyone in reach, primarily the teachers. Many of us had worked our butts off and deserved a break, however, it was clear that this view was not shared by all the stakeholders. Still, enough is enough, Andrea and I headed off for four nights camping on the Nyika Plateau, an area so remote it is reputed to be one of the safest places in the world in the event of thermo-nuclear war.

The general perception of teachers is that we spend an enormous amount of time on holiday and that this is unfair to the remainder of the population. Although many of the remarks made are done so in a jocular manner, it is clear that some needle actually exists and this sometimes extends to one's friends. To counter the remarks, I determined to calculate the time spent working during my holidays.

The results were interesting and are based on averages. I have to throw this proviso in just in case one of my good friends recalls a particular vacation when the norm did not apply. For holidays of less than two weeks, I would spend half the time working, but should point out this would often include some of the weekends. During the longer holidays, in recent times these being at Xmas (4 weeks) and over June and July (6 weeks), I would spend between one and two weeks working. Without even including the fact that most teachers work for at least a few hours over each of their weekends, what it boiled down to is that according to my calculations, teachers received an average of twenty days more holiday a year than the "average" non-teacher.

It has to be accepted that some non-teachers work during their holidays and I did so myself when working in the travel industry, although it is unquestionable that on average teachers do more. It must also be said that these calculations do not hold good for countries outside the UK, where most of my envious friends and family reside. Holidays in the United States are incredibly confusing, Japan and South Korea are minimal and in Australia, the normal rules of the working week do not seem to apply when the sun is out and the surf is up, which it is most of the time.

It is somewhat pointless becoming defensive about our long holidays when in many countries a teacher's remuneration is so low that they cannot afford to leave their homes during the breaks. Having moved into teaching from the travel industry I had faced a double whammy, not only were those perks of free flights lost, but my pay was also more than halved: was this done for an extra twenty days sitting in the garden?

Entering the world of international teaching changed everything. Typically, your average Brit, teacher or not, will take a two-week vacation in the summer and if they have the spare change, a one-week trip during the winter. The better off take more time and visit more exotic locations, whilst the worse off take less time and travel shorter distances. However, whether it is Bali or Butlins, the Seychelles or Skegness, these holidays involve travelling there and back. The beauty of being an international teacher is that you are often already there to start with.

Having been based in East Africa, Eastern Asia, the Middle East, Southern Asia and Southern Africa, we have been given access to an enormous range of destinations at relatively low prices, especially when compared to going back and forth from the United Kingdom. It would take another book to recount all the holiday adventures of the last thirty years and we have been places and done things that I could never have imagined. For this volume we will focus on the actual travelling, much of it in cars, but also on trains, planes and buses, and including those barriers that can so often be thrown in the way.

Southern Africa: 2016-2020

One reason for our return to Africa was to continue the explorations we had during our time in Tanzania, specifically to indulge in safaris into Africa's bush. Whilst Malawi itself is not the best Southern or East African country to pursue this interest it is surrounded by Tanzania, Mozambique and Zambia, whilst close neighbours are Botswana and Zimbabwe and a little further afield are South African and Namibia. That all adds up to an awfully large number of lions, leopards, elephants, buffalo and even rhino to visit. Ultimately, we did not take full advantage of what was on offer. Due to family circumstances, we twice had to cancel trips to Namibia and Botswana and we ended up only visiting South Africa for a tennis trip.

Exploring Malawi from tip to toe was fulfilled. There is beautiful scenery and a great number of animals, although sighting the few large predators proved beyond us within the country. One disadvantage with Malawi is that it is a long, thin country and whilst there are marginal alternatives, moving from place to place often involves one road, namely the M1.

Quite what inspired the nomenclature I am unsure for in my home country the prefix "M" when applied to a road, denotes a motorway. Malawi's M1 is far from that. Malawi's M1 is a 1,100 kilometre stretch of surfaced road. For most of its length, there is a northbound lane and unsurprisingly a southbound lane. At times the width of these varies considerably due to the damage done to the edge of the tarmac caused by the hail and ride minibuses and to the potholes in the centre of the carriageways themselves made by the heavy goods vehicles.

A second and even more irritating obstacle on one's journey has been the police stops. One individual posted on social media that he had been stopped by the police thirty-four times between Lilongwe and Blantyre, a journey of only 300 kilometres. In four years, we were only stopped and fined on one occasion, but in total, we must have been halted by the police many hundreds of times. The sole reason for the vast majority of these stops was for the police to extort money from the driver, a practice that is surprisingly common in Southern and Eastern Africa. On a recent trip to the far south, we were shocked to be stopped only once on a return journey totalling some 800 kilometres. That sole stop was simply so the policeman could request food from us, he made no pretence to check the vehicle, papers or driving licence.

"Hello, how are you, Ma'am?"

"I'm very well officer, thank you, how are you?" Andrea, the driver, replied.

"I am good, very good. And sir, how are you today?"

"I am good officer. Thank you."

"So, today, you know it is Eid this weekend?"

"Yes." Replied my wife, although neither of us had a clue, having had four days isolation in Majete Wildlife Reserve.

"Well, I need some food."

"Mmm, OK, hang on." I reached into the back of the car and rummaged in a bag containing a few snacks and pulled out a bag of plain crisps. "Here you are!" I said reaching over my wife towards the open window.

The policeman looked at the crisps with some disdain.

"No, you can go to the shop." He said, pointing in the direction of the local market.

"What's wrong with these," I asked, "Do you not want them?"

"Ahh. They are already food." He answered, which perplexed us both. "You can buy food in the shop."

It was starting to sink in that he wanted us to buy him the raw materials, probably including a chicken so that he could prepare the meal for Eid al-Adha. After proffering the bag of crisps one more time, he began to give up and we drove off.

The journey time wasted only amounted to five minutes, although if we had followed his desires it could have been an hour as he haggled in the market and the prices inflated with the presence of white faces. The alternative was to give him money, which is something we strongly object to when it comes to both government officials, including the police, and to children, with whom we are happy to hand over fruit, pencils and so forth.

As soon as a financial transaction of this type occurs it constitutes a bribe and if anything needs to be stamped out in Africa it is bribery. Removing corruption from the African system is a monumental task, although one that is probably more important than alleviating hunger, improving healthcare or funding education because all these three hugely important issues could be improved by taking corruption out of the equation.

One of the more irritating situations, because you have not got a leg to stand on, is when the police fine you for an actual offence. I was stopped for driving on a foreign driving licence. We had known we should have acquired Malawian driving licences after three months in the country, but it had slipped off our to-do list. The officer, a tall, unsmiling individual, bent double and leaned into the car putting his face into my own. It is at this point that you realise that you are not going to be fined by the police; you are going to be scammed by a lone policeman.

Not only did he take me for having an invalid licence, but he also claimed the insurance was then invalid, which pushed the bribe up to 25,000 kwacha (about £25 or US$30). There was no way out of this one.

Some eighteen years before we had been stopped by a Malawian policeman and asked for a receipt. He told me to go down to the local police station and pay there. After waiting an hour behind a man reporting the theft of a chicken, I went through the laborious paperwork. Back then the result was that our entire trip was delayed by twenty-four hours and on this more recent occasion that was simply not an option; I paid the bribe. There is a huge downside. Without a receipt, if you are stopped again you will go through the same process. I am not sure if it defines itself as a Catch-22 situation or a Hobson's choice, however, the police know exactly what they are doing. I am only glad that I was not the man stopped thirty-four times.

Until my age was just south of sixty years, I had never been fined for speeding nor been caught by one of the dreaded speed cameras that infested Britain for much of the Nineties and Noughties. That all came to an end in June and July of 2017.

My mother-in-law, Sandy, had dropped in for a visit and we took her down to Victoria Falls and South Luangwa National Park in Zambia. The holiday was rather good, although was marred by being stopped twice on the return journey by Zambian police with speed guns. Andrea and Sandy are from California and unbeknownst to us, there had been a series of legal cases in that US state resulting in the police having to hand in many of their speed guns. What would make the world a much safer place is if the US police were forced to hand in their real guns, however, it is not the time to drift into a fantasy works right now.

The result was that California, in their glorious and profound wisdom, had determined that the surplus speed guns could be donated to countries in Africa. For those of you who know African roads speeding is a problem, although usually because the traffic is too slow. Trucks can barely make the gradient on hills, overloaded vehicles emit clouds of diesel exhaust as they try to pull off and wandering goats make exceptionally high speeds extremely risky.

Whilst speed guns are not really what Zambia needed, they did use them. Accelerating to 115 kph approaching a hill, it was then that the copper clocked my speed. In Zambia they were much more formal than in Malawi, there were immediate receipts and it is possible that the fines did not go into the pockets of the individual policemen. I queried being stopped, however, as there were no speed signs and we believed the limit was 120 kph. The officer went to great lengths to show me that the maximum speed limit in Zambia was 100 kph, even dragging out a photocopy of some statute. The reason for my confusion is that we had earlier travelled from the Malawian border to Lusaka, the Zambian capital, where a limit of 120 kph had been posted every few miles. When this was pointed out to the officer, he simply did not believe me.

Confusion still reigned when I entered Lusaka a few hours later. They have a weird traffic control system and as you approach a whole sequence of roundabouts, each posts a limit of 60kph, followed by 40, followed by 20, at intervals of about 30 metres. With heavy traffic, it was impossible to see each speed sign and I was caught a second time in the day. Another Californian radar gun!

We returned to Malawi and, once Sandy was headed back to the Golden State, Andrea and I drove off to see the chimpanzees on Lake Tanganyika, a return trip of some 2,500 kilometres.

Crossing the border from Malawi into Tanzania at the Songwe border has to be one of the most painful experiences of almost any African crossing between nations, although Zimbabwe into Zambia at Chirundu pushes it close. At the latter, we were held up by every single agency. First, it was Interpol insisting we could not leave Zimbabwe as we did not have our copy of the car ownership document certified by a solicitor. Then it was passport control stamping our passports with transit visas when we already had a tourist visa. Finally, it was customs who claimed we could not bring the car into Zimbabwe because we had a transit visa rather than a tourist visa, which of course we had previously had. All these hold-ups cost us nothing but time, some four hours by my reckoning, caused entirely by the deliberate mistakes of the staff in a practically empty border post. Songwe was a different ball game.

At many land borders in Africa, nearly everyone at the post intends to persuade you to hire the services of a facilitator. There are always many shifty types offering to help you through the border for a fee. The fact that they do make things easier keeps them in business although their activities are entirely illegal. There is another catch to all this though, the facilitator pays backhanders to the police, immigration officials and customs, if they did not, they would not be allowed in the buildings. To ensure you progress at what could be termed a normal speed, everyone in the system has to be paid off.

Arriving at Songwe we managed to shake off the touts and entered Malawian immigration control, which to my mind should be called emigration control, as we were after all leaving the country. The only issue here is if your visa has run out and if it has, they will issue you with a large fine. I say only issue, but that is not quite true. Many Tanzanian police and border control personnel like to waste your time by berating you for not speaking Chichewa if you have lived in the country for more than six months, which has a certain irony because one of the official languages of the country is English.

However, that was the easiest bit and took no more than ten minutes. Next came the car. A few days before leaving the country with a vehicle you have to log your intended travels with Interpol and receive a letter, for a fee, which says you are the legitimate owner and you are not permanently exporting the vehicle. For us, this takes place in a very dusty, file filled room in the Malawian Police headquarters. On one occasion when I visited the room had caught fire, which delayed things somewhat, although usually, they are quite efficient at taking your money. The staff there are supposed to check to see if the car is stolen and if you have paid the necessary taxes, still, I am not sure this is anything but an extortion exercise. You would think that having crossed this hurdle it would be unnecessary to do anything at the border, you should be able to drive straight through. Well, you would be completely wrong.

At Songwe I was led into the Interpol office and shown to a chair. Next to me, writhing on the floor, in considerable discomfort, was a dishevelled and bleeding man in handcuffs. I was told to ignore him. This proved difficult because as soon as he realised there was a mzungu in the room he redirected his pleading towards me, which is somewhat ironic because I felt as much a prisoner as he appeared to be. (Mzungu has come to mean any white person, although in actual translation it means a man who wanders aimlessly.)

Many Malawians in authority enjoy making people wait. In many African states, time is not regarded as important as in western countries, an idea that permeates most of society. Having to wait for six hours to see a doctor is a fairly normal state of affairs for an African in Malawi. However, those officials with regular contact with mzungus have a good handle on the cultural differences and particularly at something like a border post, will use this knowledge to increase the wait, increase the irritation and, hopefully, the mzungu will be more inclined to provide a backhander.

It was an hour before Interpol finally approved my passing the border, but they had managed to come up with a fee, for what, I now have no idea, although it was certainly not a statutory requirement. As I would not pay them directly in cash, I was given a chit and told to visit the bank counter to pay.

The counter was little more than a window, in the corner of a room, with booths for car hire and an office entrance on either side. Simple. However, it was not. It was far from simple. Around sixty people were pressed into a solid mass, all attempting to reach the cashier to make their payments. The vast majority were lorry drivers. If there had been an orderly queue it may have taken two hours to clear, but this was no queue and there was no access; the cashier's barred window was blocked further by a phalanx of touts. The only way to pay and escape from Songwe was to pay off the touts so they could take care of the trumped-up charges for my car. Everyone in the

Songwe border control offices is entirely aware of the illegality of all that goes down there, the only conclusion that can be reached is that every single one of them is on the take.

As chance would have it, a huge Tanzanian truck driver had managed to push to the front and past the touts. He blocked the window far more effectively than they had. Unexpectedly he turned to me, some four metres back and indicated I should pass my cash and chits through a series of hands into his, an act which I undertook with some trepidation. Entirely out of the kindness of his heart this guy saved me from quite a horrible and crushing wait. When he came out of the ruck, he passed over my receipt, my exit pass if you like, with a huge smile and waved away my offer of a tip. It seems he was as pleased as I was to see the rigged system beaten.

We were three hours into the wait now, but at least we were crossing the border, little did we know that there would be another two hours eaten up on the other side. The Tanzanian officials were decided under-employed, probably because all their potential customers were held up on the Malawian side. If I remember rightly there were two fees, one for our visas and the other for a road traffic charge; the former went off without a hitch. As we had lived in Tanzania for two years, we knew that the Tanzanians were as bad as the Malawians, there was no way it could be this simple.

The road fee was a small amount, maybe twenty US dollars. We had an ample supply of US currency, Tanzanian shillings, Malawian kwacha and both Malawian and international credit cards. We could pay and started with cash.

"No, no, no. We cannot take cash."

"Why not?"

"Well, our cashier is at lunch and only he can handle cash. We have to be careful not to be accused of corruption." The guy beamed.

"OK. Well, how about a credit card then?"

"Yes. That will do very well. Come with me to the card readers."

I followed the man to an inner room, in which were four card readers on a single desk.

"Try this one?" He suggested. I did and there was no connection, in fact, no life from it at all.

"Why don't we use the card reader in Immigration, that worked perfectly?"

"No, no, no. That is for the use of Immigration only, they have a special signal."

"How about this one?" He suggested, his smile broadening as it again failed to light up. It was at this point I noticed that all but one was unplugged.

"Should we try plugging them in? I think that Immigration had theirs plugged in?"

"No, no, no. That is for the maintenance guys not for me or you. Try this one?" He passed me a card reader that was very much alive and having punched in whatever code vendors enter into those things together with the amount, we waited. It seemed like we were making progress.

Transaction - failed! In Africa, it seems there is only one response to this message.

"Failed! You have no money in your account."

"No, I have money on my bank cards and credit on my credit cards, there is no problem with my card, the problem is your machine." This is always regarded as an insult, even though, time and time again, it proves to be correct. I further examined the card reader. "Look, this is an Azania Bank machine, it even says on the bottom, 'Azania Banks Cards only'; it's not going to work." For some reason, he left the room for a few minutes and I plugged in one of the other card readers, which was working perfectly. When he returned, I asked, "Why can't we use this machine?" He glared at me.

"No, no, no. This machine has to be maintained by maintenance. Come back to the front office."

I followed him to the counter, where Andrea was waiting patiently. Well, I say patiently, although resignedly is probably the better term. We had now clocked up four hours at the border, even though all our paperwork was in order.

"How do we solve this problem?" I asked, more in hope than in any expectation there might be a solution.

"Well...you could wait until the cashier comes back." There was a long pause. "But he takes very long lunches. Or...I have a friend!" It was not clear whether I was expected to congratulate him as, by this stage, I felt it a remote prospect that anyone might befriend this little toad.

"My friend has an Azania bank card."

"Yes?"

"Well, for a fee...he might be prepared to pay your road fee and then you can pay him in US dollars!"

So, we finally got to the point. It was more elaborate than on the Malawian side, mainly because the Tanzanian government had tried to put steps in place to prevent corruption at the border, even so, the staff had found a way around it. They had engineered it to leave only one option open, that of paying with a bank card that a non-Tanzanian could not possess, leaving the only route of payment being through a tout.

Pissed off. You bet. Paid the tout. You bet. Five hours was enough.

A couple of hours up the road dusk was setting in. We were pulled over by a motorbike cop for exceedingly the speed limit. This time it was due to there being no signage and my belief that we were in a non-urban area, something which seemed blatantly obvious as there was not a building in sight. Not so apparently.

We did not argue and had a nice chat with the officer while we paid over the fine. Interestingly he told me there was no top speed limit in Tanzania unless a maximum speed was posted, something we had never known. This should have led me into a discussion about the complete lack of speed signs in the previous ten kilometres, however, I held back. He also gave us detailed directions as to how to get to our planned accommodation. The fact that we never managed to find it left me in doubt about the rest of the information he had so graciously provided.

The following day having put another 100 kilometres under our belts, we were pulled up again and once again it was for speeding. This time I was not. Definitely not. We were more than 10 kph under the 50kph limit. I argued.

This scam was wonderful. As we pulled up, the officer in charge handed his phone to one of the other officers as I continued to argue. After a few minutes, the phone was returned to him and he showed me a photo of my car with a caption plastered over the top showing 56kph. In true Victor Meldrew style, I could not believe it. I had been photoshopped.

At this point, I tried to dispute the methodology, it was so blatantly rigged. When he agreed that I had the right to protest I was somewhat surprised until he added that my complaint would need to be lodged at a police station located some one hundred kilometres to the south. It would have been necessary to backtrack two hours of our journey. No thanks. We paid the "fine".

In the space of three and a bit weeks, I had clocked up four speeding fines, never having had one before and not having had one since.

The chimpanzees were wonderful, as is Africa!

East Africa: 2001-2003

The earliest experience of transport in my first job overseas had been the journey from the airport to the school, along a fairly good road, although one that had been peppered with vertiginous speed bumps. A few weeks later I made the trip in the opposite direction going much further, this time to the nearby town of Arusha, a journey of only 80 kilometres, although one that came with some new and interesting elements. It was a local bus with maybe fifteen seats, each quite small, with little access room.

At a guess, there were over thirty passengers, but by the time they were on board, it was impossible to count. The majority were female. I was one of only two or three males on board and was certainly the only mzungu. It was also clear that the majority of the passengers were not destitute, in fact, they appeared to be relatively well off, an observation that was supported by their size. Whilst malnutrition and low body weight is a major problem in Africa, so is obesity. It appeared that my journey was to be closely accompanied by some of the heaviest ladies of the continent.

To begin with, it was not too bad. Squeezed between a woman with chickens and another with baskets of fruit is some people's idea of fun and as the journey progressed lateral pressure forced me to slip down the seat. With my left buttock lodged on the lap of the lady to the left, my face gradually slid into the cleavage of the one on the right. It was not that I did not feel I should adjust my position, it was simply that it was impossible, not a single piece of my body was controlled by my synapses, every movement was now controlled by the society I had temporarily joined. All the other passengers considered it normal. The lady whose breasts were being forced apart by my nose was engaged in a regular conversation with the one whose lap supported my buttock. The journey lasted nearly two hours, although my close neighbours certainly made the speed bumps a little more interesting.

There is only one further bus journey in Tanzania that springs to mind, that being on a luxury coach from Moshi to Dar-es-Salaam. It was considerably more comfortable than my first experience, for a start we had our own seats and to further satisfy the luxury label the bus had video facilities. The benefit of having a video playing throughout a journey is obvious, it can distract from those boring stretches, and although perhaps not as much as a pair of brown breasts, it does provide an alternative stimulus. It has to be said that watching repeated showings of the movie Annie at full volume, whilst cruising through the African countryside does not distract, it annoys. Enormously. Thankfully, the video player had broken for the return journey. It was not me. Honest!

Buying a little Suzuki four-by-four kept me off the busses after that. It was mentioned earlier that I had not received a speeding fine until 2017, however, we had been stopped before for speeding and, once again, that had been in Tanzania.

We had been returning from a two-week trip around Malawi, which was one of the reasons some fourteen years later that we chose to relocate there. It had been our first time at the Songwe border crossing, which was almost as bad in 2002 as it was fifteen years later and proved fraught travelling from Malawi into Tanzania. However, the issues had been somewhat different on this occasion. It turned out that when we had left Tanzania, some twelve days before, we had failed to fill out the required paperwork for the car. This was to cause more than a little confusion amongst the officials when we returned.

It was a perplexing hour with the police. Outside, Andrea remained in the vehicle, ensuring its contents from theft, whilst being besieged by a group of forty or fifty currency touts. It has to be pointed out that this again is an illegal activity and took place in full view of the police post where I was arguing the case for returning my car into the country. For once, the police were in a jovial mood and whilst they did not seem in any hurry to speed up the process, they had not reached that flaring of the nostrils stage that indicates they might just be about to become more draconian. I had a flash of inspiration that was only beaten in its brilliance by Andrea's quick thinking a day or two later.

"Look. The car is in Tanzania. Yes?" They nodded.

"And there is no paperwork to say it ever left Tanzania, correct?" They mumbled their agreement.

"So, how about we say that the car has stayed where it is for two weeks and we toured Malawi on foot?"

Smiles turned into grins and grins into belly laughs. It seems the idea that a vehicle would have remained in one piece after sitting in one place for twelve days was ludicrous, notwithstanding the fact it was parked outside a 24-hour police post. They roared. Apparently, this was such a stupid idea that they loved it, forgetting completely about the prospects of an earner from the mzungu, they sent me on my way. It is probably one of those stories that they will still be telling their grandchildren years from now.

Moving away from the border, although well before we met up with the speed police, we dropped into a little town where we had stayed the night before we left Malawi a fortnight previously. Our stop was at a brothel. It should be pointed out that we do not make a point of deliberately staying at brothels and this had been the first such occasion, although there have been a few since then. Quite simply, a lot of cheap hotels in developing countries perform more than one role; their owners would almost certainly prefer to call them hotels and we were not wealthy enough to take the next step up the accommodation ladder on our early travels.

We tend to travel with a backgammon set, a game of Scrabble and some cards. The night before we left Malawi, we had played Scrabble and had inadvertently left the backgammon set behind. The backgammon box was also the perfect size to house our spare cylinder head gasket.

We did not expect that our belongings would still be there, still, it was worth a try. Not only were they there, but as soon as we walked in the barman bent down and brought them up onto the bar with a huge smile on his face. We stayed and chatted for a while before leaving him with a huge tip. Africa! It is more than wonderful!

Finally, after a fairly unbroken run, we were stopped by two policemen just north of Lugoba. Astonishingly, they not only had a speed gun, but they also had a brand new, fast motorbike. Once again, I was exceeding an urban speed limit in what appeared to be a rural area and certainly, there had been no limit indicated by road signs. It has to be said that the authorities in countries throughout Africa do erect signs advising motorists of the speed limits, however, the fact is the signs are nearly all stolen, mostly to be fashioned into cooking pots.

On balance it was a fair decision to stop us and the officers were very particular in explaining both the workings of the speed gun and the display, which indicated 56kph. It then came down to the fine. We cannot remember what it amounted to, although do know we could not afford to pay it. We were 500 kilometres from home, needed another tank of petrol and a single overnight stop, which we intended to take in a tent and we had no spare cash. In Tanzania in 2002 cash was king. Between us and home, there was no opportunity to visit an ATM and nobody took credit cards, the cash in our pockets was all we had.

With the police officers trying to persuade me to come up with the money, Andrea reached into the glove compartment and pulled out a bill we paid for the fitting of a new clutch cable; we knew we had been ripped off at the time. She handed it to the policemen.

"This is the reason we have no money. Look at this!"

The coppers unfolded the bill and examined it intently. Within moments their minds were changed. To them, it was clear that we had been so comprehensively ripped off by one of their fellow countrymen that they could not possibly add insult to injury. Once again, we were waved off, leaving state officials smiling and laughing in our wake. Africa! It is incredibly wonderful!

There were other marvellous moments with that little car. Expecting to drive it onto the Lake Victoria ferry was one. I had to say my heart was in my mouth when they used a large crane to lift it and drop it into the hold; it surprised me more when they then covered the car in mattresses. Perhaps that is why, that some forty years since that vehicle was built, it is still going strong, owned by an old Tanzanian mate of mine.

The first time we crossed a land border in Africa we had my friend with us. We had been heading off to Nairobi, where he was playing in an international rugby match for Tanzania against Kenya. On that occasion, the border crossing proved to be a pretty simple affair, with one exception. He had been told that if he listed his real job, which was as a member of the support staff at the school, he would face interminable questioning from immigration. It seems the only way around it was to list his profession as a peasant. We spent the journey taking the piss out of him, especially when we found that on his passport the officials had spelled it peeasant. As I will need to put a profession on my new passport in a year or two, I would quite like to try this one. My sisters have always claimed I was a bit of a peasant and it does sound a bit more exotic than retired.

China: 2004-2010

China's transport network is now phenomenal. We were there when the country was really starting to put things together. During our time there I beat my own land speed record, riding on the maglev to and from Shanghai Airport and hitting a speed of some 431 kph, which is quite fast! Back then the train hurtled you right into the centre of the airport in magnificent efficiency, the problem was at the other end. I am not sure how this came about, but there are only two terminals, the airport and Longyang Road Station, which, to all intents and purposes, is in the middle of nowhere. Still, it is fast, so who cares where it goes.

During the six years in China, we did not drive or own a car. It was unnecessary. In both Suzhou and Guangzhou, the cities we lived in, public transport was dirt cheap and a taxi ride cost less than a bottle of beer, which itself was less than a dollar. Travelling by bus, train or plane across the country was also extremely cheap and comfortable, as long as you avoided Chinese New Year.

Booking flights could be an interesting experience. For a trip to Yunnan we had booked a midday flight, however, we were advised two days before departure that it had been moved to seven in the morning, which was inconvenient, to say the least. I asked if there was anything else available and, being told there was a midday flight, requested that our booking was changed. For this, we were given a 60% refund, which paid for nearly all the extras on our holiday. Quite astonishingly, the flight we ended up on was the one we had originally booked; we never really understood what had occurred but accepted our situation with delight.

In the school year 2009-2010, I took a sabbatical to work on a novel, but also made some cash writing articles for local English medium magazines. Surprisingly, there was nothing in the way of censorship, although as a foreign national I did feel the need to take a little care not to criticise the central government. The articles were quite successful and the editor was always asking for more, sometimes suggesting the content, at other times accepting whatever took my fancy. That was until he received an article of mine entitled, "Death on Two Legs".

The piece took a view on Suzhou's traffic from the perspective of a pedestrian, including sections such as, *"It must be remembered that over 30% of Chinese drivers have held a license for less than three years. This group is responsible for over 70% of road accident deaths. Official figures put the number of road deaths in China at over 200 a day (2008) although external agencies believe the figure could be twice that!"*

I also offered advice, *"There are standard pedestrian crossings at every junction displaying the normal green man / red man system. A green man displayed does not mean you are safe to cross. Traffic turning left or right has no indication that your light is green and will expect and take right of way or simply drive into you. There are three possible solutions to this: The first, the Chinese way, is to cross without looking anyway; this has an advantage in that you'll not know what's about to hit you. The second is to cross with your head swivelling in all directions, particularly on the lookout for turning traffic. The third, my preferred solution, is to cross on red only, just slightly further from the junction! This apparently extreme method has the advantage that you know exactly what's going on, there are no surprises and traffic is only going in two directions."*

It has to be confessed that I had become a little bored writing advice articles about how one should live in China and this topic had seemed to spice it up a little. My editor disagreed. It is possible he took it as a condemnation of Chinese driving and drivers as a whole, but more likely that he had just passed the driving test himself and regarded it as a direct, personal slur. I did not work for the magazine again.

My replacement (who I actually believe was my editor) wrote a few interesting pieces. One was headlined as "A Characteristic Restaurant" and he wrote, *"There is no fault to find with either the dining environment and the sincere and friendly service, or the incessantly renewed delicacies. If you want to have a try of the most fashionable new way of having Hamburger, you might order a "Mexican chicken meat roll", by selecting a soft and palatable Mexican pancake, fresh and dainty chicken-leg meat and lettuce, and mating them with delicious shasha paste and black-pepper mayonnaise, you'll feel a unique flavour, fresh and tasty. There is also "strongly puffed chicken meat", packed in portable small cardboard box, which is crisp, fragrant and a little chilli to eat, with strong puffing taste lingering in one's mouth."*

Indeed! It was a review of the KFC in Suzhou.

It was September 2007, and on a whim, we determined to fly up to Tianjin to watch England face the United States of America in the quarterfinals of the Women's World Cup. Internal flights in China are extremely reliable and with the fastest baggage handlers in the world, they prove to be much quicker than in many countries. There was however a problem and the problem was that our trip had been booked by an idiot, that idiot being me.

Instead of checking things out properly, I had assumed that the game was to be played in the TEDA stadium, when in fact it was to be played in the Tianjin Olympic Centre Stadium, some 40 kilometres to the West. I also assumed that we would be able to pick up tickets easily, which proved to be true, but it did not quite pan out as we had expected. The result of all this is that we were staying in a hotel in TEDA and needed both match tickets and a ride right across a city that is bigger than London.

TEDA is Tianjin's port area, made infamous in August 2015 by an enormous explosion, first of nitrocellulose and then of ammonium nitrate, which killed some 180 people and injured another 800. As I write these words, Beirut is still clearing up the debris from the port explosion there, almost exactly five years on from that in China. It is horrifying to think that the ammonium nitrate in Beirut was already in their port warehouses when the explosion in Tianjin occurred.

We eventually arranged for someone to drive us over and provide tickets, however, there was a delay; thirty minutes before kick-off we still had not left. When our driver arrived clutching the tickets, we indicated the need for speed and he complied, to the letter. Never in my wildest dreams had I thought we could be driven so fast through a major city. There were elements of a rollercoaster as we rose and descended on Tianjin's many flyovers, but it was more akin to a slalom as the driver weaved between cars moving a third of his speed. At times we were touching 150kph. With only one exception, which is outlined below, this is the closest I have ever felt to death. When he dropped us at the stadium it was already ten minutes into the match and hundreds of touts were waiting outside, selling tickets at a fraction of the price ours had cost.

However, there was a football match to watch. As we tried to run up the stairs, Andrea told me she desperately needed a pee, which is hardly surprising after our journey through town. I waited. When she came out, she said she had asked an American lady in the loo what the score was. The answer had been, "I'm not sure, it's all so complicated." It turned out it was still nil-nil.

In the end, it was hugely disappointing that England lost 3-0. Even if most of the Americans in attendance did not understand the scoring system, they did understand that they had won.

Interestingly, when I was checking the facts about this match, the attendance is listed as 29,586. The stadium's capacity is 60,000, which means it should have been half full. I know what 30,000 people look like and there were nowhere near that many, if there had been 5,000, I would have been surprised. It has to be suspected that the Chinese were massaging the numbers and had given away that many tickets, although the majority were certainly not used. And the reason for wanting good numbers? The following year China was due to host the Olympics; everything had to look good, including the attendance figures.

Bizarrely, we completely missed out on the Olympic Games, as we were starting at a new school in Guangzhou. The pressures of a new job and the additional distance to Beijing made it difficult. We did have an entire day when the roads were blocked for the Olympic torch to come through, although the streets were so packed, we could not even see the runners.

Living in China made South-east Asia imminently accessible and we travelled around Thailand, Vietnam, Cambodia, Malaysia, Indonesia, the Philippines and, to the extent that you can tour around them, Singapore, Hong Kong and Macau. We also made a long trip to Australia, New Zealand and Fiji. These visits also had to be wrapped around trips home to see friends and family; it is ideal if they can come to you, however as parents age this becomes more difficult and how many people want to spend their vacation in a country like Bangladesh for example?

If there is one argument against working overseas it is missing your friends and family. There are some close friends in England and Wales who I miss enormously and family across the United Kingdom and the west coast of the United States, who we see far less often than we would like. There is a converse, in that I have possibly seen my family in New Zealand a little more than would otherwise have been the case, but only marginally. Most of the bonds do not weaken, in fact, if anything, they have become stronger, although those that were more marginal can break and some relationships seem to fall by the wayside. As I interrupted my discussion of near-death experiences, it could also be pointed out that you are almost certainly not going to be around when close friends or family kick the bucket, this was the case with my mother, my youngest sister and a very good mate. I missed them before they died and miss them more now.

It was in Fiji that I found myself strapped in next to the pilot in a four-seater Cessna seaplane. It was a first for me and had proved a thoroughly enjoyable flight. We were flying over Nanuya Levu Island, the home to the film, the Blue Lagoon, which brought Brooke Shields to international attention at the age of fifteen, as well as earning her the award of the first-ever Golden Raspberry. I suspect the pilot had been telling me this when I spotted the fuel gauge.

Empty. Even the little red light was on. Empty. Pointing at the gauge I stuttered at the Australian pilot. "Em..em..pty!"

"Yeah," he drawled, "I need to fill her up soon."

We landed safely and determined our return journey would be by boat.

If the list of countries above ended with Fiji, it started with Thailand, the country that provided me with the biggest scares of my life. The first was scuba diving when I proved to myself that it was an activity incompatible with my understanding of life. It was our honeymoon and I had promised to try and share my spouse's love for all things underwater. I am a strong swimmer, although had always avoided scuba with excuses about my ears. As it turned out, it was not my ears that were the problem; it was my brain.

Some twenty metres down and I was cruising, starting to become comfortable with the breathing apparatus when I determined to roll over and lookup. To this day I am still unsure how it was possible to control the panic. My urgent hand signals to the instructor may not have conformed to the signing protocols that are used by these sub-marine specialists, although my meaning was clear enough, "Get me out of here!"

With a five-metre safety stop, which seemed to last an eternity, I was finally at the surface. Air. Comfort. Safety. Never again. To this day, I have no idea what the fear is. Thalassophobia or aquaphobia do not seem to be the problem, although bathophobia may be a candidate. I reckon it is far more likely that it is a type of claustrophobia, for which one of the key symptoms is a fear of suffocation, but possibly, just possibly, it is a type of acrophobia, something similar to that suffered by the student on Tioman Island. Whatever it is, it is one of only two things I have in common with Jennifer Aniston, the other being that I do not wear a bra that often.

To clear these irrational fears out of my mind, it had become important to go back to one of my more favourite pastimes, which is going up mountains. I love walking up them, although in the heat of Thailand, Andrea's suggestion of a less energetic method of ascent was probably a good idea. In a relatively flat field, somewhere to the North-west of Chang Mai, mastering a quad bike, or ATV as some are called, was enormous fun. Having grasped all the basics, we set off in a group of seven, which included two guides, up the local mountain.

We are unsure what caused us to pause, perhaps the view, for we were on a narrow contour track, which ran close to the top of a cliff. When we were called to start off again, I cranked the throttle and found the ATV was stuck. A bit more needed perhaps? Unbeknownst to me, the left-hand front wheel had dug itself under a tree root although the other three tyres still had maximum grip. You have probably never thought about the forces on a vehicle when the rider puts it into this position, basically, as the revs build and the engine kicks out quite massive torque, the entire bike spins around the trapped wheel until it is freed. The recalcitrant tyre bit and achieved forward traction just as the machine was pointing directly down the cliff.

I am sure that an airborne ATV can be enormous fun, but it is not when you are underneath, the ATV is on top and below is a vertiginous drop into a Thai forest. Every millisecond of the scenario is seared into my neurons. It has to be suspected that the knock I took to the head stamped it there permanently. Instinct kicked in and I told myself to wait before throwing myself clear, if not, the ATV would have landed directly on top of me. On hitting the ground, which as it turned out was more like a forty-five-degree slope rather than a vertical cliff, I could hear my Father's words coming back to me from the 1970s, on the occasion my sister had made a bad fall, "Spread your arms out, you might break your arms, but it could save your life." It did not break my arms, although it probably saved my life. The ATV plunged seventy metres and smacked into the trunk of a tree. I fell less than twenty metres and suffered only bumps, scratches, bruises and, oh yeah, this irrational fear of the combination of vehicles and heights!

Sylhet, Bangladesh: 2015

We did not manage to spend much time touring in Bangladesh, which is a great shame, because the people were overwhelmingly lovely. We did fly up to Sylhet, which proved a pleasant change from Dhaka, mostly visiting farms and small villages, there is little of the country that is not under concrete or the plough. However, we did make a trip to Khadimnagar National Park, which was just large enough to include a circular walk, albeit one that would only occupy a couple of hours.

As a geographer, I am a map man, I love all good maps. Unfortunately, to have taken the map with us would have involved uprooting a large wooden sign, which we did not believe was either practical or legal. Back then, neither of us had a smartphone. We followed the circular walk with the memory of the map residing in our heads, that is until we reached point nine. As point ten was the end of the loop we knew we were close but unfortunately at this point, the evidence of any suitable track disappeared. There were in fact four paths, we were at a crossroads, but none, other than the one we had come along, demonstrated any sign of recent use; they all petered out after a few tens of metres. Not to be outdone by this circumstance I checked them all out, being snarled at by what seemed to be a monkey in the process and chose the route that seemed most likely but should also bring us back on ourselves if it proved to be incorrect.

It should be pointed out that Andrea is very trusting when it comes to my sense of direction, sometimes far more than she should be. On this occasion, it seems I had dropped the ball and we ended up traversing ridge after valley after ridge, with no sign of a path at all. After an hour of blundering around, we finally decided to follow a stream downhill, on the basis that it should join the river we had followed on our entry to the park. At that point, our taxi driver called wondering where we might be, which proved a difficult question to answer.

Finally, we had made the right choice and made it back to the signpost with the map. It turned out that we had been less than thirty metres from the exit point, which left me with even more egg on my face. Notwithstanding this episode, I still maintain that my sense of direction is better than Andrea's. However, she has taught me a huge lesson as regards getting lost, a methodology that is common amongst womankind and sadly lacking amongst men; I have learned to ask for directions. Unfortunately, my newly gained skill would have been of no consequence in Khadimnagar, as there was no one to ask.

England: 1992

One major inflexibility of being a teacher is that the holidays are static. Although a little more latitude has been added in some schools over the last thirty years with the introduction of healthy days, basically your holiday dates for a year, the school year, are mapped out for a year ahead and in some countries, this could be as much as two years ahead.

As someone who had worked for major tour operators for many years and been intimately involved in pricing, one of the most important factors in determining calendar variations of prices were the school holidays and we went to great lengths to ensure we maximised our listed prices at those times. It would be fair to say that all of the profitability of travel companies in the short-haul markets was during the school holidays.

In my second year of teaching at the Westlands School, I had the temerity to ask for a couple of days off just before the October half-term Holiday. There was an invitation to join a couple of friends in Antigua and the only flights we could afford were on a Wednesday evening. At school, my request was met with the same reaction that could have been expected if I had asked to have sex with the school secretary on the stage during assembly. In the end, I managed to wangle the trip, but only after having to agree to contact a school in Antigua and to set up some sort of twinning scheme.

The trip did not go entirely as planned. I suffered a sun-burned bum on the first day after cleaning a boat naked. I almost decapitated one of my friends with a rope that swept across the boat and dumped her in the sea. Then I knocked the other out by making extravagant turns in the motorboat while he was water-skiing. Along with swimming into a swarm of jellyfish, these moments made up a memorable holiday although it was the day trip to Montserrat that could have put the icing on the cake, unfortunately, the Soufriere Hills volcano, whilst hissing and steaming on our visit, waited another eight months before it finally erupted. Not quite a narrow escape!

Qatar: 2010-2013

Qatar is not my favourite country. I had my doubts about going in the first place, had even greater doubts about extending our contracts for a year and disliked the place with a passion. The only redeeming factor was the people we worked with at the school. There was little to do there, after all, Qatar is a rocky desert promontory that sticks out some 200 kilometres into the Persian Gulf like a leprosied penis. I had a go at driving on the dunes, which was marginally safer than driving on the roads, as long as you avoided the Qataris who, without any doubt, are the most dangerous drivers on this planet. Our choice of vehicle was a Chevrolet Trailblazer, not so much for its practicality, but that it was built like a tank and would probably survive a serious collision with a Toyota Landcruiser, the car of choice for the Qataris.

The major plus point to moving to the Middle East were to be the visits to the magnificent archaeological remains scattered across Lebanon, Palestine, Syria, Jordan and Egypt. Unfortunately, almost as soon as the ink was dry on our contracts, the Arab Spring kicked off. Although we took in some of Egypt and much of Jordan, we felt it unsafe to venture further afield and places such as Syria had become off-limits.

It was finally leaving Qatar that thrilled me most. My flight to London was scheduled for late evening, my wife's flight to the USA for the following morning. All our freight had gone and we had been in a great mood all day.

At the airport, I sailed through check-in and on to immigration. It was a little puzzling when the officer waved my passport in the air and pulled across his senior.

"You may not travel."

"Sorry, why?"

"Well, you see, you have left your wife?"

"No. I haven't left my wife, she is on a flight to Washington in the morning, she is flying to the USA."

"You are leaving the country without your wife. This is not permitted. You cannot leave her here; you must go home."

My arguments about her flight leaving eight hours later than mine fell on deaf ears. The only possibility they would accept is that we should both pass through immigration at the same time and she would have to wait out the time in the airport. It was too late for that option, so I returned home.

Whilst there have been delays at borders, I have only once been prevented from crossing. This was not borderline deceleration; it was a full-on roadblock. Qatar is a primitive country, with primitive people and a primitive attitude towards humanity. I was not allowed to leave the country because I was leaving some of my belongings behind. Those "belongings" happened to be Andrea.

While we were living in Qatar a phone app[5] went onto the market, firstly in Saudi, then in Qatar and I believe in Kuwait. It was a simple app and had one function. It alerted the phone's owner if their wife, or wives, were trying to leave the country. A number was provided to call to prevent this from happening.

You would not want to lose your belongings, would you?

---

[5] The Week. '...**Saudi wife-tracker app**'. 13/2/2019

Seven: The Good, the Bad and the Ugly (Curriculum)

Here I explore my ideas on curriculum and the immense impact it has had in making the teaching profession both joyful and so frustrating. In four of my schools, issues over the curriculum have been a major cause in my leaving those institutions. It is central to good teaching and is a major factor as regards student behaviour. Students, teachers, management and parents all desire a quality curriculum.

Bishop Mackenzie International School (BMIS), Lilongwe, Malawi: November 2019

As was mentioned in chapter two and will probably be mentioned again later in this account, one thing that I am an expert in is writing curriculum. To do this it is essential to have a solid, unshifting base from which you can work, without too much prescription. As to what makes for a good curriculum and as to why some people are better at preparing it than others you have to consider a multiplicity of factors.

Firstly, the topic should interest the individual responsible for building the structure. For example, I could never write a good curriculum based on soils because the subject bores me stupid, whereas there have been colleagues who love nothing more than getting down and earthy. Secondly, the topic must have relevance to the students, not simply as something that has to be done for academic purposes. To my mind, this is where Maths and sometimes Science can become unstuck.

Then comes the curriculum carrier or carriers, the packages in which the students will find and unfold information; these are crucial and must grab the students' interest. More and more these tend to be web-based, but that is not essential and good videos, reference books, magazines and newspapers can be used in conjunction with talks from experts, field trips, interviews and so forth. Anything that is hands-on for the student leaves a more lasting impression.

There should always be new skills. These might build on previously acquired skills although it is always very satisfying to finish a course and leave students with a completely new skill set. It is ideal if these skills are cross-curricular so that the student can apply them in other subjects. Often this does not happen, for a variety of reasons, although one being that both students and teachers tend to compartmentalise subjects, building walls around them and making cross-fertilisation difficult. Two examples of skills that can apply across subjects are interviewing techniques and referencing, although there are thousands. The IBO terms them as Approaches to Learning Skills which is a typically unnecessary mouthful when the word "Skills" alone would do.

The next on the list is currently underrated by educationalists: knowledge. The reason it has been systematically downgraded is largely down to Google. If you do not know something you "Google it". This is all well and good, but as with skills, acquiring knowledge requires some prior knowledge (remember I was a secondary school teacher and have no idea how this works with tiny little kids).

There was a news item announcing with fanfare the signing of a post-Brexit trade deal between the UK, Fiji and Papua New Guinea. Some Economics students might decide to use this type of article for an assessed piece of work, yet they probably have no idea of the physical distances involved, nor how diminutive trade between the UK and these countries is. Even when it is spelt out in the article, 10,000 miles is meaningless to many students as is the sum of £369 million; many are unable to put any context on the deal. They require a knowledge base to constructively take on board further knowledge.

To continue on the same theme, students enjoy building their knowledge base and love showing it off, this is not something they wish to shun as many educationalists seem to think. In many regards, students regard the acquisition of knowledge as more important than building skills. I believe the two should go hand in hand.

The curriculum also needs to be differentiated. This is a word that trips off the tongues of all teachers. Fundamentally it means to have course materials that are accessible to a variety of ability levels. There are many ways to achieve this, however, a curriculum is written before the make-up of a class is known, therefore differentiated material has to be generic rather than specific. For example, you would not decide to write a differentiated curriculum for students with no arms, unless there was a high likelihood of having such students, whereas preparing material for students with language difficulties or cognitive disorders is more likely at an early stage as there are certainly going to be such students in the classes of an international school and probably in most city schools.

Finally, and this is where so many teachers slip up, the curriculum needs to be well documented. It is all well and good having a written curriculum that you can deliver yourself, however that bus might just mow you down tomorrow and another teacher will have to step in. My standard is to write curriculum in such a way that a non-specialist teacher could deliver it, as sadly in my subject area this is quite common. If you are lucky enough to have a specialist step into the dead man's shoes, then they will have the skill sets to modify your curriculum, the non-specialist can simply follow the instructions.

Simply fulfilling the requirements of the curriculum coordinator is never enough. They set low bars in this regard, although they set many, for the simple reason that they are usually not subject specialists. It is no coincidence that I can say the best curriculum coordinator I have come across had previously been a Humanities teacher and can appreciate that a Science teacher for example may have a similar prejudice.

By the end of the previous year, we had been given very rigid parameters that had to be fulfilled before the end of the academic year in preparation for the accreditation visit. These are the many, low bars identified in the previous paragraph. My responsibilities amounted to over fifty per cent of the Humanities courses to be delivered to the 11-16-year olds at the school. It would be fair to say, that with one other full-time teacher in the department and three part-time teachers, my individual burden was a little excessive.

The expectation was that I would be teaching the Year 7 & 9 courses with other teachers, I knew that I would be handing over the Year 10 course to others and not being involved myself. However, it had been unclear who those other teachers might be and therefore the documentation needed to be bulletproof. The Year 11 course, which was intended as a loosely based Economics unit, under the heading of Trade, Development and Trumponomics, was to be taught solely by myself.

It came as a little bit of a surprise to find that the accreditation team had found some holes in my Year 11 course. These were pointed out to me by the curriculum leader after our return from holiday. It was inexcusable. Reconstructing what had happened was quite simple, my priorities had been directed elsewhere, to assist others and assumptions were made that the paperwork for the course that only I was teaching would be fine. It was not.

In fact, it was an excellent course. There were no holes, in reality, just a few checks missed off the odd textbox and a couple of updates that were not reflected in the paperwork. However, we had been asked to go the extra mile to tick those boxes and I had failed to do so. I apologised and ticked the boxes. It seems strange to relay, but the threat for us failing to tick all the boxes was that we would lose our gratuity payments, which were worth some $6,000 per annum. This will come into focus and in more detail in chapter thirteen but management through this type of threat is far from ideal.

This bureaucracy, which I do understand the need for, can be as simple or as complicated as a school chooses. Unfortunately, we had a rather anal curriculum coordinator who chose to go down the overcomplicated route and further confused this by implying to the accreditors that our curriculum was a finished package. In my view, the less complicated something is the better and no curriculum is ever a final package; they are all works in progress. This is probably why I have tangled with curriculum coordinators over a sustained period, whether they be the good, the bad or the ugly.

For sixteen years I have worked with IBO curriculum coordinators. They have the difficult task of ensuring their school follows the IBO guidelines. As the subject content is, within certain parameters, set by the individual departments, their main task should be to ensure that the skill progression is as expected. Far too often they become bogged down in subject-specific clerical issues rather than the bigger picture. When I first taught the IBO's 11-16 programme it was very fluid, by 2020 it has become mired in complications, impenetrable terminology, unnecessary bureaucracy and teachers who were becoming more and more disillusioned. To some extent, this is the fault of the curriculum coordinator, whose job it is to minimise these difficulties.

The irony of the situation at BMIS was that it was technically possible for what happened in the classroom to be completely at odds with the written curriculum. Over a sustained period, there were no checks on this. My written curriculum might have indicated that I should be teaching a course on the Mayan civilisations, whilst I could have delivered a unit on the formation of canyons and no one would have been any the wiser. All it would take is a little sleight of hand.

Whatever its faults overall the IBO provides one of the best international educations in the world. It might surprise some people, but the most popular curriculum taught in international schools is the English National Curriculum. The US does not have a national curriculum; each state has its own and these combined come in at a distant fourth, whilst the IBO holds second place. In comparison with the IBO the English system only comes out as better in one regard, that of detailed subject knowledge, whereas the IBO Diploma Programme, is held in the highest regard in every other area, although particularly with regard to skills[6]. (This information was sourced from UK University admissions officers by World Education News and Reviews.)

There is one major flaw in the IBO's overarching ideals. Their concept of international mindedness has a distinctly liberal Western European slant, which to my mind is not that much of a problem,

---

[6] IBO. '**DP students better prepared for university**'. 4/12/2107

however, it does come into conflict with their ideal of respecting local cultures and societies. Two examples stand out like a sore thumb, one being the death penalty and the other homosexuality. This does not need spelling out, but there are countries in which IBO programmes are taught that use the death penalty as a deterrent and others where homosexuality is illegal. There is no explanation of how acceptance of local norms can be reconciled with the requirement to teach wide acceptance of individual human rights. This matter is explored to some extent in the section below focussed on Qatar.

We do not only have to consider nations such as China or Saudi Arabia, in addition, there is a growing disquiet of the IBO's liberalism in some schools in the United States, where their ideas are considered by some to be socialist or communist in nature.

Bishop Mackenzie International School (BMIS), Lilongwe, Malawi: 2016-19

On arriving in Malawi, I expected that the curriculum was in a good state, well-documented and "ready to go", having been told this was the case by the management. Nothing could be further from the truth. For the most part, one of my colleagues and I battered it into shape over three years. The fact that he was a rangy Australian, who actually has medals for being an Australian, a loose command of the English language and a tendency to bang his head on the top of door frames, endeared me to him somewhat. I love the Australians' humour mainly because it is so like that of the Brits in that they claim to enjoy being belittled. Just like many Brits they are also rather insecure and hide their pain rather than admit it. When he joined us, after my first year, I began to feel we were getting somewhere with the curriculum.

It is not that there was not a curriculum when I started in Malawi, but it was so badly documented it was hard to work out what it was. My work on it combined new elements, a few I had written previously and brought in from my last school, and some amendments to what they already had in place. One irony of the roadmap I had put together was that it had similar names to the courses that teachers had delivered previously. Thus, right now, my having left the school, teachers are digging into the scheduled work and may believe they have taught it before; they have not. It is vastly improved but does have similar labelling.

I believe that a curriculum should be spiral in nature, extending from kindergarten to college and that skills and even some knowledge, should be revisited on every turn of the spiral, each complete turn representing a year group or grade level. This allows effective teaching and learning throughout a student's progress through school. It is unfortunate that many schools do not achieve this and instead focus on each unit within the curriculum without making enough assessment of its interconnectivity.

A good example of this was when the school tried to encourage the teachers and departments to introduce a scheme called project-based learning. We were all forced to attend an online course, which was hosted by an American Design teacher. What was not considered at all was the extent to which we already had these aspects covered, how it fitted into our curriculum and the prior experience that teachers had with it.

After only two sessions the course irritated me so much that I went off and modified one of our existing Year 9 units to fit the expectations we were supposedly being introduced to. It took little time. When I unveiled the course, it was clear that it was of a far higher standard than that being espoused by both the course leader and our curriculum coordinator. In fact, it was lauded.

There was an expectation that you should finish the course to receive a certificate. I have never had much time for certificates of any sort, perhaps because one for my teaching qualification was never issued, they simply sent me a letter telling me about my qualification. Certainly, a certificate for doing what I could and did do anyway seemed entirely unwarranted. Even so, a signed certificate came through anyway even though I did not complete the course. It has to be suspected they felt they had to give me one because they had held up my curriculum writing as an exemplar.

My programme should still be running since my leaving and is intended as a culmination of the Year 9 course, which progresses through a Geography unit on the East African Rift Valley, through History units on the Industrial Revolution and Socio-political revolutions, culminating in the project-based learning, which is based on Religion. The risk is that teachers new to the programme will randomly pick out the one they find easiest and deliver that first. If they do so, it demonstrates they have little understanding of the skills progression throughout the year, which are intended to improve both the students' audio-visual and written presentation skills, each unit building on the next. The curriculum is far more complicated than taking one course at a time.

Over four years at BMIS we really did go through a cycle that frustrated me enormously. In the first year, we were asked to combine assessment tasks. The view was that there were too many assessments, particularly for the younger students. My argument was that the assessments were small and easily handled; this view was dismissed. Over three years I combined more and more as required until they eventually turned around and said the assessments were too big and complicated, could they be broken into smaller tasks. Sure, they can be broken up, although it takes us back to exactly where we started. Why was all that time and effort wasted?

The answer to this question is quite simple. It seemed that the experiences of the subject teachers, some of whom had a far greater breadth and depth of involvement with IBO programmes than the school's management, were largely ignored. It was a repeated pattern and hugely frustrating.

The time wasted in teaching is phenomenal and would never be permitted in a commercial enterprise outside that industry. Not only are pupils allowed to waste time, but teachers also waste their students' time and much of this leads to a significant number of the student body becoming bored. This pattern continues into the relationship between teachers and their managements and it is perhaps a key indicator of good management when wasted time is minimised.

There are two main reasons my curriculum writing was of such a high standard. Firstly, I tend to think like a student or at least put their needs first. Admittedly, this does have some downsides in that every now and then I act like a stroppy teenager. Secondly, I am a perfectionist particularly in terms of filing and making sure boxes are correctly completed. The downside of this is that I spend far too much time on minor issues and can sometimes make documentation overcomplicated, although always look for methods to improve systems of work and make them more efficient. In the end, I spend time to make time; it is a lesson that others could well learn.

In 2016, if we made a change to a unit two additional documents had to be updated. By 2019 that change would have to be reflected in five different documents and by 2020 the management appeared to have added a sixth. Alongside these changes in administration, the school did away with many heads of department, thus ensuring the teachers did not have an easy route to voice objections. More and more meetings turned into one-way affairs, the views of the classroom teacher were most often ignored, the power became focussed entirely around three people, all of whom had an extremely limited breadth of experience in delivering an international curriculum.

The question that needs to be asked is whether the students' learning had been enhanced by all the additional bureaucracy and, whilst this is necessarily a subjective judgement, the answer would have to be no.

Westlands School, Sittingbourne, Kent, England: 1991-1997

For eight years my role was primarily that of a Geography teacher and for six of those a head of department; this commenced at Westlands, my first school. The course content was largely prescribed by the English National Curriculum and came neatly bound in a series of age-appropriate textbooks. Although there were choices, these were limited, you could cover topics like glaciation or river features; there was no time for them both.

In my second year as a teacher, I attended a seminar on the use of ICT within Geography teaching, which exposed me for the first time to a large number of Geography teachers in one room. Publicly, I expressed my surprise at how "environmental" the subject had become and was met by sneers of derision and comments such as, "What do you think Geography is?". Clearly, I had used the wrong terminology. What I had meant to express was my surprise that the subject focus had drifted so far towards damage to the environment, without adequately explaining how our environment was formed. To my mind this shift, as early as 1992, was what has led to the virtual death of Geography as a subject; it is now rarely taken seriously, particularly in an international context.

I was thoroughly engaged in teaching environmental concerns, even incorporating Ben Elton sketches into my lessons to make the point, but what were we teaching? Topics that could be taught in English, Science, ICT, Current Affairs, whatever. If one or two of my students from that period have chosen not to live on a river floodplain, have weighed up the consequences of owning a home on an eroding cliff or have made sensible choices regarding watching and understanding weather forecasts, I would be happy. Otherwise, it is not clear that what my students learned in my lessons will have been of any use at all as there was too little focus on skills.

Priory Special School, Spalding, Lincolnshire, England 2000-2001

Quite strangely, being required to teach many subjects is what eventually led to my employment overseas. The special school in which I ended my career in the UK was a school for secondary age students, yet was set up similarly to a primary school, where a teacher would take the same class of students for most subjects. Where you have a lot of students who are challenged academically, in many cases a generalist teacher will be able to cope with the required levels of complexity, although this is not always the case.

Art was taught separately, which was something of a plus for me. My artistic ability confines itself to drawing maps and the odd field sketch. On many occasions, I have had to cover an Art lesson and when no work had been left, my skill set could handle the topic of vanishing points, but that is about all. In my ten years of teaching in the UK, I must have covered as many as fifty art classes; for some reason, Art teachers seem to take more time off sick than other specialists. In over half of those lessons, the instruction left by the Art teacher was that the students should draw a training shoe. Quite why this is I am unsure, although it could be to do with the availability of training shoes, sitting as they do on most kids' feet. Man, are they difficult to draw, in a class of thirty you might come up with one good offering and at the end of the lesson when you compile the kids' work to put into a drawer, you would find thousands of other examples of terribly executed drawings of training shoes. In addition, it made Art studios very smelly places to be. Is it possible that all art teachers are sadists?

My Art teacher was. I remember he was an exceptionally short man who drove a TR6. I also remember he hit me quite a lot. Back in the early Seventies, this was quite normal; if you transgressed you were whacked. However, he did not hit me for breaking the rules, he hit me solely for being a bad artist. Looking around some of those Art classes I covered over the years it has to be thought that he would have belted the vast majority of the kids.

Technology was another subject that did not come under my remit, I think you need a special qualification to be put in charge of sharp tools and thankfully languages were also excluded. However, my teaching load included Science, Maths, English, Humanities, including my first History teaching and P.E. the last of which occupied a full day of my week, proved thoroughly enjoyable and improved my level of fitness.

When it came time for me to move on and apply for my first jobs overseas, my curriculum vitae was as broad as was possible for a UK secondary school teacher at that time, but what I failed to realise was that I had slowly been losing my specialist skills and this was particularly the case for the higher-level work for the older students. Looking back now this was the time when I ceased to be a Geography teacher. Whilst maintaining a passion for geographical issues, I had developed a broader passion for teaching and more importantly, a passion for enhanced learning.

International School of Moshi (ISM), Moshi, Tanzania: 2001-03

It was impressive how they managed to utilise all that experience in Moshi. I taught students from age 11-18, the upper limit being Geography to IB Diploma level, for which I simply did not have the skill sets to cope. Fortunately, there was an experienced Geographer there and she saw me through. For the younger kids, I was teaching History, Geography, Religion, Life Skills and English; some of those students saw an awful lot of me during their week.

It was also my first experience of teaching with almost no written curriculum. This is not such a bad state of affairs in your specialist subject, but it was decidedly unsettling in something like English. The parents at ISM were my most enthusiastic supporters. A Swiss-German guy collared me on one occasion and asked if I remembered the lesson I had delivered to his son's class on 12th September. As I had no recollection of the subject, let alone the lesson, I had to admit ignorance. His son, a very low-level user of English, had come home and delivered a one-hour lecture about the differences between a handful of terrorists and the huge peace-loving Muslim communities. It is wonderful to have the time to go off-topic, fantastic that a student should have taken it in and better still that he had developed the skills to express himself. If we had been following a tight curriculum this may not have occurred.

For two years I coped teaching multiple subjects, a Year 12 World Affairs course being added to my timetable in the second year. In the end, I had requested that my workload should be more focused to persuade me to stay for the third year.

Staffing complexities are notoriously difficult in international schools, as I was to find out. For what would have been my third year, a P.E. teacher was leaving and they had chosen to fill this position with a guy who had worked at the school previously. They believed the only other subject he was capable of teaching was Geography, which meant my only option was to continue in the role as a jack of all trades. It was not a tenable position and I chose to move on.

Suzhou Singapore International School (SSIS), Suzhou & Utahloy International School (UIS), Guangzhou, China: 2004-09

Back in 2004, the International Baccalaureate's programme for 11-16-year olds was an educational model that was designed for me. I guess this sunk in when teaching a class about European explorers in the fifteenth and sixteenth centuries. At SSIS a Year 8 girl raised her hand and said, "What about Zheng He?"

They were the four words that changed me forever as a teacher. I had never heard of Zheng He and had always been confident that the answer to any question a younger kid would ask would reside somewhere in my mental database. The realisation that my classes were full of kids with quite different experiences, with completely different mindsets and who were actively educating themselves, was so far distanced from my experiences in the UK that it blew my mind.

Of course, there had been some exposure to this in Tanzania, although for the most part they then operated loosely within the English National Curriculum. For three years in Suzhou and one in Guangzhou, I was able to open up the world to my classes with less formal teaching styles and learning styles that suited the students.

Arriving in Guangzhou, in 2007, took it one stage further when, supported by an incredibly good secondary headteacher, and a helpful head of department, I was able to take the ideas I had been putting together and structure all my classes into a laptop-based course. It was incredibly helpful being able to focus on only Years 8 & 9 and there was a decent amount of time available for curriculum development.

It was at UIS that my name changed. Never having enjoyed being called, Mister Whitworth, or even worse, Sir, my adopted moniker became Mister Mark and it stuck. From that point right up to my retirement, I abandoned my surname; it seemed to further improve my relationship with my students and certainly never caused any problems. A few teachers took issue with the change, but there again many teachers take issue with any change.

UIS was almost my ideal job. Unfortunately, we left after one year, having renegotiated a reduction in our contract, simply because my wife's working conditions were untenable. It was a necessary decision, but one that I regret enormously in terms of my teaching and the progress I was making in terms of curriculum development.

However, I left behind an enduring legacy, which came about due to my lack of experience as a history teacher. At the start of the year, I ordered an incredibly cheap set of textbooks on American history, perhaps fifty books. What I had missed was the fact that this particular book had been written in the 1890s and about the only thing that had been updated was the cover. My excuse, and it was the only one I could come up with, is that the book could be used as a primary source of information; the students would get an idea of what the views were of people from that time. It was never a plausible explanation and I am sure that the head of department was left confused. He probably has that set of books somewhere in a cupboard waiting for his replacement to find a couple of years from now.

We returned to SSIS, who were keen to have us back. They were implementing a full Mac school system, which was finally up and running by the January of 2008. Although I have never been a Mac lover, it did seem a step in almost the right direction, however, it came bundled with some of the very worst school management I have ever been subjected to.

On the verge of solidifying my ideas on curriculum using a slick ICT based programme with distance teaching capabilities, working with tried and tested colleagues, some of whom were, in fact, good friends, comfortable with the living environment and feeling extremely positive about the direction I was headed, it seemed all was hunky-dory.

It was then that the secondary headteacher chose to drive a massive wedge in between some of her staff. The fallout was immense. I lost one good friend forever; we never spoke again. I lost another for a while and although we are now corresponding, it is unlikely we will ever be as close as we were. And I resigned from my job, which was messy and took a year off while my wife continued at the school for another year. It has been suggested that this should be explained in more detail, but that is impossible because I simply do not know what happened. It has to be suspected that the three of us were all given different information about each other and our actions by the headteacher. Less than a year before my two friends had acted the roles of best man and father of the bride at our wedding party, we had been exceptionally close. If I did anything remiss then I apologise sincerely, although cannot for the life of me think what it might have been.

Eventually, SSIS managed to rid itself of that management team and the school once again returned to the high standards it had previously held. We need to remind ourselves that it does not matter how hard you work, how competent you are, how well you build relationships with other teachers, at the end of the day the whole thing can be brought down by someone who has been put into a position that they believe they can execute, but that they simply did not have the capabilities to fulfil.

International School of London Qatar (ISLQ), Doha, Qatar: 2010-2013

We worked with some fine people in Qatar, both the teachers and the management were pretty sound, although it felt I was stepping back somewhat in terms of curriculum development.

The other concern was the ever-present Supreme Education Council (SEC). Qatar is not a democratic state and is effectively run by a single-family. There was more censorship in Qatar than in any other country we have worked in, much more so than in China. The body responsible for ensuring that schools conformed to their requirements was in every way "supreme" and you certainly could not argue with them.

The SEC first came into my life when a parents' complaint bounced into our department. As usual, it had been directed from parent to government, rather than to the school management and with little opportunity for discussion we were told to burn a set of textbooks. Any decent human being would be rattled by this order, let alone teachers committed to exposing kids to as much diverse information as possible and I chose to investigate the problem rather than act immediately.

The problem regarded an English language textbook regarding religions. Unsurprisingly, it was the chapter on Islam that had raised the ire of our student's father. On one of the pages was an explanation of what the Hadiths were and a quoted example. I have no idea why the author or publisher managed to come up with the hadith that had been chosen, but it was one of several that identify the Prophet Muhammad as having had sexual congress with all nine of his wives in a single night.

In school textbooks, aimed at 11-14-year olds, this is probably not the hadith to have chosen; there are thousands of others more appropriate. Research showed me that many Muslims were particularly sensitive about this particular set of hadiths and certainly it was one of the least popular in terms of promoting Islam in the early twenty-first century. Only a mad man, or someone trying to make a point, would have chosen this hadith and remember, this textbook had been written for use in the UK, which has a significant Muslim minority.

Whilst the content was not untrue, in fact, it was remarkably accurate, you could see the point of the complainant. However, burning books is not something to be undertaken lightly. I believe it was my idea, although am prepared to accept, I may have appropriated it, but the suggestion was that we glue the offending pages together. It was accepted and the books were not burned.

One of the most hilarious decisions of the SEC was to introduce the requirement to teach two hours of Qatari history, each week, for the entire year, to every year group. To anyone with even the faintest idea about Gulf history and the influence that Islam has on that history, the requirement was preposterous. If they had asked us to do a ten-week course of two hours per week to a single year group, we might have managed.

Qatari history is, to put it bluntly, fairly boring and extremely limited in scope. It does not help that everything before the advent of Islam is almost disregarded, because that would have been quite interesting, however Qatari history is the tale of one Saudi tribe who migrated a few kilometres from one hostile desert area to another and ended up being put in control of the state by the British, who deliberately enlarged the mineral rights, to try to keep some control over Gulf oil and gas. The actual result was that Qataris seem to now own half of London including the Shard and the North-west of Mayfair, which is now known as the Qatari Quarter.

It is unclear why it was me that attended the meeting given by the SEC to introduce these requirements, but I was accompanied by at least one other international teacher and one of our Arabic speaking staff. I had a whole slew of questions prepared. Looking back through my notes from the meeting a few items stand out:

Nothing to be taught that is *"contradictory with Islamic teachings and community values..."*

"The Flag, national anthem and Emir's face are very important, must be at the front of every Qatari history document."

The whole school *"timetabling should include, Arabic – 3/4 hours/week, Islamic Studies – 2 hours/week, Qatari History – 2 hours/week."*

In my notes, I make repeated reference to the impossibilities of the situation, in trying to combine IBO requirements with those of the SEC. This was in terms of both practicality, there was not enough time, nor staff with expertise and in philosophical terms, where the IBO was liberal and questioning and the SEC completely dogmatic. I also recall there were some restrictions on Science and would suspect this would be concerning human evolution, which of course DID NOT HAPPEN and to Mathematics, although about this I cannot even speculate on the detail.

We were advised that they were putting together a series of Qatari History textbooks, one for each year group, which to their credit they did, albeit a month or two late. Unfortunately, each one was little more than an enlarged pamphlet and completely inadequate for teaching a class for a year. The books themselves not only included some inaccuracies, but they also included some potential pitfalls, and a pitfall for a teacher in Qatar is almost anything that might upset any of the ruling families and something that could easily land a teacher in gaol.

My favourite item in one of their books was a link to a website. Seemingly quite innocuous, it focussed on the migration of the Qatari people from central Saudi. However, on the website was another link and this led me to a long dissertation regarding the Qataris, who went by another name back then and who were disdained by righteous Muslims. I have been unable to backtrack and find the source of this material and have no idea if it is accurate or not, although it is absolutely clear that if one of my Qatari students had followed the links and then reported it to his Dad, this would have been passed to the SEC and I could have ended up in a cell. (Please note that the last sentence was written entirely in the male gender. This was deliberate. It is highly unlikely the complaint would ever be taken as seriously if made by a female student.)

There was an event that shook many ex-pat teachers in the Gulf, although I am unsure if it was publicised very much in the Western press. It was not the curriculum that put the teacher, Dorje Gurung in prison, but a handful of young students. This item is from the Washington Post[7]:

---

[7] Anup Kaphle. '**Qatar jails a Nepali teacher...**'. Washington Post. 9/5/2103

"On Monday, April 22, Gurung said he had a sit-down chat with three 12-year-old boys who were making fun of him. Among other things, the seventh graders poked fun at his appearance, calling him "Jackie Chan," a famous Chinese actor.

On Tuesday, April 23, the mocking again began in earnest while Gurung was in line for lunch. At first, he said the teasing was light-hearted, but then one student put his hand on Gurung's shoulder and a finger in his nose. At this point, Gurung grew agitated and said remarks to the effect of, how would you like to be stereotyped i.e. called a terrorist?"

Gurung has no legal representation, but the Nepali embassy is seeking permission from the Kathmandu government to meet with Gurung, Doha News reports. Without a lawyer, Gurung's friends fear he would not get a fair trial. The court would rely on the complaints from Qatar Academy's students, they said."

There was a massive international outcry within the teaching profession and eventually, the Qataris had to capitulate. Dorje Gurung was released after two weeks and deported to his home state of Nepal. However, he has been advised never to transit the Gulf and the charge of insulting Islam has not been dropped. At the time, as teachers within Qatar, we were advised not to show any support for Dorje Gurung, because of concerns for our own safety. We were told the necessary complaints should all come from overseas for fear of someone else being banged up.

I would certainly fight to stop someone mutilating my curriculum, although it certainly is not worth going to prison for. I would have spoken to those boys at the Qatar Academy and because of my race, may have got away with it, because westerners came higher in Qatar's apartheid hierarchy than southern Asians. However, it is not possible to teach day after day with this type of threat hanging over you and when you are likely to become a target at any moment. Best to leave.

International School of Dhaka (ISD), Dhaka, Bangladesh: 2013-16

At ISD, just as in Malawi, they also tried to get rid of the heads of department. At least they were brave enough to admit the new system did not work and the posts were effectively reinstituted before we left. I have had both good and bad heads of department; however, the worst of all worlds is not having one. It is not that I feel hierarchy is wonderful or have the desire to avoid responsibility, it is simply better to have a single individual arrange and chair meetings, order stock for the department, control the budget and represent the views of the department in regular meetings. In addition, it is always good to have someone to bounce ideas off; you cannot expect busy teachers to do this at the drop of a hat. Long live heads of departments in schools, I have never jealously eyed their reduced timetables and the slight increase in their stipends.

The first sign that they are going to do away with them is when they stop having heads of department meetings. It might take a few years, but the axe is already coming down. This process is generally only halted if the head of secondary changes, which is exactly what happened in Bangladesh, except the other way around.

It was a tall order, introducing a comprehensive change to the IBO's programme, a review supposedly designed to bring their secondary structure into greater alignment with their programmes for primary age students and those pursuing the Diploma Programme. What it did was to introduce a great deal more jargon, with an expectation that students would come to terms with it. Six years on and this remains a major problem, especially with the younger secondary students and those for whom English is not their first language.

In my second year in Bangladesh, a new head arrived, supposedly an expert in IBO programmes for secondary schools. It took her a while and towards the end of that year, she started to make some fundamental changes. For me, the final straw was her reducing the hours devoted to the Diploma Programme subjects, to a level some 30% below the advised minimum. As I was teaching Diploma Economics at the time this would have had an immediate impact on learning and there would have been a lowering of the grades the students would attain. I made it clear that my third year there would be my last.

Although I primarily consider myself as a teacher of 11-16-year-olds, I found teaching older students interesting and generally achieved good results. Economics is an involved subject and allows you to bring in any number of current issues. In Malawi, I introduced a course on Trumponomics, which went down very well. However, what is more frustrating is the extent to which the course content is prescribed, which is not the case for the kids in the 11-16 bracket.

It is more fun to deliver integrated Humanities courses, rather than units focussing only on one of Geography, History or Economics. To my surprise, I found that the book Sapiens, by Yuval Noah Harari, mirrors much of my course content, in his exploration of Anthropology, History and our relationship with our environment. Colleagues from schools earlier in my career, when our focus was on separate subject areas, may be surprised by the extent to which I have managed to put together integrated courses.

It helps me that my main qualification is in Geography, my secondary qualification is in Economics, I followed university courses for two years in Economic History and one of my hobbies is History. Many teachers in Humanities have a strong bias towards one of the component subjects, particularly the Historians, who will feign backache rather than pick up a Geography textbook.

In Bangladesh, I had the pleasure to work with a fellow Economics teacher, far better qualified than I and it benefitted me enormously. On balance, I suspect I was the better teacher and she was the better Economist; the dynamic was sound. Having management who understood the importance of teaching Economics in a developing country was a huge help; there was pressure to introduce Business and Management, although it did not detract from the importance of the Economics courses.

On the other hand, I find working with many History teachers is slightly weird. There is an obsession within their ranks that the skills of interpreting history are paramount and have absolute dominance over understanding the process of history. Thus, there is no need for the students to develop an overview of history, simply being able to analyse a historical event gives the kids transferable skills and then, supposedly, they can access any history they wish.

I see the point, but do not agree. At the end of the day, learning about historical events has to be fun. The way to make it fun is to allow the students to make connections. If history is taught as a series of independent, unconnected events, half the fun has gone.

Two main strands come out of this chapter.

The first is that I am an arrogant individual who believes he knows more about the teaching of Humanities subjects than anyone else. Clearly, in this, I am misguided, to say the least. There are fantastic teachers in this subject area and I have worked with a few of the best.

The second is mentioned albeit briefly in the paragraph above. Lessons must be fun if you are to engage students throughout the rest of their schooling and hopefully afterwards. You can have the best teachers in the world, but if they focus on the older kids and minimise the importance of those in younger age groups, they will lose those students' long-term interest.

The curriculum must be fun!

Eight: Wherever I Lay My Hat

(Living Spaces)

This section deals with the subject of homes. Since commencing teaching, I have lived in five different homes in the UK and ten overseas, although some for only a few months. I have sold two properties in the UK and together we have bought a retirement property in Mexico.

Lilongwe, Malawi: January 2020

We had spent our Christmas vacation apart, Andrea in the USA and I in the UK, both seeing our respective families. We had enjoyed completely different experiences on our return journeys. I had been upgraded to Business Class and with only a two-hour time difference was feeling pretty fresh. Andrea, with an eleven-hour time difference and an extremely crowded journey in the back of the plane from

Washington, was seriously jetlagged. We were both trying to get our heads around returning for the first week back in school and had only one day remaining to do so.

The rainy season in Lilongwe extends from late November until mid-April, although this is usually split into the little rains, in late November and early December, and the big rains, which commence in January. It was therefore the start of the big rains. The name itself is apt, the downpour is torrential. To cope with the run-off, the open storm drain that runs in front of our house is a metre and a half in both width and depth. With massive differentials between the surface temperatures and those in the upper layers of the troposphere, thunder and lightning are commonplace, sometimes appearing to simply run downwards and at others wrapping around half of the sky, unzipping the clouds in a sawing horizontal motion.

It is unclear whether it was the vertical or horizontal version of the lightning that hit the house. The explosion was deafening and when we had both gathered our senses, we bumped into each other in a pitch-black hallway. It was not as if we did not know what had happened, more as if we were both considering whether we were still alive.

Our house was well equipped for blackouts. There were candles with matches, solar camping lights, my wife had a flashlight and I had a torch, these are of course identical items, although we have stuck with our roots somewhat when it comes down to nomenclature and do have the occasional incomprehensible conversation. However, more than anything else, allowing a little light into our night-time world was our set of solar panels, batteries and the inverter. We had gone two and a half years without losing household power, which in Malawi is unheard of.

After the lightning strike, it was clear something was wrong. It did not take long to find out that all the breakers had been thrown, but as all our electrical equipment is additionally defended with surge protectors, it seemed there was no lasting damage. However, the power did not come back even with the breakers returned to their normal positions. As the mains electricity was out, the fully charged batteries should have kicked in. They did not.

It was a few hours before our mains electricity provider, restored power, a period we could survive easily with portable battery packs that kept the Internet running amongst other things. The gas cooker provided our meal, with a little help from ourselves. When the lights came back on, it was clear we had a bigger problem as a huge pool of water had collected on the kitchen floor.

At this point only one course of action made sense...make everything safe and go to bed.

Rather than drag the tale out further, the results of the lightning strike were that the inverter had blown some circuits and the copper hot water tank above the kitchen had been hit so forcefully that both its intake and out-take pipes had been blown off. No wonder there was a great deal more water that greeted us when we rose. There was no other significant damage.

In our home we have some $7,000 worth of electrical equipment, all of it had been safeguarded by the surge protectors, for which I must say a huge thank you to Belkin. Later investigation proved it would have been impossible to protect the inverter and it ended up costing me $500 for it to be repaired. The re-plumbing of the hot water tank was undertaken and paid for by our employer, as part of our housing contract.

In that first week back, we were running around like blue-arsed flies and it was fortunate that I was allowed a couple of days off work to sort out the mess. There are some benefits to living in accommodation that is provided, although sometimes these are outweighed by the disadvantages.

Around the World

When we determined to buy a home in Mexico, we undertook almost six months of research, although once we were there, it took less than a week for us to buy a property. This decision was made with lightning speed, it was my first visit to Mexico and we hope that it was the right choice, however, there were reasons we felt able to make such a bold move. For the last twenty years, we have been moving into new countries for new jobs. We had not visited Tanzania, China, Qatar, or Bangladesh before we accepted jobs in those states and whilst we had visited Malawi previously, we had not been to Lilongwe.

These moves, to new lands and new jobs, are exhilarating. To make the transition somewhat easier for you, many international schools provide accommodation, this was the case in all of our moves together. You get what you get and you learn to live with it; this applies to the job and the country and its people, although sometimes you have to do something about the accommodation.

One week in Mexico was more than enough, when previously we had no opportunity to be choosy about where we were to live. It is just one of those roulette wheels on which international teachers dance their lives away.

Lilongwe, Malawi: 2016-2020

The solar system mentioned above does not mean the planetary grouping in which we reside, but the panels, batteries and inverters that kept us comfortable in our house. There are more details below, however, the solar is what turned this house into a home, one in which we ended up spending five years. If we had felt we would be moved around each year it would have made investing in a solar power system less advantageous.

When the missus arrived, back in 2016, she was alone, as I was held up in Dubai. The school administrative staff brought her to the house and went through a few of the things she needed to know. In fact, all she wanted to know was where the bed was, as it was difficult to locate in the dark and yet again she was jet-lagged after the journey from the States. Andrea had no idea of the extent of the property nor who the strange guys were hanging around; it was probably a little disorientating. We spent much of the first eight months learning to live with constant lengthy power outages.

Although only eleven per cent of homes in Malawi are connected to mains electricity, the actual demand for the stuff is fifty-per cent higher than the supply. As in many African countries, the result is "load shedding", which means power is cut for long periods each day to those homes that are connected. In addition there is a seasonal aspect to this, in that nearly all the electricity is supplied from hydro-electric plants, which do not have enough water running through them from May to December and often in January there is too much water, with too much debris in it and they become blocked. Electricity can also be bought from Zambia and Mozambique, although it has to be suspected the reticence of Malawi's monopoly electricity supplier to undertake such purchases is that it would find fewer funds available to be slipped into the pockets of their management.

In 2016/17 we were lucky if our power cuts lasted for less than eight hours a day; they were often much longer. In the first three months, the record was a 37-hour blackout and that starts to become very inconvenient, negating any benefits of having a fridge, freezer or an electric cooker. However, the load shedding was not evenly spread across the town. Many teacher's homes and the school itself are located in Area 3, whilst our own home was in Area 9; these residential areas are adjacent. However, the Vice-president's official home is located in Area 3, which is therefore given priority as regards electricity supply and their power cuts were always far shorter than our own.

At some point, the school determined it would buy generators for the teachers. Although they are noisy and dirty, at least it would give us some backup. In a logic that can only have originated in Africa, they installed the gensets in the teachers' houses commencing with Area 3, on the basis that it was closest to the school. There were fifty-odd machines to wire in and I believe we were the forty-ninth, receiving our backup supply just in time for the Christmas holiday.

The generators were the wrong solution, administered in the wrong way and were costly to buy, probably a total bill of around $30,000 in total, additionally, they were expensive to run. Needless to say, it was the individual teachers who paid for the fuel. Not all teachers needed them, in fact, many in Area 3 never used them. Particularly because of the noise, we minimised our usage and searched for more sensible alternatives.

Eight months in and we had conquered the problem. A gas cooker, fed from an LPG tank, an inverter and four large solar panels with matching batteries did the trick. Sure, it cost us, although every penny spent was worthwhile. In over four years we were only inconvenienced twice by blackouts, once was when the lightning struck and the other when I forgot to make a technical adjustment to the system. No more meltdowns from the freezer, candles only when we wanted them, TV and Internet as required, cooked food on demand, basically all those things which most people take for granted. For an outlay of $4,000, which included the cooker, it has turned a version of hell into something almost heavenly, because this is a wonderful home and has been the best we have lived in throughout our semi-nomadic existence.

We did not expect an extensive garden, but we had one, the boundaries are sixty by sixty metres and we used about five-hundred square metres of that for food crops. There are also fourteen mango trees, a couple of banana plants, papaya, avocado, several large, mature shade trees and an extensive lawn. We had a comfortable, although somewhat dated, three-bedroomed bungalow, with an extensive veranda, where we spent much of our leisure time. There is a carport, a large, surfaced car parking space and a scullery area. There are quarters for staff, separate from the main building and these are also wired and plumbed in.

It is a struggle to find downsides, although I guess these are as follows. The electric fence atop the two-metre wall that surrounds the property is somewhat unsightly. We had a group of Bangladeshi electricians living next door, from Sylhet, who were quite lovely, however, they generate noise almost constantly. Towards the end it was their guard dog, previously it was an electric saw, sometimes phone calls and one of them had a huge bass speaker that was so loud his comrades eventually forced him to get rid of it. Bangladeshis have a hard time being quiet, we should know.

Without any doubt, the biggest downside was the cost. Notwithstanding the fruit and vegetable production, the running costs were high. Many of the teachers at the school have outgoings of less than $75 a month, covering power, water, guards, gardening, TV, Internet and so forth. Our bills for the same have been as high as ten times that. Occasionally we add up how much more we could have saved if we had opted for one of the smaller properties and over five years it comes out to around $35,000. Even so, it has been worth it.

When we had arrived, the school were employing three guys as guards and gardeners to the property, which had been empty for four months. Following the advice of our employers, we took on all three and one of their wives to work as a cleaner. Two of the lads we employed as night guards and the other as a gardener. The gardener and the cleaner moved into the staff accommodation on the property and within six months had produced a lovely baby boy, who we think of as a grandchild.

It became clear over the first year that the school had been paying the workers subsistence wages, which we had continued. In that first May, we decided to double their pay. All four remained with us for a further three years, however when I began spending more time at home, we dropped down to two staff, the night guards had reached the end of their contracts and we let them go. Terminating their employment was not without difficulties. Although they had twelve months warning, only one made proper alternative arrangements, the other is now unemployed. Unfortunately, he is still hung around, asking for money, it is sometimes difficult to know what to do.

We have always tried to ensure that people who pass through our acquaintance come out of the experience much better off than when we first met. Three of our staff have now built themselves homes and a fourth has bought a substantial piece of land for his family; they would have been unable to do so if we had not been prepared to pay them substantially more than we could have got away with. Whilst it would be too much to say that we are friends, we are both pleased that there is a substantial and continued level of respect between us.

One wonderful aspect of our garden was that it was always full of birds. This is less wonderful when they eat the tomatoes and peppers. Huge kites soar overhead, we had sparrow hawks, owls and cuckoos adding to the predators, mousebirds, bulbuls, cordon-bleu birds, warblers, pied crows, sunbirds, tropical boubous, drongos, weaver birds, orioles and hoopoes are all residents or regular visitors, whilst swallows and bats flit across the garden as dusk approaches. Add in the agama lizards, skinks and geckoes and we had a full ensemble of entertainment. And then there are the snakes.

If you have ever wondered why so many African houses have an area around them scraped bare of vegetation, there are two reasons. Firstly, the goats eat everything, including the roots and secondly, it is kept completely bare so that snakes cannot approach without detection. We have had the odd snake in the garden and more recently sightings became quite regular; one specimen appeared to be living below the veranda. I will confess to not being particularly fond of snakes, but would rather follow a policy of live and let live, an ideal that was blown out of the water when we concluded that the addition to our menagerie could well be a Mozambique spitting cobra.

This is the advice given by Kapama Game Reserve[8] in South Africa, *"It is considered one of the most dangerous snakes in Africa.*

---

[8] Kapama River Lodge. '**The Mozambique Spitting Cobra**' 1/2/2013

The snake can quite accurately spit its venom up to two to three meters. Its bite causes severe local tissue destruction (similar to that of the puff adder). Venom to the eyes can also cause impaired vision and if left untreated could cause blindness. This snake is highly nervous and when confronted can rear up to as much as two-thirds of its body length, spread its long narrow hood and will readily "spit" in defence."

To my shame I killed it, using a long heavy stick to knock it out and then to crush its skull. I may not be keen on snakes but do not like killing anything, except mosquitoes and the odd cockroach, however you do not want one of those spitting cobras disturbing your cold beer in the evening.

Moshi, Tanzania: 2001-2003

In Moshi, as Andrea and I had been employed separately and did not become an item for some time, we each had our own home, although they were identical and only one hundred metres apart. They were basic two-bedroomed semi-detached bungalows, although I seem to recall they termed them duplexes, with a small amount of land around each. I believe there were eight units in all and they were all on the school campus, albeit separated from the school itself by two rugby pitches. The walk to work was fewer than four hundred metres and to the north of our path towered Kilimanjaro, it was possibly the shortest and most beautiful journey to work that either of us had experienced.

It is in Moshi that we became used to coping with the difficulties of intermittent services such as power and the Internet. As we were less dependent on electricity and digital communication back then, we seemed to cope quite well. One advantage of being on campus was that we were on the same electrical grid as the school, which had boarders and there was a massive generator to keep them happy. The downside was that they did not switch it on if the kids were on holiday, the teachers were second-class citizens.

It was a romantic place to be and both of us remember it fondly for our first kiss, the stars blazing, moonlight reflecting off Kilimanjaro's glaciers and a gin and tonic in hand.

There were very few downsides. It was a little too far to walk into town regularly, there were not many good places to eat, health services were basic and there was some petty crime, but the school had a fence and guards, which kept most of the undesirable elements out.

One such undesirable element that did get in was the most frightening animal I came across in Africa...a rabid dog. The poor thing was obviously in the later stages and had gone completely mad. I almost wrote barking mad and thought better of it. I kept it at bay with a large stick and eventually retreated into the safety of Andrea's house. The guards, who were even less well-armed and with no secure shelter, did the only thing they could. We found the dog on the rugby pitch on our walk to work the following morning; it had been stoned to death.

Another undesirable would have had short shrift with a fence. It appeared just as I was about to get into the bath, so it had an advantage over me in that I was naked. A huge furry ball with eight legs, two of which were lifted towards me in the air. Spiders and I do not get on very well although I am not keen on killing them. Reaching for a broom I tried to guide the arachnid towards the door. In the back of my mind there was a clear voice telling me it would be best to be wearing clothes, but this I ignored. It only took one touch with the broom head and the creature seemed to explode into a thousand pieces, each scurrying off as fast as they could for the darkness offered by my furniture. I am afraid that I morphed into a naked mass murderer within seconds, out came the Doom aerosol and an act of genocide followed.

It was amazing to watch what I considered to be a birth, although I have since learned that the mother carries the babies, I had never seen anything like it. I just wish it had been outside, then I could have allowed nature to take its course. I also put the dying mother out of her misery, but I regarded it as a mercy killing rather than anything else. I kept on telling myself that it did not look like a good spider, but I know it is an extremely poor excuse.

The school fence might have saved me from burglary, however, it almost proved my undoing a few months later. It was two in the morning when I heard a massive commotion from the house just outside our perimeter. Rushing out I was joined by two guards and we were just in time to see two thieves running from the house opposite, one carrying a large TV set. We were quite helpless; the entrance gate was too far away for us to readily step in and we could only shout at the men through the fence as they made off with my neighbour's belongings. A few moments later a third ran out, armed with a half-metre panga, a heavy twin-edged hacking knife, which presented no danger to us on the other side of the chain link, although what came next was rather scary. My neighbour, half-dressed, rather bruised and battered, came out after the intruders shouldering a hunting rifle, which he preceded to aim directly at myself and the guards, mistakenly thinking we were the thieves. We ducked then shouted and shouted. Eventually, he lowered his weapon towards the floor.

When we managed to get to him, it was clear he had been knocked around quite a bit. As I dressed his wounds, having pulled enough grit out of his back to surface a small road, his head cleared and he filled me in on the details. They had broken in while he was asleep and he had caught them as they were trying to unplug the television. Overpowering and then pinning him to the floor they proceeded to beat him across his bare back with the panga. It was quite clear they took enormous care to ensure they did not cause serious harm, it would have been easy enough to kill him, but they used the flat side of the panga for their blows. Even so, his back was a mess and it was two hours or so before I felt I had cleaned all the wounds sufficiently. Around six o'clock we drove down to the local doctor.

One irony of this burglary, or I suppose robbery, as violence was used, is that they took little more than the television. Sat on the table, in plain sight was his laptop, worth five times the value of the TV and clearly far more portable. It seems the thieves did not know what it was.

The guards on the ISM campus were very poorly paid, even worse dressed and had little in the way of shelter, however, they did try to fulfil their jobs to the letter. They were called askari, which means guard but is also the word used for both a warrior and a roundworm infection. One of the gates to the campus was swept away in a storm. As the gates were always kept locked at night, this presented something of a problem. The askari came up with a novel solution however and continued to lock the gate, even though it was lying ten metres away from the gateposts. This really does deserve a "blind dedication to duty award" and is up there with some of the tasks that teachers have to do when preparing for OFSTED inspections.

Rejects: Suzhou, China: 2004. Doha, Qatar: 2010. Dhaka, Bangladesh: 2013

It makes eminent sense to group these. You arrive in a new land, a new city and with a new job and you are put into completely unsuitable accommodation. This happened everywhere except for our African homes and we are not particularly fussy!

In Suzhou, we were initially given an oddly interesting apartment. It was large, full of bold colours such as bright orange, had a back projector TV set, that for 2004 was enormous, came equipped with a full karaoke system and had a huge empty aquarium that we were told leaked. Admittedly, it was on the third floor and there was no lift, although we were relatively young and even less relatively fit, so that was not too much of a disadvantage.

We could have coped with these idiosyncrasies, we might even have belted out a few songs on the karaoke, however, we could not sleep. The apartment was directly above the main gate of the complex. Not only was the gate noisy, but every car driver that came up to it saw fit to sound their horn. We were suffering from advanced sleep deprivation by the time we found out that the previous occupant, a fellow teacher, had demanded to be moved out at the end of the previous year.

It took another month of complaining and finally, we were moved. In nearly every sense, the leadership of the school at that time were magnificent, it was a single slip. How did they allow new staff to be moved into accommodation rejected by existing staff; it made no sense.

In Qatar, we were initially happy with our ninth-floor apartment, in the Al Mana Twin Towers, although there again, we had arrived without our freight. My first concerns were regarding storage, we were moving from a three bedroomed apartment in Suzhou and this had only one, in addition, there was minimal cupboard space; I just could not see how we would cope when our container arrived. The second concern was when Andrea became seriously ill.

The apartment was hermetically sealed and air-conditioned. It was possible to open the windows, although, with temperatures of up to fifty degrees Celsius outside, the result was that the floor became covered in condensation and resembled an ice rink within seconds. I guess it was these conditions that had led to the build-up of virulent mould. Only when Andrea was admitted to hospital, remaining bedridden for two weeks with what turned out the be pneumonia, were we offered alternative housing. What a difference. It turned out that we had been given a one-bedroomed apartment because the administrative wing of the school was under the impression that only one of us was teaching. There were reasonable apartments in that block, with a second bedroom and without mould, we had just been unlucky, more significantly, the school had screwed up.

Arriving in Dhaka was also interesting. A messy, sprawling noisy city of nearly 20 million souls it was certainly the largest metropolis I have ever lived in. We were taken to our apartment directly from the airport by the school's CEO, a wonderful and friendly man. Entering the apartment, it was not the look of disappointment on our faces that was the biggest concern, it was the look of disappointment on his, but to give him his due, he tried to make the best of it. After a few weeks, when we requested a move, he was totally supportive.

The apartment was huge. Bangladeshi culture expects that a home should have a large reception room and that this is cut off from all the other, private rooms. Large...you could have landed a light aircraft in it! The reception room stretched from the back to front of the building, the length of a cricket pitch and was about five metres wide, it was featureless and completely unfurnished. There were rooms to each side, I believe six in all, five intended as bedrooms, although only one was furnished as such and a kitchen that was so small only one person could occupy it at a time. The only room with air conditioning and mosquito nets was the master bedroom.

It was hard to see how it would be possible to function in the property and, to be honest, we did not. We found out that the previous occupant, a single teacher, had used the master bedroom to crash occasionally, although to all intents and purposes, had lived with his girlfriend elsewhere. (To emphasise the incestuous nature of the world of international teachers, this guy married his girlfriend and is due to move into the house we vacated in Malawi in 2021. It's a small world!) It would have required enormous expense to furnish the place and it would still have been uncomfortable. However, it was only on a technicality that our move was granted; there was no cooker.

My wife is still unsure what a cooker is, so for any American readers here is a quote from Wikipedia, *"A kitchen stove, often called simply a stove or a cooker, is a kitchen appliance designed for the purpose of cooking food"*. Got it?

The CEO had noticed this when he introduced us to our new home. There was a double gas burner, with two cooking rings and nothing more. When we first asked for a move, the school told us they would ask the owner to fit a cooker instead. This would have been enormously difficult as there was so little space and it would probably have had to join the fridge in the aircraft hangar that was our lounge. We were delighted when the owner refused, as suddenly we were free to move somewhere else. However, remember the lack of nets? One of us, and it was not me, was bitten by an errant mosquito and ended up spending two and a half weeks off school with Dengue Fever. The other one in the partnership, me, was tasked with finding a new and satisfactory apartment, which I did.

Dhaka, Bangladesh: 2013-2016

The apartment I found was so good that when Andrea first walked in, she said, "Ugh! I don't like that wall."

I put this down to the after-effects of Dengue because except for one weirdly patterned blue wall it was an excellent apartment in nearly every way. It had everything the aircraft hangar did not and the only downsides were that the balcony was tiny and there were bars on all the windows. It should be pointed out that nearly all Dhaka apartments have bars, to deter burglars and these are even fitted in the highest of high-rise homes.

We remained in the apartment, very happily, for nearly two years and were disappointed when we were told we had to move. It turned out to be the strangest removal exercise I have ever undertaken; we moved three metres.

The owner of our apartment had lived below us and had sold the one we were in. He wanted to keep us as tenants and also wished to move closer to his work. As a result, we moved into his apartment one floor below.

Over our two years of occupancy, the owner's wife had been nagging our cleaner to come and work for her and when we moved, we found out why. In the original apartment, we had the odd big cockroach, although nothing that was bothersome. When we moved, we found out where our visitors had been coming from; their kitchen was infested and everything was covered by thick layers of grease. The clean-up task was huge and it took weeks to finally rid ourselves of the roaches.

A page or so back I mentioned public spaces in Bangladeshi homes, I also mentioned a small kitchen. It seems that just as visitors do not move out of the public space, so no one other than the females in the household and the maid, if there is one, enters the kitchen, which is why they are so small. Our landlord, who was a lovely guy, had probably never been in his own kitchen, he had no idea what a mess it was. When we finally left Bangladesh that kitchen was pristine.

Doha, Qatar: 2010-2013

We moved into our replacement accommodation while Andrea was still in hospital. She was brought to our new home and immediately spent a further week in bed while the antibiotics did their business. If you have started to believe that my missus is sick all the time, this is completely untrue. She has quite an excellent record of good health, punctuated three times by dengue, pneumonia and malaria.

It was a pleasant three-bedroomed house standing at the corner of a compound in which there were nineteen other identical homes. Being a corner plot, it had a significantly larger backyard than most of the other properties. We enjoyed the house and even managed to "green" the yard, although this was only possible for eight months of the year.

It is the only place we have ever lived where we needed the air conditioning 24/7 throughout the year. Qatar's climate is unpleasant and shade is essential, however, we were able to put a pool table into the yard and held irregular dart's tournaments there, surrounded by our potted tomato crop and some flowering plants.

We did struggle for a while to reach the house. Returning from work one day we found the road blocked with large pieces of concrete. It seems there was a new development just to the south of us and no one had considered that we might need continuous vehicular access. This is quite typical, rather than strange, whatever they say, the Qatar government gives no one any rights unless they are Qatari. There was one route out, which required only ten metres off-road, but this involved a round trip motorway journey of some fifteen kilometres, which seems a bit excessive when all you want is to get to work. The only sensible alternative was to cut across the desert for a mile or so, this section was hard and rocky, so there was no problem with sand, but there were sharp pieces of metal that could take out a tyre; care was needed. This situation continued for some months until the error was accidentally rather than deliberately rectified.

Within the compound three-quarters of the homes were occupied by teachers from our school; this has some huge advantages, although it also makes life somewhat claustrophobic. I will say that however pleasant the house, we would leave the country at every possible opportunity, which ate into a significant amount of our income.

Strange as it might seem, we know the family who live in the house today, having worked with them in Bangladesh. The area is more built up now, being as it is on the northern edge of Doha and adjacent to the newly built city of Lusail. This might mean the sand that used to be blown into the house every day might now have been replaced with building dust.

Guangzhou, China: 2007-2008

We had some interesting apartments in China; however, it would be rather boring to list them all. The older ones had been influenced by some interesting state regulations, such as buildings of five storeys or less did not need a lift, or that heating was required North of the Yangtze and air conditioning recommended South of the Yangtze. Quite how many of these were actual rules and how many anecdotal is a different matter. Our Guangzhou apartment was on the sixth floor. Whilst it did have a lift and it did have air conditioning, it did not have heating and became mighty cold for a few days in the winter.

I had quite a lot of contact with bats in China, much more than most people, one flew directly into the centre of my chest as I was walking down a city street. Another flew into our apartment and it proved extremely difficult to encourage the mammal to leave. One morning we woke to find that a banana sitting on the dining room table had been half-eaten; I immediately assumed it must have been a fruit bat. At this stage, halfway through this book, you have probably concluded that I am not very bright. This assumption is correct. After a few control tests, which only meant shutting the windows, I had to back down and admit the culprit could not be a bat. Then we met it. Remove the B and substitute an R. Rat.

The rodent's access point proved to be a small square hole in a pane of glass; I am unsure as to why it existed, possibly for an extractor fan that had been removed. To reach the access point the rat had to tiptoe along a couple of metres of narrow pipe and jump half a metre, it then had to reverse the process when it left. It should be remembered that this was all conducted some twenty metres above a busy urban street. Whilst I was amazed that the rat used such a precarious route, I was gobsmacked that it had discovered the way in.

The solution came courtesy of Microsoft, who used to sell their products on disks in boxes. The Windows Vista plastic box provided a perfect seal. In nearly every single respect Vista was a dreadful operating system, although I was delighted with the quality of the packaging. We never saw the rat again, I don't know whether it jumped, bounced and fell to its death or whether it was simply deterred from gaining entry; it is one of those mysteries that will never be satisfactorily answered.

Suzhou, China: 2007-2008

Returning to Suzhou, we were allocated an apartment on the nineteenth floor. As Andrea does not have a good head for heights this did have its challenges, although it should be added that mosquitoes have the same problem as she, the only ones we had in our home ascended in the lift. Acrophobia is also a problem of mine, although I am generally fine holding onto something immovable such as a rail; the result is that I move from one anchor point to the next when on a high balcony. Two memories stand out, one concerning the idea of being too low and the other of being too high.

The first was when a blimp, lost in the fog, flew past our balcony, so close I could have thrown a ball into the passenger compartment. Several eyes, wide open in fear, stared back at me. If the blimp had hit the structure, they would all have certainly perished. I am unclear as to what the damage to the apartment would have been.

The second concerned a guy who came to fix a faulty air conditioner. It was clear he would have to go outside the building, although I had expected him to be better equipped than he was. He had a short length of frayed rope and a normal trouser belt, using these two items to secure himself he edged around a section of the building and jumped onto the A/C platform.

The nineteenth floor is approximately sixty metres above the ground. My heart was pounding every second he remained outside and there was worse to come. He fixed the air conditioner, which only needed the coolant topping up, and then chose a different route for his return, this being through the window at which I was standing. First, he passed over his tools, then his can of refrigerant, then the rope. My heart sank. Lifting his arms, he motioned for me to give him a lift up. Holy shit! It is a good job he was light.

I never, ever, ever want to hold somebody above a drop of certain death again.

Nine: Stayin' Alive

(Health)

Below is a discourse on the health difficulties facing a teacher, from the simple issues of dealing with dental problems to injuries caused by colleagues and mental meltdowns. Certainly, these matters become more complex when you are living overseas and, normally, employers will provide health insurance to cover most eventualities. I always find it amusing that most of these insurance policies exclude death.

Lilongwe, Malawi: February 2020

The lightning strike delayed a much-needed visit to the dentist. One of my two bridges had come loose, some fifteen years after being fitted and it was beginning to play havoc with the left-hand side of my mouth. I remember being somewhat upset when having to have two molars extracted before my fortieth birthday. However, in our time in

China, I had been able to afford the bridgework required to give the impression that a full set of teeth sat in my mouth. Now one of them had worn out.

Unfortunately, the prognosis was not good. Both the lower left wisdom tooth and the first molar, the teeth supporting the bridge were rotten, requiring extraction. It would leave me with a row of three missing teeth. Even now, I have still not determined what should be done about this, unfashionable false teeth or implants? The answer to this question is dependent upon how long I expect to live and if you finish this chapter it might be possible to draw some conclusions regarding this matter.

The dentist we used in Lilongwe is excellent. By western standards, I guess her equipment is a little dated, but she knows her stuff. So much so, that upon my arrival for the extractions, she had a guest. When asked what her newfound assistant's role was to be, she explained he was an extraction expert and had more muscles than herself, which did not exactly calm me down. However, they did such a good job that in a break when asked if they had removed the first of the teeth, they told me that both were out. Good work.

However, a double tooth extraction, particularly with one being a wisdom tooth, is not pleasant. I returned to work, dropping in on the boss to tell him of my return. You might have thought that some sympathy might have been expressed. No. The following day I had to talk my way through over thirty ten-minute parent-teacher meetings, it was hell. I received enormous sympathy from the parents and even from the kids, however, not once did anyone in the management team ask about my wellbeing. Something is seriously wrong in an organisation when this sort of thing happens.

Following my time with the dentist, I started to become concerned about all those other things that start to go wrong with your body when you are pushing sixty-two years of age. The trouble is that I had started to compile a list and it had grown longer and longer and although knowing that doctors do not like patients walking in with more than one ailment, it seemed this might be necessary.

Although my mates seem to think I am sick all the time, these tend to be mild ailments, generally connected to my nose and exacerbated by my allergies. Their favourite phrase is to say that I have, "…seen the world through the veil of a handkerchief" and there may be some truth in this. Lilongwe is not a great place to suffer from allergic reactions and the tree pollen and the dust were the main catalysts for my problems. Quite what is in the dust that causes the issues I am unsure, but with the wet season having lots of pollen followed by a lengthy dry season with lots of dust, it plays hell with my sinuses. However, notwithstanding these issues, my attendance record throughout my entire time in employment has been excellent.

In my twenties, having visited a doctor twice in a couple of months, I expressed concern about becoming a hypochondriac. She lifted my file, it was all paper in those days and waved it at me.

"This is you," she said, "and this" lifting a doorstep of a file from the floor, "is a hypochondriac." Some doctors know how to make you feel better without drugs.

However, it was time to go and have a once over and to my delight I found a sensible, clear thinking Dutch doctor at our local clinic, the ABC. Yet another acronym and one that stands for the African Bible College, which is also a medical clinic.

If you arrive at ABC at the wrong time you will find you are involved in a prayer meeting in the waiting room. As an atheist since my early teens, this is not the sort of place I am comfortable. My shunning of a heavenly entity all those years back coincided with my taking up smoking and I had never stopped. Fifty years of smoking outweighed fifty years of atheism and I was quite happy to be administered to by a hard-line Christian because she proved to be such a cracking hard-line doctor. She was also the mother of one of my students, which meant that my appointments with her tended to focus on my physical state first and her daughter's educational progress towards the end. This is more than normal in an ex-pat community.

We were beginning to put together a strategy for improving my health when things were brought to an abrupt halt by the appearance on the international scene of Covid-19, something that sent Andrea and me into self-isolation and my doctor back to the Netherlands to cope with the pandemic there.

Medical facilities in Malawi are not of a high standard, even if some of the doctors, both ex-pat and local, are excellent. Many Malawian nurses work in the UK, three of the early Covid-19 deaths in the UK were Malawian. Trained medical professionals, migrating mainly to the UK, Saudi and South Africa, has left Malawi acutely short of skilled staff.

If staffing is one issue, then technology and power are another. Although hospitals and clinics sometimes have priority for electricity supply, this does not mean there are no power cuts. There may also be insufficient funds for fuel to turn on the backup generator. Statistics that put this into perspective are the infant mortality rate, which is ten times higher than in Europe, life expectancy, which is twenty years less than Europe and the number of physicians per 100,000 of population, a statistic in which Malawi falls in the bottom three in the world.

If there is a serious problem, teachers and many other ex-pats will be taken to Johannesburg to be hospitalised and treated there. As I write this, all scheduled flights in and out of Malawi are cancelled, it is Covid-19 causing the present issues, although the bigger problem will be if you go down with another serious medical ailment, for example, a stroke or a cardiac arrest and cannot get out of the country to be treated.

One thing that I will leave Malawi with is a little more medical knowledge than when I arrived. It became apparent that at some stage I might have to perform CPR and thought it prudent to refresh my knowledge if not my practical skills. In the process, I found that the Bee Gees song "Stayin' Alive" has an ideal beat, 104 per minute, to perform chest compressions on a heart attack victim. We are all lifelong learners.

Dhaka, Bangladesh: 2013-2016

I was fifty-seven years of age when I spent my first night in hospital, which is quite a remarkable statistic and was admitted with suspected dengue fever. Dengue is exceptionally unpleasant and I know this not only from extensive reading but because of experiencing Andrea being terribly ill when she had contracted it. When you go down with the symptoms of dengue fever the medical professionals treat you for that complaint. It is also known as breakbone fever, for the good reason that it makes you feel as if your bones are breaking. There is little in the way of treatment, it is not a curable disease, it is more a question of minimising the chances of dying.

Dengue fever is a mosquito-borne disease and it is spread by diurnal mosquitoes, unlike malaria, which is spread by nocturnal ones. In addition, it is more of a city or sewer mosquito than those that spread malaria, which tend to be more rural. Basically, it lowers or stops the production of blood platelets. If this continues dengue haemorrhagic fever sets in and it can be fatal. Because most painkillers also harm the production of blood cells, the use of them in cases of suspected dengue is limited; it is painful and you cannot take anything significant to reduce that pain.

They tested me and then treated me for dengue fever for two days, whereupon they discovered my test was negative. According to the doctor, the most likely condition was that of chikungunya, which is rarely a killer. I immediately demanded paracetamol. They kept me in for a third night, which I suspect was more to do with revenue maximisation than anything else, and it was during that evening that I discovered that my slipped disks were playing up.

Around three in the morning, I woke to find a strange man sponging my face and neck. Not having a clue who it was I reacted somewhat abruptly and rudely. The following morning when I was being taken for my MRI scan, I discovered I was being accused of racism, the sponging orderly having been Bangladeshi. I will confess, it was not racism, but probably, to my shame, a touch of latent homophobia, it is unlikely I would have reacted as I did if my rest had been disturbed by a female wiping me down.

They offered to operate on me to solve the disk problem, however, I was not having any of it. What a great free and online service NHS Direct provides, it took two months of careful exercise and with the help of their website, the problem was solved without involving anybody else. It was becoming increasingly clear that the hospital, which sat directly opposite the school and was part of the same company as ISD, was magnifying the extent of health issues and maximising the amount of revenue, without real concern for the long term health of their patients, who in this case happened to be group employees. This led me to a somewhat different interpretation of the hospital's approach to its patients.

Whilst still in Dhaka I also had a chest complaint. The specialist at the hospital suggested a bronchoscopy. I asked if an MRI or CT scan would be a more appropriate method of identifying a problem; we were particularly concerned about the possible ramifications of my smoking habit. I am a little innocent as regards the medical profession and infrastructure and did not have the background knowledge to do anything but accept his reasoning when he advised me that the bronchoscopy would be less invasive. To my mind, a bronchoscopy, which involves pushing a tube up your nose and down into your lungs, is only marginally less invasive than a colonoscopy. He explained what he meant by saying that the radiation entering your body from a scan was itself more invasive and more harmful. To cut a long story short, I accepted his explanation, however from further reading, his planned procedures were not in sync with modern practices.

It only became clear from the billing what the reasoning was. If a CT or MRI scan were involved the Radiography Department would have received the main payment, whereas the doctor would only have received a consulting fee. Whereas if the doctor performed the bronchoscopy himself, he would receive the fee for the procedure. Got it…personal profit before hospital profit before patient's health.

As it turned out, Dhaka, as well as giving me my first experience of overnighting in a hospital with suspected dengue, also quite unexpectedly gave me my first experience of a general anaesthetic. Although I had been told not to eat before the bronchoscopy, the first I learned that they were going to knock me out was precisely two minutes before they did so. I woke an hour or so later and within two hours had walked the 400 metres back into school, where the deputy head took one look at me and summoned a driver to take me home. The biopsy proved negative by the way.

Having been brought up in the UK with the National Health Service, you tend to take it for granted that doctors or consultants will act in your best interests. You also understand that fundamentally the service is free, although prescription charges are payable and gradually some other services are necessitating a payment; I believe in vitro fertilisation is one, but only in some regions. Having experienced medical care at different levels and for various reasons in Bangladesh, Malaysia, Austria, France, the USA, Tanzania, New Zealand, China, Malawi and Qatar, out of preference I would pick the UK's NHS. Long may it live!

Sittingbourne, Kent, England: 1991-1997

In my first years of teaching, I tried hard to engage in after school activities with other teachers, even though this was a little difficult because of living so far from work. On one such occasion, the teachers were to play a football match. I would love to be able to tell you who we were playing, but it will become clear why that information has escaped me.

It was a windy, rainswept night and the game was on Astroturf under floodlights. I remember that bit. I also remember a team member, a close colleague, receiving a head injury, although he played on. My last memory is of jumping to head a ball and instead head-butting a seriously hard object that happened to get in the way. I was out cold. Later I learned that the previously concussed teacher in his confused state had jumped for the same ball as me and our heads collided. I also remember it the first and only time I had been in an ambulance. Do not ask me what the score was.

Medway General Hospital A & E was busy, it was a Friday night. I saw the triage nurse quite quickly, but clearly, a gaping wound on my forehead was of lower priority than the various stabbings and comatose drunks that surrounded me. The waiting area had a huge glass door through which the wind howled carrying regular soakings from the incessant rain; it was November and it was cold.

In the only act of pleasantness I can ever recall him making toward me, the deputy-head who had disliked my presence in the school so much, turned up to see how I was, he had also contacted the woman who was my wife at that time. It proved a little unfortunate that he had not told her which hospital I had been taken to and it took her several hours to track me down.

Eventually, I was called and a good looking, cocky resident doctor took me over to surgery with a little gaggle of the best-looking nurses surrounding him. Everything about this guy shouted, "Don't let him touch you!" as he preened and teased with girls. As it turned out, his flashy showing off with a few butterfly stitches was not really up to scratch. His last advice to me was to keep the wound dry.

An hour later, back in the wet and windy waiting room, with only a damp football kit to keep the elements from my shivering frame, I noticed blood dripping between my football boots. I processed slowly. Blood is wet. He said do not allow the wound to get wet. The wound is now wet. I called for a nurse.

Two nurses came to my assistance, took one look at the re-opened gash and tutted. They freely expressed the opinion that all doctors were wankers, should not be allowed near open wounds and that they would undertake the job of stitching me up properly. They were not the same cute young nurses that came with Doctor Butterfly, they were the real deal. Nine proper stitches later, the bleeding had stopped and my partner had arrived, waiting to take me home. My head hurt.

The next morning, it still hurt, in addition, I could not move my leg. It took a second visit to A & E, this time one more local to my home, to establish much of the skin and flesh had been ripped off from just below my right knee. I had sat in Medway A & E for something like five hours, wearing a pair of football shorts and no one had noticed. OK, the NHS does have its faults; you have to tell them what is wrong with you, not the other way about.

The following Monday there were two of us who turned up at school with seriously damaged faces. I had taken off my dressing so that the nine stitches and the coagulated scar were prominent above my two black eyes and Neanderthal eyebrows. My colleague had massive bruising and swelling covering the entire left-hand side of his face. Fortunately, he appeared to have recovered from his concussion, although it is sometimes hard to tell with PE teachers. Separately we both told our classes that we had got into a fight with each other; they swallowed the story for at least twenty-four hours!

Spalding, Lincolnshire, England: 1999-2001

The sun streamed through her tangled blonde hair. Her lips parted, small twitchy movements. She knelt semi-naked on the side of the bed, toes wriggling in frustration and pushed her pointed face closer to my own. She kissed me. It was 8 a.m. on Thursday 16th August 2001, little did I know I would never see her again.

She changed my life, but not in the manner which she would have approved.

She leaned forward again and whispered something. She was having great difficulty making herself understood; I could not hear a word she was saying. Perhaps it was best that way. It seemed I had woken profoundly deaf.

Looking back, if I had to narrow it down, the period 1st January 2000 to 31st August 2001, represented the most fundamental upheaval in my life. The erroneous idea that the new millennium commenced with the year 2000[9] had been swallowed by the vast majority of the globe's population, the 31st December had been the biggest party night the world had seen. At 23.56hrs, on goes Prince's epic track, the stereo screaming, "Tonight we're gonna party like it's 1999!"

On comes the television for the chimes of Big Ben. Hugs and kisses all around. Back to the stereo and U2's New Year's Day blasts out, "I want to be with you. Be with you night and day. Nothing changes on New Year's Day." However, it did.

A more ominous line from Bono's lyrics reads, "I will begin again…"

---

[9] Konstantin Bikos. '**When Did the 21st Century Start?**'. Time and Date. 1995-2020

On New Year's Day 2000 I owned a four-bedroom home, with a double garage, believed I was happily married, gainfully employed, performed DIY and gardening chores as a matter of course, had a large number of very good friends and was finally content that my country was going in the right direction again, after almost two decades of Thatcherism. My life was turning out as my parents might have hoped for and even to the satisfaction of my in-laws. I appeared to be happy.

The wheels came off one by one.

By New Year's Day 2001, which was the actual commencement of the new millennium, I was separated from my wife, no longer owned a house or car, had become obsessive about my job, was having trouble keeping in touch with my mates, was drinking heavily and had knocked myself out twice in the space of a couple of months. Tony Blair and Gordon Brown, whilst being an improvement on the previous administration, were not pursuing a socialist agenda and the world's future seemed a much darker place. Life had not turned out how my parents had hoped and my in-laws were no longer speaking to me. I was distinctly unhappy.

Something better change.

For some, I have learned, this means an attempt to go back, to attempt to rebuild what was; these thoughts occurred to me. However, the fact is, I had never wanted the four-bedroomed house, I had never wanted the gardening, I wanted to remain a perpetual twenty-something with few responsibilities. The problem was that I was forty-two.

It was this slide that led me to awake in that Lincolnshire bedroom on 16th August 2001. It was the start of the recovery that led me to meet my future wife five days later, in Moshi, Tanzania. I wrote at the time, "...this is not a loneliness, it is more like my soul being scraped across a cheese grater." Almost around the same time as the world went into its mid-life crisis, with the events of 11th September 2001, my own very suddenly became a lot brighter. It seemed very odd, sitting in the heart of Africa, looking up at unknown constellations, with a Californian girl, drinking gin and tonic.

If I was in a mid-life crisis, this was not the end, but it was the beginning of the end, or certainly the beginning of a new outlook on life. Maybe my whole life has been a crisis.

As it turned out, I had not gone deaf. One ear had been pressed very firmly into a pillow and the other had been completely blocked by wax. A quick trip to the doctors sorted me out, which was a good thing for I left for Africa three days later.

The girl's voice followed me on a few international phone calls before being abruptly silenced. Just as suddenly, I began to find my own voice and it began singing songs I had not sung before, the songs of the naked man on the couch.

Moshi, Tanzania: 2001-2003

What Moshi did for me was to return me to health, mental health. It did not happen overnight and it was not clear to me at the time that anything was wrong. I was ascribing responsibility for faults in my life to others and denying personal responsibility for any problems. Reading through my diaries of the time, some of the thoughts were excruciating and that was at a time when I had determined to send them as group emails to my friends and family back home. Some people thought I was mad and extended metaphorical hands to assist, others cut off contact, a few permanently.

Meeting the woman who I would eventually marry was a big step in moving on, she would not put up with my navel-gazing, she wanted to have fun.

Fun is one of the best medicines and with it came fresh air, wide-open skies, wild Africa, a simpler, less cluttered life and a clearer route forward. If I was unable to grasp it immediately, I did eventually and have no regrets over the paths Andrea and I have trodden together over these last twenty years.

My one regret from my time in Moshi was caused by another football injury. As you get a bit older you think a little bit more and for a tad longer. Unfortunately, this is not always the best thing to do when you are playing in goal and a big Tanzanian centre-forward breaks your defensive line. If I had thrown myself at his feet immediately, I would have been unhurt, as it was, a millisecond too late I took the ball off his feet and he collided with me. At least I had saved a certain goal. Being knocked out again was not too bad, simultaneously having my medial ligaments permanently damaged, was a disaster, it meant I would never climb Kilimanjaro.

If there was regret there was also an event that brings cheer every time it comes to mind. The school received a call from the local hospital requesting blood donations from anyone with O negative blood, which is a rarity in Africa. An African woman was about to go into labour. She was severely anaemic, carrying only a tenth of the normal haemoglobin; they believed she would die immediately after birth without a major blood transfusion. Four teachers set off for KCMC, the local hospital, three being experienced blood donors, although for the PE teacher it was his first time.

We were met at the door and immediately led to the blood donor unit. The hospital was cleaner than I had expected and the little shop was doing a roaring trade selling "In Sympathy" cards, which left one with an ever so slightly dry throat! We had a weigh-in, a blood test and the standard blood pressure test; each was satisfactory.

We had promised to look after the PE teacher, but when we were ushered in they took three of us in at one time and left him until last; hospitals and blood were not his scene at all. The equipment was all new and sterile, even if the surroundings were not and my blood gushed out at its normal, double-quick speed. The headteacher had a real gusher as they took the needle out, his blood spread quickly and soon his sheet was covered with a large crimson stain. This is what the PE teacher had to walk into and it made him even more queasy. I am not sure how much blood they managed to extract from him. The following day we were told that our donation had been needed, that the woman had survived and her baby was doing fine. This made us feel good, but perhaps not quite as good as she and her family. You do not get that sort of feedback in the UK.

Suzhou, China: 2004-2007 & 2008-2010

A line in an old Lonely Planet guide had told me that, *"As elsewhere in Asia, the Chinese do not have Rh-negative blood and their blood banks don't store it."*

Oh! Poo! It was fortunate that during my time in China I did not need any of the red stuff. It was a little worrying that the precious liquid that keeps your author alive and kicking on this planet was completely unavailable. Many of you will appreciate the significance of this. We proud bearers of the blood type "O neg" can donate to one and all with a dash of class that sets us aside from any other types, we are in demand from Anchorage to Zanzibar and fulfil our responsibilities to mankind with joy in our hearts and a song on our lips. On the downside we can only receive "O neg" and when native groups are overwhelmingly of a differing type, for example in Asia and Africa, there is a potentially deadly problem.

On our initial medical on arriving in China, a nurse completed my medical card simply as "O", as they do not seem to recognize you might need a little dash after the letter. This is disturbing; for six years I carried an ID card that would have condemned me to death if I had needed a transfusion.

My first visit to a doctor in China was at a hospital in downtown Suzhou. I have only a vague idea as to the reasons for my presence there, although it was something to do with my guts and a gas build-up. What became immediately apparent is that the waiting and the consultations took place in the same room, which meant everyone got to hear and sometimes see, what other peoples' ailments were. This was early on in our residence in Suzhou and my spoken Chinese was limited to the basic, "hello", "yes" or "no", I did not have a clue what was being said in any conversation, however, there were some interesting boils on display.

It is worth pointing out two facts here. Firstly, that my ability with languages other than my own, is seriously deficient. I can go back to my school days when the French Department, so disturbed by my lack of proficiency after having been taught French for seven years, requested that Whitworth be taken off the "O" level course. It turned out I was the first student in the school's fifty-year history to be allowed to drop what was a compulsory subject. Their intentions were honourable; they did not want me damaging the progress of the other students in the class. I have never achieved anywhere near competence in another language, notwithstanding my residing and visiting so many foreign lands. The exception is going to be Spanish, although the use of the future tense should be noted.

Secondly, Chinese is not what it seems. Sure, the country has a single written language, although Hong Kong and Taiwan use the more convoluted traditional text and on a technical basis, Mandarin is the spoken lingua franca, but it does not help an ex-pat to find that the geographical varieties of dialect are only partially intelligible with the knowledge of the standard language. Put simply, someone from Sichuan may not understand a word that someone from Tianjin says. I believe there is even quite a big difference between the dialects of Shanghai and Suzhou, even though they are only eighty kilometres apart. As a foreign national living in China, which one are you supposed to learn, the one used on your local street or the central government's version?

Due to my complete inability to communicate, my school had sent along a member of the Chinese language department to assist me at the doctor's. This is all well and good until you realise that your most intimate medical secrets are to be shared with a teacher you will see every day at work. It was not until the doctor called me over and asked what the problem was that I realised I was not simply sharing my problem with the interpreter and the doc; every single person in the room leaned forward, almost cupping their ears, to find out what was ailing the Gweilo, the details spelt out loudly and clearly by my colleague. There were smiles, nods and minor conversations breaking out all around the room when everyone discovered I had gas.

Gweilo, by the way, is the Chinese nickname for white Europeans and means ghost man. It is not, although it can be, intended as rude in normal use. I think I probably looked like a ghost man when I left the doctor clutching my instructions for a diagnostic ultrasound. Everyone in the room waved a cheerful goodbye to me.

The scan itself turned out to be almost as entertaining. Two young nurses conducted the procedure and it became clear they had found something unusual when they started whispering to each other and pointing. On this occasion I was unaccompanied and, fortunately, one of them had a little English. She pointed to a blob that appeared on the screen and asked me if I had eaten. I had not, which caused them to become more perturbed. Eventually, they asked what I had to drink, which solved the problem completely…milk. I had been asked not to eat and had followed the instructions to the letter being completely unaware that a drink of milk could have thrown them. I guess it turns into some sort of yoghurt-like ball in your gut. The long and the short of it was that there was nothing wrong with me, which made both the two nurses and me extremely happy.

A few years later, in my second stay in Suzhou, I attended a doctor's clinic that had been set up for ex-pats. This meant that language was not a problem and they followed some of the western norms regarding privacy. There was a small cyst that was bothering me on my eyelid and the doctor agreed they would cut it out. There is nothing I like less than having anyone touch my eyes, particularly with a sharp knife, however, the procedure was undertaken so perfectly that I asked the doctor about a second cyst that was on my scrotum.

The deal was done and I found myself lying on the same surgical bed a week or so later. The doctor was great and worked with the assistance of a nurse, who turned out to be the same young girl that had attended the work on my eye. She was a much-changed character. Clearly, she was scared to death about seeing, let alone touching, any part of me that would normally be covered by my underpants. She tried to hide at the head of the bed, passing instruments to the doctor without looking. It could have been amusing, but I felt so sorry for her. I could see her going home that evening and telling her Mother that the Gweilo do indeed have 多毛的白色生殖器 (hairy white genitals).

Any time you admit to having lived in China the question is always asked, "How did you cope with the pollution?"

For five of our six years we lived in Suzhou, which has comparatively low pollution compared to many Chinese cities; in Guangzhou, particularly living in the centre, it was pretty bad. However, whilst we were there, I had some time to conduct some research and check a few things out. In amongst all those scientific papers regarding China's part in destroying our planet, there were a few, written by Westerners, that were much more optimistic.

Today it is quite clear what can be done with man-made atmospheric pollution in China, we have all seen the satellite photos taken while the Chinese were in lockdown. What is less clear is what can be done with China's natural pollution, admittedly exacerbated by man, that of the dust-filled storms that sweep off the loess regions, particularly around the Yellow River catchment.

What was being pointed out by those outlier environmentalists, was that the People's Republic of China was not only well aware of the problem, but it was also in a position to be able to act far more quickly than the democratic west in sorting out some of the fundamental issues. Far too often the West point a damning finger in a Chinese direction and there is a commonly held belief that China has bad governance, bad systems and that they are not necessarily educated enough to understand global issues. This is not only wrong it is extremely rude. China has excellent scientists, it has people, amongst them politicians, who care hugely about their own and the global environment.

China's water supply and to some extent their electricity supply is dependent upon the normal flow of two rivers, the Yangtze and the

Yellow River. Both rise on the Tibetan Plateau and are fed by glacial meltwaters. This may go some way to explaining why China is not any time soon going to "free" Tibet but also explains why China has an intense interest in the state of the Himalayan and Tibetan glaciers.

The argument goes that China will be more able to take swifter action on the environment because it has the political apparatus to command such a thing. This is true. It is also in a position that almost two-thirds of its land area is unsuitable for either agriculture or large urban development. In addition, it has a large, relatively cheap labour force, together with the technological capability to manufacture large scale apparatus. Combining these elements means that there are resources that can be easily applied to greening their energy policy.

If we want evidence of China's ability to act swiftly, decisively and comprehensively, we need to look no further than the statistics for the spread, or containment, of Covid-19. For all the criticism levelled at China, they did a far better job of controlling the pandemic than the USA, UK, India, or Brazil and to do this they used authoritarian force.

On two trips around China, one to the far west in 2008 and the other after we had left the country in 2012, I was astonished at the massive scale of the wind and solar farms. On the second of these two trips, I was also shocked by the amount of reforestation, one prime intent of which was to reduce the dust storms that plague north-eastern China.

It is not the case that China is not bothered about the environment, it is not the case that they march on regardless of the damaging effects of coal-fired power stations, it is the case that they are taking very serious and costly action to ameliorate the effects on climate change and it is the case that this will take time to have an impact. It is quite likely that in twenty years, we may well look back on this period and see that China's actions were more effective than those of the West and we may have to thank them for their attempts to stem the decline in Earth's health.

China is key to the Earth's future and every one of us needs to understand that.

Ten: The Exorcist

(Discipline)

This essay deals with discipline. Not only the discipline of students by their teachers and their schools but also the discipline of teachers by the school management. It seems to me that very often double standards are at work regarding the two, specifically as regards written rules and regulations. Conversely, it is quite common to see school management, who are almost invariably comprised of promoted teachers, treating their own teaching staff in a similar manner to that with which they treat students and nobody, least of all a teacher, likes the dunce's cap!

Bishop Mackenzie International School (BMIS), Lilongwe, Malawi: February 2020

On Friday 28th February, I was quite astonished to have the secondary headteacher come into my room. The reason for my surprise was that over three and a half years I could only remember him being there once before. It was second-guessing when I mentioned an email recently sent to him and for a minute or two we discussed my planning suggestion. He then came to the real point of his visit, which shocked me further.

It seemed there had been a complaint, from a parent, about my treatment of her son during the first period of the day. Clearly, as it had only been an hour or two previously, I remembered precisely what had occurred and it seemed to me to be an insignificant incident. The boy had been messing around with two other students, low level, although irritating behaviour and it was preventing all three of them from working; I had told him to move to another desk.

While he was moving, I explained what the problem was and how there was now an expectation that he now progresses at a faster pace. All this was done very calmly and quietly. At this point the boy turned to me and held out his arms, palms upwards and poses in a "What have I done?" shrug. My standards do not allow a student to take this sort of action without a consequence and I asked him to wait outside the room, the intent being to go and talk to him about it. At this point, the rest of the class became aware something was going on, although they would have been unsure of precisely what.

On leaving the room, I asked him what he meant by his gesturing and did so by imitating the gesture, having no idea what it would be called. With no answer, I asked a second time. It was clear the boy was upset and having resolved to have word with him after the lesson, I sent him back inside. As they were supposed to be working on their laptops, I was unaware that the lad was no longer working at all, for it was at this point he had started to send emails to his mother.

It seems they were along the lines of his being fed up with BMIS, wanting to leave, always being picked on and there were a series of messages in the same vein. It was this the headteacher wanted to talk to me about.

It will be clear to anyone reading this that the student was not directing his complaints toward me, however, that is not how the headteacher saw it. Following his visit I fired off an email outlining the incident, explaining I had followed normal classroom practice, had not raised my voice, had not been angry and also pointing out that I had been a little amused by the gesture the boy made, I had every expectation that the matter would be laid to rest.

It had not and I received a threatening email later in the day, *"There seems (sic) to be regular problems coming through at the moment with you Mark, and you need to sort this out. I'm afraid further problems would need to be handled following disciplinary procedures."*

The whole incident seemed so bizarre, particularly the comment about "regular problems" as to my recollection there were none. It seemed best to completely ignore his email, his points were not based on any form of rationality and if there were a series of similar circumstances these should have been dealt with in a face to face meeting. However, there was another line in his email that bothered me. He said he had spoken to other students in the class and they said, "*...you lose your temper included (sic) when the power goes off. A couple of students said you slammed a ruler on a desk after one such incident. They mentioned that you often apologise to the class after losing your temper.*"

For whatever reason, he was linking my staged fits when all power is lost in the classroom (which is a particularly irritating fact of life in Malawi and the fits are quite comical) with a student complaining about being disciplined in the classroom. All the evidence seemed to point out that there had not been a serious issue in the lesson that morning and, as there is a video camera filming outside my classroom door, he could have checked the tape to verify my version of events.

It has to be suspected that he had checked the tape and had found nothing contrary to what I had said; if he had he would have used it against me. The whole incident started me thinking, what was bugging him? Clearly, it was something to do with getting angry. It slowly dawned on me where the problem lay.

Just before the Xmas break I had cause to complain about a member of the management team. I had carefully weighed up the best approach and had made an informal complaint. If I had made a formal complaint, the headteacher would have been obliged to act, the lesser route gave him a bit more leeway. Besides, I had never made a formal complaint about a colleague in thirty years and it was not my plan to start in my final year.

It had been an issue with the same class. I often wait outside the door for groups, although on this earlier occasion, when they were to have a formal test, it was even more important to do so to ensure a quiet and orderly approach to the examination. They were late. Not five minutes, not ten minutes, but fifteen minutes. Something like this is not the fault of the students, it had to be a teacher holding them up.

And so it proved. As the kids started to dribble in, they were soon followed by an irate curriculum coordinator. It seems she was concerned that the students had not been given notice of the test and had spent fifteen minutes questioning them about it. She only determined to speak to me when she had already delayed proceedings and had not checked our work management system nor students' homework diaries. If I had been able to see the funny side of it, I should have pointed out that this particular class had been with me for the last lesson of the previous day, during which I had gone through the entire contents of their test with them. I could have pointed out that the test had been posted on the student management system for two weeks, that they had received an email message concerning it on the previous day and that they had been told to make a note of it in their planners.

However, her manner was appalling and I became furious. I was so angry that it was difficult to speak. Not angry with the kids, but with her. All she had to have done was to check. She had not. I believe that this was the incident that the headteacher referred to as regards losing my temper.

Any reasonable manager, with a modicum of common sense, should have done something about this, but it was akin to a scene from The Office. Because I was so angry, I did not feel fit to go back in and supervise 11-year olds and this should have been evident to her. Instead, I had to listen to her raging on, while I tried to work out how to calm myself and manage the job at hand: a lesson and a test that would now have to spill over into the following week.

This particular incident was certainly the most appalling act of mismanagement I have ever had directed at me in front of students. Even if I had been in the wrong, which was not the case, the matter was handled in the worst possible fashion. I mention elsewhere the lack of breadth of management experience at the school and feel that this episode showed it at its very worst.

So, this was what the headteacher was referring to in his email and this was the payback for complaining about one of the management team. Astonishingly, neither the headteacher nor the curriculum coordinator apologised to me for their respective outbursts, even when it had become clear that they were in the wrong.

It is normal that if a teacher is thought to have breached their contract, then there should be a presumption of innocence until sufficient evidence is gathered to prove otherwise. Whereas, if a student breaks the rules, there is often a presumption of guilt, until it is proved otherwise. I question whether either of these maxims is entirely valid, however in my last year of teaching it was absolutely clear that the management of the school had completely reversed them; they had lost trust in their teachers, largely because the teachers had long since lost any trust in them. This was most clearly evidenced by the fact that twice in three years entire departments had left on mass due to destructive mismanagement.

The consequence of their attempts to intervene with my classroom management is that I failed to fulfil my aims with one particular group. My adage had always been that I do not mind if the students do not like me at the start, because by the end of the school year they will have developed a respect for me and a realisation that their advancement through the year has been substantial. It is a policy that has worked year after year after year and is reflected in the high esteem in which I am held by the pupils. Perhaps the management was jealous? I know for a fact that I was far, far more popular with kids and parents than anyone on their team.

Bishop Mackenzie International School (BMIS), Lilongwe, Malawi: 2016-2020

We can go back to October 2017 to unearth the beginnings of my realisation that something was wrong with the control systems at the school. Andrea and I had been asked to indicate if we would like to renew our contracts for a further two years. This is done some ten months before the new contract will commence, largely due to the difficulties in hiring overseas staff.

We considered it a formality but were then called into a meeting with the CEO and secondary headteacher. The CEO advised that they were not going to offer us contracts although he would reconsider his position in December. We were astonished. He used the phrase, "I think you may have boarded the wrong bus."

It was a knock to our systems, nothing like this had ever occurred before. It was clear the criticism was directed solely at myself and that Andrea had become caught up in the crosshairs. Although what precisely had I done? It seemed that criticisms of my performance were made by only two people and that those criticisms were not about my teaching, but about my arguing points of view, largely regarding curriculum.

In December I was told that the situation had been fully investigated and that all the criticisms had been unfounded. Ah! Well, OK then, you put us through ten weeks of hell only to tell us that we were doing a good job, something that we knew to start with. Maybe we were on the right bus, it just seemed to have rather a poor driver, the controller had set him off on the wrong route and that two conductors were making up stories while peeing off the edge of the platform.

My performance dipped substantially in those ten weeks, as did Andrea's; we were nowhere near as effective as teachers. However, having been reassessed during that period, it was found that we were not on the wrong bus. How the hell were we on the right bus when we were performing poorly, but on the wrong bus when performing at the highest level. It made no sense and if one were to wish to point fingers it was absolutely clear where the fingers should be pointed.

There had been no apology on this occasion either. Andrea was not even told directly that the decision had been reversed, she had to find out from me.

Crass management.

A policy that the secondary school was developing around that time, one that only got into full swing a year or so later, was that teachers should not have direct email contact with parents or, to be more specific, they could have direct contact, however, their email had been approved first. If anyone wanted to devise a policy that would cause long-term harm to students, parents, teachers and to the school itself, this was it. As a result, over a long period, teachers would flout the rule, find alternative means of communication or, and this was the most worrying aspect, reduce their communication with parents.

There are only so many metaphorical sticks you can use to persuade students to behave. Having the parents onside is an enormous asset, but this is not automatic. In most international schools the parents are committed to their kids' educations and are supportive of the teaching staff. There are always a handful of parents who are somewhat more problematic but generally, they can be brought around with sound communication from their offspring's teachers.

In the English state schools I taught in this was more of a problem. Although the majority of parents were supportive, a significant minority appeared to have carried their own problems with educational establishments with them into parenthood. Not only did these parents have an anti-establishment attitude themselves, but they also instilled it in their children from a young age.

What had become noticeably clear as I entered my last two years, was that there had been a breakdown in the relationship between BMIS and some parents. It was to mend this situation that the management had introduced the parent-teacher vetted emails policy. However, what was even clearer was that there was not a breakdown in teacher-parent relationships, the breakdown was between the management and parents. In introducing vetting or censorship in communication, reducing the quality of dialogue and in some cases preventing it, the management piled themselves deeper and deeper into the mire.

In the final chapter, when I examine the fallout of 2019-20, this will be elaborated on further.

Around the World

Here is a short list of some breaches of school rules from Guyana[10].

- Wearing shirt unbuttoned low down.
- Smoking in class or on the school compound.
- Eating and spitting in the classroom.
- Not attending assembly.

---

[10] Ministry of Education. Guyana.

They seem fair enough, even when you find out these are not the rules for students, they are for the teachers. All four have the consequences of a first and second warning followed by suspension or dismissal.

It is obvious that teachers need rules and further guidelines, however for most teachers these are automatic, there is no need for them to be spelt out.

In terms of dress, I have worn virtually the same type of clothing for my entire time as a teacher; a pair of shoes, smart chinos and a button-up or button-down shirt. If you want to know the difference between the two shirts, it is easy enough to look them up. If it were cold, I would wear a sports jacket, although not one with patched elbows, and if the management were particularly anal, I would have to wear a tie. Easy.

Working in the Tropics the one thing you do not want to hear is, "Gentlemen, ties please!" This sort of phrase comes out for parents' evenings particularly, although at some schools the Headteachers regard ties as a requisite of the job. Note the sexism. Except for bans on open-toed sandals, I have never, ever heard an instruction to female teachers about their dress. The difference between what male teachers are allowed to wear and what female teachers are allowed to wear is enormous.

For male teachers, it is a variation on the theme I outlined above, although it can extend as far as suits. T-shirts, polo shirts, shorts, hoodies and so on, are completely unacceptable, which is fine. I am not sure why it is, but in my experience female teachers get away with almost anything. This is fine to a point. Whereas a male teacher might be spoken to for wearing a polo shirt, a female teacher is not for wearing a t-shirt. A male teacher would certainly be spoken to about having a shirt undone exceptionally low, although nothing is said to the females about semi-exposed breasts and skirts showing an enormous amount of thigh, which to my mind is distracting not only for the students but also for fellow teachers. I am sure there are schools where this is properly sorted out and there is some fairness for men and women, although I have yet to work in one.

There are then the rules for teachers that are so obvious they are not even written down. You would have thought that the idea that the teacher should deliver the prescribed curriculum would be more or less written in stone, however, it is not. I have come across many teachers who openly ignore their own subject department's instructions on content and skills delivery and there are as many excuses as there are examples. Internationally, I have yet to see any other action taken on this other than a refusal of a contract renewal.

Likewise, with the discipline of students. If it is prescribed that a student who is late, even by a second, should be given a late mark, then this should happen, however stupid it might be. Unfortunately, some teachers fail to see the bigger picture on many aspects of student discipline and bend and break rules as suits the situation. I know this because I have been there and so have most of my colleagues.

Rules for the students are written down and there are many of them. The rules are designed to prevent kids from misbehaving, largely to ensure their educational progress is not disrupted.

What is misbehaviour? Clearly, stabbing a teacher falls into this category, but should submitting work late also be included? Is wearing a hoodie to school an indication of an errant child or do they have to be selling amphetamines in the toilets? Arriving late to school is not helpful, but where does this fall on a scale that includes physical and cyberbullying or dancing on the desks during a lesson.

By far the largest problem for the kids is bullying, however, by far the largest problem for many teachers is work being submitted late or not at all. The gulf between the two is immense.

Bullying is a massive issue and statistics from both the USA[11] and the UK[12] bear this out. In the USA, gang-related incidents in schools are measured separately, although to my mind gang culture is just an example of more organised bullying; as students move from Middle School to High School, "bullying" reduces and "gang" offences increase, giving more or less the same figures overall. In similar, if not directly comparable figures, the UK has a lower level of bullying than the USA, although it is clear that cyberbullying is at its highest in the Middle School years.

Those examples are for students bullying students, how about students bullying teachers? Some quite shocking figures from the USA[13] suggest that approximately 20% of public school teachers

---

[11] Statista. '**Percentage of U.S. public schools with selected discipline problems...**' 2020

[12] National Centre for Education Statistics. '**Discipline Problems Reported by Public Schools**'. July 2020

[13] American Psychological Association. '**Violence Against Teachers**'. 2016

reported being verbally abused, 10% reported being physically threatened and 5% reported being physically attacked in schools. In similar, although not directly comparable figures, the UK has around 18% of teachers reporting abuse. Perhaps of far greater concern is that in the UK in 2017-18 around 3% of schools reported that widespread disorder in the classroom occurred at least once a week. Whilst it is not spelt out in the figures, most teachers are aware that these incidents are largely focussed on a sub-group of their members, not all teachers, thus becoming persistent identifiable bullying by students.

I have been attacked by a student once, physically threatened twice and verbally abused a few times, although probably many more times when I was out of hearing. As for widespread disorder in the classroom: twice. Except for one case of verbal abuse all these instances occurred in the UK.

Clifton School, Rotherham, England: 2003-2004

In early musings, I mentioned returning to the UK for a year to take on a difficult role in a difficult school. It was my second day. On the first day, I had my first lesson with a particular class, however, three students were missing. When the three came in the next day, I took them into a classroom separately from the others, who were then supervised by another teacher. The intention had been to introduce myself, chat with them and make us all comfortable. As soon as I was by myself in the room, the three kids stood up on the desks and started to walk around the classroom a metre from the floor.

It was behaviour I had not witnessed before and I will confess to being a little perplexed. However, experience kicked in and I allowed them to wear themselves out. We eventually had our little chat. This is an example of widespread disorder in the classroom. It was not particularly dangerous, although certainly if one of them had been hurt falling off a desk, you can guess whose fault it would have been. I could have reacted, called the deputy-head, or started haranguing them, however, there was little point; they needed to come to terms with me and I with them. Not one of those three repeated the stunt with me. There was a similar case a couple of months later with another student I was talking to. By then I had found out that the desk walking stunt was quite common at the school. When I pointed out that he was standing on some exam papers and the print of his shoe would easily identify him, he climbed down and carefully cleaned off the papers.

It is strange how students blow hot and cold. The same sixteen-year-old asked if he could stay in one lunchtime to talk to me about sex. His question concerned the practicality of sex with a female who was menstruating, although that was not quite how he phrased it. As he was Muslim, I pointed out that what he was asking about was haram, that he should bear this in mind and then went on to give him the ups and downs of sexual intercourse during menstruation. He listened carefully, asked some valid questions and was thoroughly polite. One hour later, in normal lesson time, he was as objectionable as possible, presumably to maintain his image in front of his peers.

Other Schools, Lincolnshire, England: 1990

I was called in as a supply teacher for the odd day at a school near The Wash. It was one of the worst run schools I can remember. Having been taken to my class by the headteacher, once he walked out the kids stopped work and started arsing about. There was nothing that could be said or done to stop them, I tried everything and I was about as well-versed as anyone back then in dealing with awkward kids. The only thing that worked was to call the headteacher back in again, but as soon as he left, we had the same thing. It turned out that it was the same throughout the school and in many classes, it was just aggravated somewhat by my being a supply teacher.

When the only person who can apply direct control to a bunch of kids is the "manager" then management has failed. After two days working there, I told them to stop calling me; there was plenty of other work.

The next day I received a call from a school ten kilometres down the road from the "bad" one. What a difference: kids sweet as pie, no disorder and everyone was polite to each other, including the teachers. The two school's catchment areas abutted each other and were similar.

Whilst what happened next does not fit in a chapter on discipline, it does highlight the difference in the schools.

I walked into the classroom, five minutes ahead of time. There is a note pinned to the desk outlining the cover work and a classroom assistant ready to help.

"Read them the rules of Quidditch and then ask them to explain them in their own words."

"What?" The second question to the classroom assistant was, "What is Quidditch?", followed by, "What is Harry Potter and the Philosopher's Stone?" I had never heard of Harry Potter.

The kids had arrived while I rapidly tried to absorb two pages of a fantasy game in a fantasy book played by wizards; the students were brilliant. The one-hour lesson simply whisked by with not a word spoken out of place. There were probably more rules in the first of these two schools, there were probably more punishments meted out, although there was no doubt which of the two was more disciplined. That is what a good headteacher can deliver, however, I never had cause to meet or speak to that individual. It would have been a nice touch to have passed on my congratulations.

Suzhou Singapore International School (SSIS), Suzhou, China: 2004-2010

The majority of the remainder of this chapter focuses on the UK, largely because there have been so few discipline issues of note since I started working overseas. However, two items from China are worth mentioning.

The first was a 2008 newspaper article about the death of eight school kids in Xiangxiang, which is in central southern China. The students were crushed in a stairwell when they stampeded out of an evening lesson. This was not the first time it had happened in China and I believe 2002 had been the last such incident.

What is this to do with discipline? One requirement, when I was training as a teacher, was to be at the door when the students arrived and to be there again when they leave. In this manner, the teacher has some control over what goes on immediately outside their classroom. Even though it has been almost entirely unnecessary in the last twenty years of working overseas, it is still a habit I like to keep. If the teacher in Xiangxiang had done this it is possible those deaths could have been avoided, instead, those kids were mourned across China.

When I first started teaching, I was lent a little book of helpful tips, including the one about standing at the classroom door. Accidentally the guide stayed with me and two years ago I, in turn, lent it to a trainee teacher. She, like myself so many years ago, has yet to return it and just this moment I called to ask for it back. The book is "The Craft of the Classroom", the author, Michael Marland. The edition I have, from 1975, is extremely dated, referring to corporal punishment and suchlike, although most of the advice in it holds good today. I believe the final updated edition was produced in 2002.

This is the first time I have publicly admitted responsibility for an action in China that could have resulted in my dismissal. In my career I have only twice lied to headteachers and, in denying my involvement in the construction of a sweepstake, this was one of those occasions. I was asked directly if it had been me that put it together and when my answer was no, was promptly told that it could not have been me anyway because it was far too clever and compiling it would have involved knowing things outside my potential sphere of knowledge.

Hmm! I guess their misunderstanding of our capabilities was one reason for the sweepstake.

Each year we ran a sweep on how long the director's speech would be at the annual all-staff meeting. I was thoroughly pissed off with a few things going down and created a super sweep, taking great care to disguise my identity, such as writing it with a New Zealand English spellcheck, using a random printer, destroying soft copies, wearing gloves to circulate it, which meant leaving it in a few obscure pigeonholes and on a desk in a storage area. It was very soon within the hands of every single teacher, amongst whom it was received with a high degree of mirth. However, the shit hit the fan when the management team got hold of it, which is probably the second reason I had put it together; they had no sense of humour.

It was to take the mickey out of the management and board. There were four sections and you were supposed to pick a "likely" announcement in the meeting from each section. Section four gave six extremely unlikely events to choose from:

- Resignation of the board with immediate effect.
- Introduction of a cap on the numbers of students of a single nationality.
- Remuneration package to increase by over 20%.
- Publication of accurate end of year accounts.
- Flying pigs to be found on the menu for all canteen lunches.
- An administrator breaks into "Papa Was a Rollin' Stone" but forgets the words.

As you will identify immediately, some of these choices were so specific to the school itself that no outsider could have understood what it was about. At the bottom of the page, there was a space for a name (where it suggested you wrote someone else's) and for your preferred choice of a new employer.

Having failed dismally to identify the culprit, a group of three administrators, to their great credit, tried to ride it out with an acapella version of Papa Was a Rollin' Stone. Unfortunately, there were four of them on the stage and they had failed to tell the fourth what they were doing.

And I guess that was the third reason I was taking the piss out of them: Poor communication.

An extremely special school, Leicestershire, England: 2000

Leicestershire does not appear on the list of jobs I have held down for a good reason; I was at the school for only a month. It had been agreed as a two-year contract, but I could not hack it. Simple as that. I had landed a job in an extremely special school. It was so special that the fees were higher than at any of the public schools in the country, even Eton or Harrow. (In the UK, public schools are, in fact, private schools.) It was the only job I had ever failed in.

Throughout my early career, I had shifted closer and closer to a focus on special needs kids and this school was right at the apex of special needs. It had been established to take on the very most difficult kids, those who had been expelled multiple times from normal schools. It was the Local Education Authorities that paid the fees, the last chance saloon for most of the students. I cannot remember the exact figures, although the school's remit was to keep these kids out of prison; they had a low success rate purely because of the intake, but they did manage with some.

The teachers and other staff at the school, which was a rural boarding school, isolated in stunning countryside, were fantastic, the management was wonderful and the kids were exceptionally difficult.

The classrooms had doors that opened up to woodland. I arrived for my first solo lesson and was surprised to find no students waiting. After waiting probably five minutes I heard a rustling in the tree above me; it was one of the kids. I asked him if he wanted to come down and have a fun lesson, to which he replied that the "others" were waiting to beat him up. I told him there was no one there and he slid down the tree. As I unlocked the door he sidled through and from nowhere sprung five other students, diving through the door and piling atop the first lad. It is quite easy to wrestle a twelve-year-old, although six of them, all punching, biting and kicking, is a bit more of a handful. It took ten minutes or so to subdue them and then I had to ask for the assistance of one of the support staff to take a couple of them away to calm down.

Having to physically restrain kids daily is what got to me. I had learned safe arm and neck locks, however, when you are told you have to crank up an arm lock to stop the kid kicking you, this is applying pain to restrain. It might be necessary, but it is not nice. All the staff were warned to expect to be suspended during the year and each kid had a social worker who was duty-bound to report any incident, which was then passed to the police; this was the norm and they staffed the school to cope with it.

On another occasion, I kept back a student to talk to him about his behaviour in class. He was not at all keen on this idea, so I stood in the doorway, preventing him from leaving. He backed up the whole length of the classroom, maybe six metres or so before beginning to charge me. As I braced for the impact, there was the realisation that he was firstly veering to the left and secondly launching himself into a karate jump kick, his objective being the closed window next to me. I had no time to react and could only watch in horror as his small form flew feet first towards the glass.

He bounced. No one had bothered to tell me that bulletproof glass was fitted in all the windows. As he picked himself up, I stood to one side, it was not worth trying to stop him from leaving.

At the end of each day, I would have quite a long car journey home. Each day I would find myself crying and it was clear I was not up to the task. When I went in to see the headteacher he was enormously sympathetic and understanding. He told me they had something like half of their new teachers leave within a few weeks, I was not the first and would not be the last. He also admitted that they did not think it would be me (two of us had been taken on at the same time) and told me he was impressed with what I had done. In the aftermath, he gave me a glowing reference and I suffered no vocational damage from my truncated stay at his school. Whether or not I left there in a sound emotional state was a different matter.

Westlands School, Sittingbourne, Kent, England: 1991-1997

In my first year of teaching, I shared a classroom with a newly qualified teacher, a P.E. specialist, who used my teaching room to register her class and for a few lessons each week. She was a young girl, fresh out of the system that sees teachers progress from school to college and back to school again, without any exposure to the outside world. An entirely different path from my curriculum vitae.

Right from the start, I managed to nail classroom discipline. I have no idea how this came naturally to me and had very few of the normal settling in issues. Perhaps my age helped, as I was in my mid-thirties, perhaps it was my face, which is always pretty unsmiling, but I believe it was more down to my expectations. I did not expect my students to misbehave and made it clear where the lines were; this has continued throughout my career. But at the same time, the prime intent within my lessons is that the students should have fun, because if they are enjoying themselves, they learn much, much more. Having these two guiding principles meant that most students would enjoy my lessons. If they know that you can deliberately deliver a lesson that is boring, and will do so if provoked, they are far less likely to push at those lines.

I believe some call this psychology but it seems to me it is simply common sense.

Unfortunately, the young P.E. teacher did not find it natural at all and her unease quickly filtered through to the students, who made it more and more difficult for her every week. Kids are like that; it seems to be an inbuilt trait and even the nicest pupils can rachet up the pressure. When I was at school, we regularly made one of our English teachers cry and each time we went back in with the intent of making it worse. Why?

The P.E. teacher was also the only black member of staff in the school, perhaps the first, although I am unsure of that. She received some support, although to my mind it was never enough. Whilst I do not believe it was overt racism that prevented the school from doing more, this may have been a subliminal factor, the area the school was in was white, white and white. I lived in South London in a very mixed-race environment, however, nearly all the other teachers lived in the monoculture of mid-Kent and I think they were simply ill-prepared for the issues that arose.

Towards the end of that first year, I was asked to go and supervise a P.E. class which the young teacher was taking; the school had completely lost confidence in her. The whole thing was somewhat embarrassing. There was me, an unqualified teacher (as it would take another year for me to receive my certification) supervising a qualified teacher taking her normal class; I did not like it at all and had enormous sympathy for the girl.

There were plenty of incidents at my first school, although in general, discipline was fairly good. I did split up a knife fight, but the kids acquiesced reasonably easily. The same character from the Canterbury field trip, the school hard man, once came at me with a metal pipe, although he backed off when it came to laying it on me.

However, one of the funniest incidents occurred in one of the morning staff meetings.

As the briefing was coming to an end, all the female teachers were asked to wait behind. Speculation was rife and there were plenty of staff at the school with a wicked sense of humour. We, the male staff, found out that they had all received a dressing down concerning the state of the women's toilets, not the girls' toilets but those of the staff. It took a while for the truth to leak out. It turned out a student had gone into the loo, swinging a heavily bloodied tampon around her head. Quite why the management would ever think that the female staff would have made that sort of mess was unclear. Over the years I have always argued that the users of workplace men's toilets maintain them more hygienically than their female counterparts and this had seemed to prove the point. It is a shame the truth came out!

Parents meetings are normally quiet, intense and a serious attempt is made by both the teachers and the parents to get inside the heads of their hormonally addled charges. Normally.

It was six-thirty, the hall was packed and I had just finished my twentieth interview. The table jerked violently against my leg. Directly to my left was an astonishing scene that I had inadvertently become a part of. One of my Geography teachers had his hands around the throat of a parent who was attempting to smack him over the head. This is a particularly difficult scenario when you realise there are upwards of one hundred teachers, two hundred students and possibly even more parents in the room; what fun it would have been if a bar brawl had resulted. As his head of department, I was aware that the teacher was a black belt in karate and knew whose side it would be good to be on.

After calming them down, both the teacher and the parent had to go to see the headteacher and we got on with the meetings as best we could. The following morning the teacher explained to me what had occurred. Apparently, the student had moved up into a higher ability set, leaving his class. However, before he had done so, he had completed some homework. Because of the move, the marked work had never been returned. This is a seemingly minor issue, easily rectified and it seemed astonishing that it could have led to what was, to all intents and purposes, a fight. Unsurprisingly, it was the parent that had started it, the teacher merely trying to fend him off. The issue? The unmarked homework had been completed by the parent, not the kid and the dad was desperate to find out what his score was.

In my entire career, there was never a point when I had been threatened with either a verbal or written warning, that is until 28th February 2020. However, that is not to say there were not times when I thought that action should be taken, such as for taking a child on a field trip without a parental permission slip or producing literature to deliberately wind up the management. As an example of how badly things can go wrong, and go wrong very quickly, an incident with Year 9 students in my last year at Westlands springs to mind.

I was having a chat with two kids at the back of the class. It was towards the end of term and towards the end of the day, everything was relaxed and we were having a laugh. I have no idea what caused me to do this, but I leaned forwards and faked to cuff both of them on the head. The result was quite unexpected. Both ducked away from the arm swipe, directly towards each other, smashing the sides of their skulls as their momentum came to a sudden halt. The only thing that stopped this from being a serious disciplinary issue is that neither suffered concussion nor fracture, in fact, other than a little bruising they were unmarked, and neither made any complaint, both knew there had been no intent.

I was able to go to the school management and explain the incident because I trusted them and they accepted the explanation because they trusted me. What a concept, teachers trusted by management and, to be honest, that is how it works in most schools. I am desperate to find out why this principle has not found its way into the management manual at BMIS.

Priory Special School, Spalding, Lincolnshire, England: 2000-2001

I have only been responsible for one expulsion in my life. I do not like students being permanently excluded from a school and would wish it had been different.

He was a fifteen-year-old, difficult and had Asperger's Syndrome. Much of the time he could be socially inept, although he tried to form some closer bonds with teachers; I was one. I have no idea what caused him to lose his temper in the changing rooms at the leisure centre, just as we were readying for class. It could have been a comment from another student; I just do not know. The first I was aware there was an issue is when he came at me wielding a baseball bat.

The kid was capable, he knew what he was doing, but with a weapon like a baseball bat there is a certain momentum after a swipe that leaves gaps in your defence. It was into one of those gaps I jumped and floored him.

After several interviews with the headteacher, social workers and other teachers it was still not determined why he had taken a sudden and surprising dislike to me. He served a short exclusion and was then allowed back to school, although was restricted in his movements and pleasingly he was kept away from me. When he was finally allowed to reintegrate into the whole school it was discovered he was carrying a catapult. He did not use it, but that was enough for me.

You can protect yourself from a student carrying a stick, knife or baseball bat, however, when you are on duty in the playground, you have no idea if someone is lining you up with an arrow, gun or catapult. It was not worth the risk; I asked that he be expelled permanently and he was.

A month later I bumped into the kid walking down the street; it has to be suspected he had set it up so this would happen. The boy was friendly and chatty, we talked about his expulsion. His argument with me was gone, he did not disagree with his punishment. I am not sure why he sought me out, although I think it was to say sorry. Maybe his condition made that difficult for him. After that, I never saw the lad again.

Around the World

Fundamentally, the best way to apply classroom discipline is with a raised eyebrow, finger or perhaps the palm of your hand. There is little point in shouting, there is almost no excuse for becoming angry and punishment is rarely beneficial. All teachers know these basics and all teachers fail to abide by them from time to time. The worst-case scenario is when the teacher is having a bad day, a kid is also having a bad day and, often over a minor issue, there is an eruption.

The teacher does not exist who can walk into any classroom, in any school, in any country and command immediate respect from the students, although carrying an Uzi they might just do it. The building of relationships with the kids is a long-term process and it is handed down, almost like folklore, from student to student, year to year or class to class within a school. It is wonderful to have a good relationship with the students and this does not have to happen on day one, but if you have not nailed it by day two hundred it is time to leave the profession (many international schools have around 200 schooldays per year).

My view of classroom discipline is somewhat at odds with the Buddhist philosophies that are becoming more and more prevalent in schools. I would not say irreconcilable, although some would. Having just read an article by an American in-school suspension teacher[14], her

---

[14] Amy Roter. '**Types of School Discipline Policies and Their Long-Term Impact**'. 20/10/2015

focus is entirely on positive reinforcement and replacement techniques and she almost dismisses any other form of discipline. I agree wholeheartedly that her principles are extremely important, although she deflates her argument when she points out that the least intense punishment that works is the one to apply. This I also agree with, but in itself, this contradicts her desire for zero punishment.

Every sane schoolteacher in the world would love to operate in a world requiring zero punishment, as would every sane parent. However, we do not, which is why we, as adults, can face fines or prison sentences in Europe, capital punishment in more backwards states of the USA and both corporal and capital punishment in Saudi Arabia.

If there are to be rules (and the only school that supposedly and infamously had none was Summerhill, founded by A.S. Neill) these rules have to have an enforcement mechanism. Is it possible to run a school with no rules?

In Summerhill's General Policy Statement on Community Life[15], it is admitted that they have more than four hundred school rules today, protecting individuals, the welfare of the school, the property and the school's reputation. Almost certainly there has been a greater requirement on Summerhill to apply more conventional regulations, although they have still managed to maintain their beliefs in optional attendance of lessons. At the core of the present set-up is that the students make the rules, or at least appear to. Perhaps not to

---

[15] Summerhill. '**Questions and Answers**'. 2020

the same extent, but many international schools have similar intent; if you have to have rules, allow the stakeholders to feel they have a share in their construct.

In New Zealand, one of Auckland's primary schools, the Swanson School has "free" play[16]; the idea being that kids can go out and do what they want in break times. If they get hurt, then so be it. This is a great idea and is probably a much better learning experience than in schools where snowball fights are banned. However, it sounds an almost ludicrous proposition if your perspective is from that of a litigation prone country.

The Swanson School received a great deal of media attention for this policy, although it is quite limited in scope. It is interesting to view their website. In one photograph a sign can be seen on a neighbour's fence, one that abuts the play area, it says, "BEWARE OF DOG" (sic). In another, it shows the climbing frames with the standard softwood chip beneath them. So, the kids are protected from at least some risks then.

However, you then look further on their website. They have uniforms, a timetabled day, homework, an internet safety agreement, a head boy and girl, they follow the New Zealand Curriculum, closed footwear for "technicraft", rules about bullying, action regarding lateness. However, the school also encourages students to take responsibility for their actions. These are standard guides for many schools; what does the Swanson School do when the rules are broken?

---

[16] Swanson School. '**Free Play** '. 2019

Therein lies the problem. If there are rules, then there is rule-breaking and if there is rule-breaking there are consequences, it does not matter if it is Summerhill or Swanson School. Children are, after all, proto-adults and we are trying to develop civic behaviour and responsibility in them. At the same time, we are trying to allow them to learn from their mistakes and whilst punitive action may not be ideal in this regard, just like the laws applied to adults, it is needed as a backstop.

The key is in attempting never to arrive at that punitive sanction. Every teacher knows this deep down, however as our behaviours as teachers are so variable, it is sometimes difficult for the students to understand where the lines are drawn. I have witnessed a student excluded because a teacher complained he touched her shoulder, yet I was taken out massively in football training and given a dead leg for three weeks by a fourteen-year-old boy and I did not even give the kid a yellow card.

To avoid discrepancies between teachers and to ensure students are clear where the lines are drawn, schools understandably come up with standardised rules. It is unfortunate that as these rules propagate, as rules do, as a rule, they begin to impinge on the methodology of individual teachers in the classroom, most of whom are perfectly capable of policing their patch.

My approach is to be tough with the little rules. It might sound petty, but if you have a short list of little rules and expect the students to follow them, there is far less chance of them going off the rails with the big rules. Thus, I have always been a stickler for timekeeping. Kids rush to my classes for fear of being late, even though the only thing that happens to them if they are is a hard stare and a quiet word. I have an enviable record for having students' work in on time, although once again the consequence of the students not meeting the deadline is little more than a little chat and encouragement. However, if the school rules were to be applied every time, there would be formal repercussions, letters home, details logged in the management's books and indelible stains on the student's record.

These, of course, are all necessary steps, but only once the classroom teacher has had their chance to sort the situation out. Keeping discipline in the classroom is the best way to minimise breaches of discipline, in and out of the classroom. Any student who has learned to understand that a teacher is firm but fair is far more responsive to a quiet word, be it whilst beating up Alison in the playground or copying from Peter in a test. More often than not, the beating and the copying both stop short the moment they see that teacher.

Management that can minimise its interference in the classroom, whilst knowing precisely what is going on in there, is the best form of school management. Management that allows full interaction between teachers and parents before they need to be involved themselves has confidence. Management that saves their energy for the exceptions, those few cases where it does need to be taken further, is helping both the students and teachers grow their skills. A management that does this will reap long-term rewards from improved behaviour and improved relationships between all the stakeholders.

Clearly, at a certain point, supportive parents become all-important and those parents that side with their offspring against the school are usually on the road to causing permanent damage to their children and probably have already.

As I write I can visualise hordes of teachers from rough inner-city schools rubbing their hands and saying, "Yeah. Let that bastard come and teach at our school. Then he'll change his tune!" However, I will not. No, I no longer want to do the jobs you are doing and feel sure that today I would be torn to pieces by your kids, although the song remains the same and you know it.

I have been invited, on several occasions, to beat children. These invitations have come from parents, usually in the course of relatively positive parent-teacher conferences. To date, in my entire life, I have only hit one child and then only once. It was my three-year-old godchild, who was crunching up my Weetabix. It was only a tiny little tap on the calf, but he screamed the house down.

I learned my lesson!

Eleven: The Big Chill

(Playtime)

This focuses on events outside school, both as a private individual and as a teacher involved in non-academic school-related activities. Teachers are human, although this is not always obvious to students, parents, or school management, and we occupy our spare time engaged in a variety of activities. However, in the bubble surrounding some international teaching jobs sometimes the line between school and leisure is blurred.

Lilongwe, Malawi: Saturday 14th March 2020

It was the final day of the rugby championships. England stood poised to lift the trophy, having an easy run out against Italy in Rome, whilst France hosted Ireland, a much tougher prospect. We could look back on three years of rugby parties, including the World Cup and the annual Six Nations tournaments. There was a hardcore of eight of us, although numbers attending usually ran between ten and twenty. In March 2020, with five of the hardcore leaving, this was likely to be one of the last such events.

The culmination of the Six Nations nearly always coincides with my birthday, which being the day after St. Patrick's Day is very often a non-event. Having the concluding fixtures a few days early meant I could celebrate without having to consume Guinness, wear a stupid hat or anything green. I had looked forward to the event for two months.

Of course, all the matches were cancelled due to the Covid-19 pandemic. They say postponed, however, for me it was effectively a cancellation and a great disappointment. As there were no games there was no get together and my sixty-second birthday, the last before my retirement, passed unnoticed.

One of the ironies of working in Africa, where few countries play rugby or cricket (and only one to the highest international standard) is that the pan-African broadcaster (DSTV) features nearly every rugby and cricket international from around the world. In addition, every match from the national football leagues of Germany, Italy, Spain and England are featured, which from my point of view makes it well worth having. As far as I can work out, DSTV premium comes out at a similar price to the Sky TV + Sports package in the UK.

The problem in Lilongwe is that I had turned into an armchair sports fan and by the time we entered 2020 was not playing any sports myself. I was becoming fatter and less fit by the day.

Doha, Qatar: Sunday 27th February 2011

There is, of course, a time and place for TV sport and when you are unable to join the other 88,000 fans filling Wembley Stadium, then the second-best must be the Shehrazad Lounge Bar & Terrace in the Radisson Blu in Doha. The event was the rare appearance of Birmingham City in a major English football tournament, the League Cup, against Arsenal.

For the uninitiated, it is important to explain the difference between the two clubs. Arsenal has won 13 league titles, 14 FA Cups and 2 League Cups and finished the 2010-11 season in fourth place in the Premiership. On the other hand, Birmingham City's trophy cabinet contains no league titles, no FA Cups and, before this final, only one League Cup; they finished the 2010-11 season in eighteenth place and were relegated, having scored the fewest goals of any club in the division. The club I have supported since I was eight are minnows and their trophy cabinet, if anyone could find it, could be mistaken for a rabbit hutch.

It had not been with any great expectation of victory that we rolled up at the Shehrazad Lounge Bar that evening in Doha, but hundreds of Arsenal fans had. The disparity in support in the bar was only clear when Birmingham City took the lead and only two people celebrated. Before half-time Arsenal had equalised and were looking dominant, much to the pleasure of the quaffing masses. However, with the second half at a stalemate and with one minute to go, there was an enormous cock up between the Arsenal goalkeeper and a defender. The Birmingham City substitute, Martins, pounced on the ball and slid it into the net. Game over. 2-1! Of course, the two of us thoroughly enjoyed the game and I do not care that our four hundred drinking companions did not.

So, there are places in Doha where you can watch a game of footie and enjoy a beer. If you are exceptionally lucky, you might just see Birmingham City lift another trophy. On balance, I would much rather have been at Wembley Stadium.

Suzhou Singapore International School (SSIS), Suzhou, China: 2004-2007

In my first spell at SSIS, the opportunity arose to fulfil a lifelong ambition and mount the stage as a stand-up comedian. It was only a ten-minute slot, but like most star-struck kids, to me, it seemed as if it was a possible opening to another world. Although it was staff only, it was a school event and the headteacher had to permit each of the acts.

I was up half of the night before the performance, putting the material together and trying to learn it; in all, it took over seven hours of preparation time and what was produced had the remarkable effect of at least making Andrea smile. You know what they say, "If you can conquer the American market, you can conquer the world. It was not Billy Connelly, but at least it would have allowed a few people to laugh at me if nothing else.

The organisation on the night proved chaotic and it was not until quite late on that I was given a start time. Just before I was due on the headteacher came over and said, "What's this I hear...". In a desperate attempt to get on with things I offered to give him the most contentious line from the act, this was,

"You can put the S into SSIS, but you can't take the P out of Singapore."

I was immediately pulled from the schedule.

I cannot blame the headteacher, I can only blame the girl who did not listen when I said she should pass it by him first. He had to make an on the spot decision and to his mind dissing Singaporeans was a bit like allowing a suicide bomber into the party. What did piss me off was that I had taken all the good, really meaty stuff out, to allow for a mixed and relatively conservative audience. The headteacher admitted that when he first heard I was going to do stand-up he believed I was joking. Hey, in that case, I must be really funny, unfortunately, none of us ever found out.

As a teenager I had been introduced to volleyball and had risen to quite a high standard, eventually attending England trials. Let me put this into context a bit: England has never been a volleyball nation and attending trials for England might mean that in most countries they would make you responsible for blowing up the balls or wiping sweat from the court.

While I had been in Tanzania, I had been envious of the school volleyball coaching, although had been too nervous to ask to be involved. Our arrival in Suzhou opened a few doors, as they were short of willing teachers to take practice sessions.

My first experience was co-coaching the SSIS boys' senior team. My partner was the Head of PE, a lovely guy, but his position gave him seniority in our relationship. We had managed to reach the final of the schools' tournament, a game that was played at our campus. Everything was going swimmingly; we were two sets up and playing what seemed certain to be the last set.

It was then that my co-coach decided he wanted to put on one of our weaker players, just to give him a run-out. The lad was not even an average player, he was poor and I argued that we should wait until we had a completely commanding lead, but was overruled. We lost the third set, our team started to decompose and we went on to lose the next two sets as well, throwing a certain trophy triumph away.

My resolve was that I should drop out of coaching the boys' team for the following season, due to too many differences in approach to my colleague. My coaching style is something akin to that of Brian Clough (a hugely successful and somewhat unorthodox football manager of the seventies, eighties and nineties), although certainly not in his league and my techniques have not been admired by many. However, they bring results, make the kids happy, which to my mind is complete justification, and I have been as well-loved as a volleyball coach as has been the case as a classroom teacher.

It was hugely unfortunate how I ended up coaching the girls' team. We had a Kiwi Economics teacher at the school who had supervised the girls' volleyball team, but who died a few days into our second year there. It was heartbreaking; he was a nice guy. Not only did I pick up the coaching role; I also took over some of his Economics lessons for four months.

In my first season, we attended the Association of China and Mongolia International Schools tournament in Tianjin, where we came out of it near the bottom of the pile. It was an interesting competition, the first time I had been involved in a double-elimination event and a huge learning curve. Every other coach present was from their school's PE staff and was probably qualified to coach volleyball, which I was not. I felt a bit out of the loop when they took their downtimes and chatted about the things that PE staff do, although I should have felt at home as these conversations tend to revolve around beer and injuries.

We did have a somewhat nerve-wracking moment at the hotel. Two of our senior girls were approached by two Arabic guys in the lobby who wanted to pay them for sex. To the girls' credit, they remained calm about it, came and told us and thereafter we kept a much closer eye on our charges.

By this point, even though success seemed a long way off, our CEO, when asked about sports at the school, had started referring to our institution as a volleyball school. This was a major plaudit and inspired us to take it to the next level. Coaching intensified, we played plenty of friendlies and I ran the volleyball club throughout the year, whereas previously it had been seasonal.

The following year we went back to Tianjin for more.

In an exciting tournament, we finished up winning the trophy, notwithstanding an injury to our star player which kept her out of the final and the fact that we were not allowed to take our second-best player with us at all. We were also hampered by an error on my behalf when I allowed the wrong team sheet to be submitted before the final set of the final match. This caused the girls to have to play out of position, so they were somewhat confused, and it also caused the opposition coach to go apoplectic. I have no idea why their coach became so cross, his team benefitted enormously from the cock-up, but I suspect that in the aftermath he passed some of his ire on to our PE Department.

We had a new American sports' director who did not seem keen on what had been going on with the volleyball and kept creating obstacles for us. A little Finnish girl had joined the school and as she had been on the verge of national honours, she quickly became our second-best player. Her mother was very keen to have her involved in our first team because it was the only way she could play to the standard she was accustomed to. Although she was younger than the other players, they looked after her exceptionally well and she was regarded as something of a superstar.

Our sports' director banned her from the tournament trip on the grounds of age. She was twelve years old. The tournament did not have an age limit, the inter-schools organisation did not have an age limit and my team already had some thirteen-year-old players. I can only think that he did not want us to succeed and his later actions made this even more evident.

After winning the tournament we were due to play another championship in Shanghai. There had been a qualifying knockout which we had won, although the sports' director accepted another school's argument that we had failed to post the result and we were put into the losers' pool. I argued this but was told in no uncertain terms that if I did not accept the decision or even brought it up again, I would be removed as coach. What was irritating was that I had filled out and signed the scorecard and had then given it to the coach of the opposing team; it was his job to submit the scorecard to the organisers, yet he was the one complaining it had not been submitted. I was thoroughly confused and demotivated. However, at that stage the school was in a complete state of disarray on all fronts, Andrea and I had already determined we were leaving anyway and the sports' director was simply symptomatic of a wider malaise. I saw my team through that last tournament; it was so sad that they were heartbroken and failed to perform.

Utahloy International School (UIS), Guangzhou, China: 2007-2008

Moving south to Guangzhou allowed me to take up responsibility for the UIS junior girls' team. Nearly the entire squad were in Year 8 and nearly every other team we played the girls were in Year 9; my team were tiny and short, whereas all our opponents were tall and muscular.

However, if I had been impressed by the team in my last year in Suzhou, I was dumbfounded by the Guangzhou team. They started with few team skills, but we built them up quickly; they were hardworking and enthusiastic.

One unfortunate aspect of volleyball is that you have to be a certain height to be able to jump high enough to hit the ball downwards; not one of our players could do so. If they were incapable of mounting a punishing attack, in defence they were awesome.

We went off for a tournament in Hong Kong and to everyone's surprise, reached the final. The two sides of the draw had been played in different sports halls and the one we played in had a higher ceiling; the hall for the final was lower. In the end, the reason we lost is that too many of our serves hit the ceiling, I simply could not get our girls to adapt and serve lower.

What a game it was. For one of the points, the ball crossed the net sixty times and for my team that meant ninety shots, although for the other team it was less, as they did not always play three touch volleyball. The team and I were congratulated by everyone at the tournament. The girls' smiles were wider than their faces and, as they were walking on air, they looked a great deal taller than normal.

What an exceptional group of kids. When I left the school, they presented me with a signed volleyball which meant the world to me. It still sits above the fireplace in pride of place.

Earlier in this book I pointed out that I was sad to leave Guangzhou because the academic set-up suited me, that was true, however, I was gutted to leave my team as the following year we would have been all-conquering.

We returned to Suzhou where I found that an excellent coach had taken my spot and was leading the girl's team to new heights, which was probably something I could not have done. My happiness at their success hid my personal disappointment which was also tinged with envy.

Bishop Mackenzie International School (BMIS), Lilongwe, Malawi: 2016-2019

Although I had done a little volleyball coaching in Bangladesh, by the time we reached Malawi, I was beginning to suffer from arthritic fingers, which is almost certainly a consequence of both genetics (my father has the same problem) and playing so much volleyball as a setter when I was younger. My knees were also failing me, something worsened by the insistence in Lilongwe that we play on sand courts.

However, there was some enthusiasm for the sport amongst the kids and I ran a weekly training session for a couple of years. I had a pleasant mixed squad and eventually, we were asked to play a tournament. Admittedly, it ended up with only one other team in the competition and we went on to win the trophy. Any rugby, basketball, netball, or swimming wins, and even some losses, were heralded, our own was allowed to pass almost unnoticed. The only previous competitions the school had ever won were in swimming.

There was not a great deal of support from the PE department for the game. They were obsessed with rugby and volleyball was hardly thought of as a sport. I was told at one point that although kids who were fasting for Ramadan were excused from all sports, this would not be the case for volleyball because it was not very strenuous. Bollocks!

We ended the first year by playing a match against the staff. Apparently, after the game, two staff members complained about my coaching methods. One of the things they objected to was that I substituted a boy on and when I realised he was staring into the car park rather than at the server, I immediately substituted him off before he had touched the ball. They thought I was being mean.

I was spoken to, at length, by the Head of PE, who admitted the complaint had been passed down the whole chain of command from the very top.

The next year we had no competitive matches, although I kept the training going. Again, we ended the year with a staff versus students' match. It was unfortunate that this match was scheduled in such a way that I could not attend, although I saw a little of it from nearly 100 metres away. My team absolutely stuffed the teachers. Apparently, it was the first time in the history of the school that the students had beaten the staff at any sport. My team were ecstatic, I was over the moon, but had determined to retire as a volleyball coach and did so.

At the final assembly that year, to enormous cheers from the student body, I was presented with a signed volleyball. Déjà vu!

Birmingham & Yorkshire, England: 1975-76

Volleyball had given me enormously increased confidence when I was a student, so much so that by seventeen I was becoming involved in school productions. I have never been much of an actor, although managed to gain myself a reputation around the school after playing an American in a restaurant scene. My stage calls of "Waiter! Waiter!" were repeated behind my back around the school corridors by younger kids for a month.

Not many people know this, but Kevin Costner and I have something in common. Both of us played the parts of dead people in our early roles. I had to lie on a stage and look dead for thirty minutes, which is harder than it sounds. Kevin did not do as well as I, his part in The Big Chill, a magnificent film from 1983, was cut so much that only a quick clip of his severed wrists appeared, whereas my whole body featured on stage, albeit my head was behind a sofa. It is appropriate that the opening song from The Big Chill is the Rolling Stones' "You Can't Always Get What You Want", although I suppose he was paid and I had to make do as an amateur.

After leaving school, a friend and I applied for jobs at Butlin's Holiday Camps and we eventually ended up as stagehands at their resort in Filey, North Yorkshire. We were exposed to an awful lot of things in that job, including the dancers' breasts and came out of it as pretty competent backstage hands.

To put this into context, Filey's Gaiety Theatre had the second biggest stage in the whole country. It had a revolving section some five metres across and an auditorium that seated over 6,000 guests.

There were shows every night and in addition, there were matinee performances and a kids' show. On top of our work in the Gaiety Theatre, we were also expected to work occasionally at their smaller repertory theatre and once a week on the limes for the late-night cabaret evenings, when we worked with stars such as Bob Monkhouse, Freddie Parrot Face Davis and Warren Mitchell. It was full-on.

The reason we had been taken on as stagehands is that one of the previous occupants of the job, had been fired, he seemed to have made a real name for himself. There was a mattress in the orchestra bit, positioned so that one of the Red Coats could dive onto it during the finale of their show. One night, this lad had taken one of the dancers into the pit for a rather vigorous physical workout. The mattress had moved substantially and the next show saw the flying Red Coat crash landing onto bare boards. There was also a rumour that while he was working the limes for Warren Mitchell, he became bored, as the comedian did not move around much during his act. So, he leaves the limes, heads off to the front of the stage and calls to the comedian, "Hey, Warren. I'm from the limes and I'm off for a piss and a pint, do you mind staying where you are for a while?".

Westlands School, Sittingbourne, Kent: 1991-1997

When I first started teaching, the drama teacher put out a flyer to all staff, it was paper in those days, asking what theatre skills we had. I returned the document, which asked you to differentiate between work you had done as an amateur and as a professional. My entry had a whole list of ticks in the professional column: Sound, lighting board, limes, stagehand. The list went on, but I omitted to include my spur of the moment fame in the spotlight when I waltzed onto the stage as Frosty the Snowman in the middle of one of our last Butlin's shows.

I heard nothing from the drama teacher, nothing at all, and found out later that he was one of those who objected to my presence in the school. A few years later I did work with him, very closely and we got on well; he was one of those who apologised.

I ended up doing a production at the school, as stage manager and seem to recall it went very well. My only slip was to have been too harsh in telling the dancers to keep quiet, which is a tough achievement on a silent stage and I had to apologise to the extras for my excess.

The Gleed School, Spalding, Lincolnshire, England: 1997-1999

Two moments spring out when I consider the Gleed School's performance of Bugsy Malone. The first was typical of a school production, the second almost completely random, but both shared both natural and farcical comedic quality that only youngsters can manage.

There are several scenes in Bugsy Malone, or at least in the version we put on, where four gangsters slide onto the stage and begin to blast everyone with custard pies. The four gangsters had been specially selected from Year 7 as their parts required minimal preparation, no lines and were a bit of easy fun. The gangsters were beautifully dressed in grey pinstripe suits with wide lapels, topped off with matching fedoras. Each carried a passing replica of a Thompson sub-machine gun and the obligatory custard pies.

This was a co-production with the local girls' school, who I believe were responsible for all the costumes and sets. The boys' school took responsibility for the lighting and sound and I was stage manager. If that sounds sexist, then so it was. The school system was sexist, the town was sexist and the county was sexist; they still are.

As stage manager, there were two tasks that I could not delegate to the stagehands. One was ensuring the gangsters entered the stage at the right place and the right time, as they were completely incapable of organising themselves and would not listen to anyone else. The performance ran for three nights, thus twelve gangster entrances; they nailed it just once. They managed every conceivable mistake, to the point where it looked as if they were doing it on purpose; they were not. Tripping over was a highlight, although when they all managed to then trip over the lead gangster and all four of them sprawled on the stage, it did have some impromptu comedic quality. On one occasion they were simply not there, on another just two of them, who went ahead but edged onto the stage in a nervous bewildered state. Finally, at the last attempt, they were in the right place, all four of them. They moved on stage with menacing presence and perfect timing, they followed the choreography to the letter and in a coordinated fashion. At last…success…something to be proud of. No. They had forgotten their custard pies.

Of course, I can only blame myself.

The other task that could not be delegated was to open the tabs, the main stage curtains. I had a perfectly capable assistant stage manager (ASM), a sixteen-year-old with great enthusiasm for the stage, although neither he nor the other stagehands were strong enough to open the tabs, which took me enormous effort.

It was the opening of the third night's performance. On the second night Blousey's voice had broken down and she had been fitted up with a radio mike for this last performance. I did the final check before rolling the tabs; glancing across downstage, over at backstage right, everyone ready. I then flicked my gaze upstage left and froze.

In the semi-darkness I could make out Blousey, standing, bent fully over at the waist, with her skirts pulled over her head; she could have been mooning, her buttocks pointed directly at me. However, she was not. Knelt behind her, with his hands in her knickers, was the ASM.

This was a somewhat unexpected sight and needed careful thought. Certainly, I could not open the curtains as a quarter of the audience would have had an eyeful. The one thing that did cross my mind is that I was pretty certain the ASM was gay, although I would not have voiced that belief, especially in Lincolnshire.

"What the hell are you doing?" I whispered as loudly as I dared. The fiddling in the knickers went on.

"What are you doing?" Louder this time. The ASM turned his head toward me.

315

"I'm turning her on." This is the last thing a teacher needs to hear when confronted with a student with his hands down the pants of another.

"What?"

"They put the battery pack for the microphone in her pants and forget to turn it on. That's what I'm doing."

Ahhh! All's well that ends well. He turned her on and we got on with the show, which was perfect except, of course, for the gangsters.

Apart from dabbling with The Witches, which as previously mentioned was a staged read through rather than a play, I had to save my next encounters with the world of theatre for Africa.

Moshi, Tanzania: 2001-2003

The Moshi amateur dramatic society put on Tony Hancock's The Lift, in May 2002 and I played the lift operator, who is the butt of many of the Hancock character's jokes. Hancock himself was played by a lovely, diminutive Dutchman, who brought exactly the right amount of Hancockian pathos to the part.

The only problem was that it was extremely short, the original TV sitcom episode being less than thirty minutes long. There were some discussions about what we could add to the end, as the scripted version's finale is a bit flat. I suggested we perform Always Look on the Bright Side of Life, which did not go down at all well.

It seems I had underestimated the strength of feeling generated by the song amongst the town's evangelical Christians, of whom there were many. We put the show on twice, once on the small outdoor music stage at the school and then up on the rooftop of a local hotel, where it went down well. On the second occasion, a few of us did an impromptu version of the Monty Python song anyway. A year later I would find my own play becoming unravelled for upsetting one of the same Christians.

Between November 2002 and June 2003, I was involved in two more stage performances and produced and directed two school plays. Without a doubt, those eight months were the most intense period of theatre or theatricals, I had been involved in since working backstage at the Gaiety Theatre in Butlins.

The first was the school play, Across the Barricades, set in Northern Ireland and following the stories of a Roman Catholic Romeo and a Protestant Juliet. For some reason, and I think it was to do with the hall being used for exams, we staged it in the art studio. This was cramped, there was no real backstage and a room to the side of the auditorium served as both a changing room and to launch actors on and off stage. The term "auditorium" is laughable. We managed to cram in around a hundred seats although those at the back had to almost crawl into their places.

What an intense show! I believe we banned all younger kids from the audience because the noise levels of the shootings and explosions were too extreme. We played it in semi-darkness, with warnings about flashing strobes and the scene changes were conducted by a band of four Year 7 students, visible in the gloom to the audience, all armed with fake Uzi submachine guns.

If there is a sense of déjà vu regarding four Year 7s with guns, I do not believe I consciously used the Bugsy Malone experience to deploy the stagehands in such a manner. There was a huge gulf in their competence levels anyway and I do not recall a single mistake being made by the stage crew on Across the Barricades. We operated in a tiny stage space, with split scenery to make transitioning between scenes quicker. It did not make it simpler for the crew, especially working in the dark, although they handled it admirably.

The level of performance across the cast and crew was of an unbelievable standard, not only in the three performances but also during rehearsal. It was a small group of only thirteen with about half as many again making up the backstage crew.

By this time, I was in a relationship with Andrea and she performed the role of stage manager. The strain between myself, as director and she, was so immense that it almost caused a terminal breakdown. She vowed never to work with me again on a production, which was a shame because having witnessed the reaction of the audience, crew and cast to this performance, I already had the next one in mind.

We were already in rehearsals for the school play Scream, when I took back to the stage in Whose Life is it Anyway? Again, it was performed by the local amateur dramatic society and this was a much bigger and more serious affair than The Lift.

The story revolves around a hospitalised paraplegic who wants to die, played by a teacher of Physics at our school, the same one to have starred in The Lift. In real life, he was extremely animated and the shortest man to have ever called the Netherlands home. I was given the part of a Cockney Jamaican porter who was into calypso. As this proved way out of my league in terms of acting ability and I was clearly not black, I chose to play the character as a Brummie punk, which went down well.

There was some criticism, from two of the more serious actors, that I was stealing the limelight with some of my antics, such as sitting with my feet up on the Sister's desk, smoking and playing with desk ornaments while a serious scene was being enacted in the next "room". However, the director liked it as he wanted the offset of slapstick with the black humour of the piece; it worked.

However, for a man of limited acting experience, I was being typecast. I could not and still cannot act, corpses apart. It is as simple as that. Whilst I knew I could not act, I was convinced that I could write, produce and direct; maybe I still can.

Scream was staged in June 2003; it was a re-write of Midsummer Night's Dream. I engaged one of my students to re-write most of the Mechanicals scenes, although she drew the line at changing a single word of the Pyramus and Thisbe play and insisted it remained as is. I did not take issue and her insistence proved to be spot on. I re-wrote all the remainder and incorporated mentions of well-known characters in the school, a rock band, fairies dressed as Liverpool players, the Mechanicals as skateboarders and a demented and lusting female IRA terrorist, which was a link back to Across the Barricades.

In casting the play, I upset one person and in writing the play I upset another, both quite seriously. The Dutchman, having been in Across the Barricades and who had probably starred in every play that had been put on in Moshi for several years, wanted the role of Bottom. As a believer that school plays are for school kids, I demurred. He was extremely upset and I do not believe he ever forgave me.

We were deep into rehearsals when the second complaint came in. Hermia was being played by a lovely girl whose father not only happened to be a teacher at the school but also turned out to be a very heavy-duty Christian. He had picked up the script that his daughter had been learning and must have gone through line by line. What he objected to, to the extent that he was going to withdraw his daughter from the cast, were the lines:

King: I had better have a chat with God and see where that gets us.

Eggy: Mister White is away right now, but if you don't sort this out...

What the teacher did not like was the suggestion that Mister White, the secondary headteacher, could be compared to God.

Keiron White, was almost as flummoxed as I; he had been the one who had checked the script for anything unsuitable. He only had an issue with one line I had written and swore blind that an especially sneaky double-entendre had been included. I never understood what he was getting at, whatever it was I had certainly not tried to be devious. I should have asked him again about the double meaning he thought I had included because almost twenty years on it still mystifies me.

We solved the God problem by simply changing the line from *"...chat with God..."* to *"...a chat with the gods..."* That kept the Christian happy because it was now referring to the pantheon of Greek gods, which was not his concern. He was also quite content with all the references to sex, drugs, rock 'n' roll, violence and death, but I guess that was more in line with Shakespeare's original content. It did not stop him from trying to disrupt my band rehearsals, pulling out vocalists regularly to avoid straining their voices, as they were supposed to be competing in a classical singing competition shortly after Scream.

We took the risk of staging Scream outdoors and though there was a threat of rain on the final night, fortunately, it held off. We had bare stage blocks, costumes that developed from night to night, fairies sitting in the trees around the stage, a band, cast and crew of over forty and assistance from as many as ten parents and teachers. We sold out every night and still they kept coming in and so we added more and more chairs each night, emptying the classrooms. All in all, upwards of a thousand people probably watched that show.

And they loved it. Big time. Even the complaining Christian teacher came and congratulated me at the end. He was effusive.

The stars were obviously the kids and their shining eyes stayed lit until the end of the school year. I do not use this word often, although it appears twice in this chapter; they were awesome. I believe the reason I never put on a school play after this is that I did not think I could improve on my work and did not believe I would ever again work with such a wonderful group of students.

By the end of my time in Moshi, I was extremely popular with the kids and thought I should go out with a bang. After eight months of treading the boards with a bit part, as a fall guy, writing, taking rehearsals and casting sessions, coercing kids into performances and then letting them take the stage, I wanted to be the star for my leaving shot. With a little bit of persuading, the musicians in the rock band from Scream reformed for a single new song.

We were due to perform at an end of year variety show and when the organisers saw the act, they insisted on putting us on last, as headliners. They also insisted that we cut the gunfire out of the introduction, as there would be young children in the audience. I thought that was a shame.

I left Moshi with the rifling drumbeat, thudding bass and jarring guitar of Should I Stay or Should I Go? At last, I had fronted a rock band and it was one hell of a good way to go out. I hope The Clash would have been impressed because the kids certainly were.

And that is how you leave a country!

Dhaka, Bangladesh: 2013-2016

It had always felt that my life had been full of little successes and larger failures. It is in the nature of an eternal pessimist to look back on events in the same way they look forward. If it were to be properly analysed, I suppose there had been significant successes, but my superego was always on hand to downplay those. Whether my successes or my failures had the larger influence on my life's trajectory remains an unanswered question. To this day and particularly whilst writing this book, it has been easier for me to spin out the tales of defeat or distress than to elaborate on the high points of my career, perhaps it is a case of being too British.

Undoubtedly, my attempts at becoming a reasonable tennis player resulted in a string of failures. It is a sport I have always enjoyed playing since my teenage years, but other than a big serve, which was also hugely erratic, my only half-decent shot was my drop shot.

We played tennis in Tanzania, my better half taking lessons while I stuck with my tried and tested awfulness; Andrea improved considerably and I did not. Dhaka did not cure my maladies on the tennis court either, although it did somewhat improve my play and unexpectedly brought significant success.

Nearly all the international clubs had tennis courts, many had two, the BAGHA had one. They also had two coaches and two "ball boys" on their staff, although the ball boys were very handy players and could assist with the coaching. The attitude in the tennis section of the club was first-rate and everyone was encouraged to play. Eventually, we found ourselves caught up in the web and were attending regular coaching sessions.

Andrea improved enormously and I to some extent. We played in the league matches from our second year, these being competitions against the other international clubs. All the matches were doubles games and sometimes we partnered with each other, sometimes with others and we even managed to win a light-hearted tournament together. This is not to say we were of a high standard. I was firmly rooted in the C team, whilst my better half was sometimes asked to turn out for the B team. In our third year there I was somewhat surprised to be asked to captain the C team, probably only because there was not a D team.

Most of my players, if asked, would have said quite freely that I was one of the worst players in our squad; this was true. However, in a season that was disrupted somewhat by the ongoing political street violence, we completed our matches with only one loss (ironically against one of the weaker teams) and finished the season heading into the playoff finals, having won our league.

One of the best things about the team was that except for Andrea and me, none of them worked at our school. This is not to suggest for one moment that our fellow teachers were not great people to be with, however, it is refreshing to be outside the bubble. Most of the people we played tennis with were from the ready-made garments industry, one was a hydrologist, another a diplomat. It brought much greater width to our time in Dhaka, something that we had been unable to find as easily in any of our other positions.

In chapter two I mentioned the British High Commission (BHC) and their superior attitude; our semi-final opponents were BHC 1. I struggled to arrange the fixture as they were coming out with all sorts of excuses to change the date of the match and to change the venue from our home court to theirs. It became so silly that I had to get the league organisers to put their foot down. The semi-final was played in the worst spirit of any of our games. Still, we thrashed them and they sloped off, not even staying for a beer afterwards. Then we found out who our opponents for the final were: BHC 2!

To have reached the final was something of a triumph as the BAGHA had not reached such heights for years. On a beautiful day towards the end of February, one of the best days Dhaka could offer, with unusually clear skies and a slight cooling breeze, I took my team to the Nordic Club, the neutral venue for our last match. The only thing missing was our most consistent player, the hydrologist.

To be honest, if our star had been there, I would have had to drop myself from the team, something I was not keen to do but had done a couple of times during the season. Instead, I played alongside Demi, a great Nigerian guy and whilst we had a torrid three games in the middle of our match, we came through with a win. Everyone else performed at the top of their game and the cup was ours.

I have had a few sporting highlights in my life however this was one of the best. The BHC 2 team turned out to be a much nicer bunch of guys than the other lot and accepted defeat with good grace. For the little BAGHA outfit to have come through against all the big boys was wonderful. My thanks to every single one of our players and the four-member coaching team at the BAGHA.

And that is another way to leave a country!

Twelve: The Usual Suspects

(Online Teaching)

This covers the period from March to June 2020 with only minor references to previous employment. These were my last three months of school teaching and coincided with the growing Covid-19 pandemic. The main focus is that of distance learning or teaching online as some might call it. The only flashback covers the period we spent in Bangladesh, where the political violence led us to implement distance learning in the period 2013-2016.

Bishop Mackenzie International School (BMIS), Lilongwe, Malawi: March 2020

The gathering storm of Covid-19, which was officially renamed as such on 11th February, was beginning to feature prominently even in the local news by the start of March. It was something of a surprise therefore that two school trips were allowed to depart Malawi heading for the Netherlands and the French Alps, respectively. The first of these trips was additionally hazardous because students were attending a Model United Nations conference and had a great deal of contact with students from schools around the world. The second trip was a skiing holiday that had no academic content, although its proximity to the Italian border should have raised a red flag.

The teachers supervising these visits were given some formal training in reducing the risk of contracting Covid-19, however, the information available at that time was not what it is today. Questions were asked by teachers before the trips as to whether they were warranted and I am sure that parents were consulted at length. However, the priority appeared to be to ensure that no monies were lost on the bookings. It should be pointed out that these trips had been paid for by the parents, not the school, but it seemed there was concern that if the school cancelled the trips, the parents would then blame them for losing the money that had been paid out. It appears there was no prospect of claiming a cancellation on insurance at that stage.

Fortunately, no one visiting Europe from BMIS contracted Covid-19, although by the time both trips concluded the Malawian government requested that all the returning students and staff should go into self-isolation for two weeks. It appeared that the school had approached the government on this matter and whilst all the other passengers on the flight were not told to self-isolate, the students and teachers were, which is quite strange and remains an unexplained situation.

The challenge for the teachers had begun. If our travelling students had not been on sanctioned school trips it is unlikely we would have been asked to start hybrid teaching, however, because they had the school was then obliged to ensure their learning continued at home. Hybrid teaching has come to mean when some students are taught at school whilst others are simultaneously taught at home. It is possibly the toughest of all online teaching situations and one we had experienced in Bangladesh a few years previously.

There were other similarities. Malawi had run parliamentary and presidential elections in May 2019. The latter had been overturned by the Supreme Court on the basis that there were too many irregularities for them to be regarded as free and fair. Between the 2019 election and the re-run on 23rd June 2020, the country suffered a series of serious protests including rioting, loss of life, closure of businesses, a couple of days when the school had to be closed and several days when parents refused to send their offspring in for lessons due to the danger on the streets. This also was a repeat of the experiences we had faced in Bangladesh, although the Bangladeshis could have taught the Malawians a great deal about how to excel at organised street violence.

International School of Dhaka (ISD), Dhaka, Bangladesh: 2013-2016

From the start of 2014 to the time we left Dhaka, a period of 30 months, there were over 2,300 major incidences of political unrest, nearly 25,000 people injured and 450 deaths.[17] At the core of these incidents was the hartal.

The dictionary definition of a hartal is a mass protest, often involving a total shutdown of workplaces, offices, shops and courts of law; it is a form of civil disobedience similar to a labour strike. It was originally intended as a peaceful protest. In Bangladesh, hartals were generally violent and involved the blocking of roads, forcing businesses to close with violent confrontations, engaging both the police and political groupings, with deaths on the street a regular occurrence.

To avoid these events it was necessary to watch the news, visit websites that monitored the hartal activity or follow the advice issued regularly by the school. Between Monday and Friday, the last of these was the obvious choice as ISD sent out a brave motorcyclist to go and check out the hotspots.

Once it was established where the hartal was focussed it was possible to identify which roads would be blocked. In most cities this would then involve a detour, however, Dhaka is not quite like that and there are chokepoints on the city's roads that are almost unavoidable; often it would be a case of abandoning your plans to go out. One cunning method to avoid hartal danger was to hire an ambulance for your journey, which became a common practice amongst wealthy Bangladeshis. The one vehicle the rioters would invariably allow

---

[17] Ain o Salish Kendra. '**Political Deaths**'. 2020

through the roadblocks were ambulances, indicating that at least some of the rioters had morals, although it could also be said that some of the rioters were easily duped or bribed.

As in Malawi, the hartals were most often led by the major political parties, who would pay for the rioters to act. So, the majority of the people protesting on the streets were not extremists, they were mercenaries, although there was an exception. The most feared group was Jamaat-e-Islami who were banned as a political party at the time of our arrival in the country in August 2013 and whose ex-leader was executed just before we left Bangladesh on 11th May 2016.

Jamaat-e-Islami was a hard-line Islamist group that additionally supported the massively unpopular reunion of Bangladesh with Pakistan. Likely, some of their members were intimately tied to the terrorist group, Jamaat-ul-Mujahideen, that was responsible for the assassinations of an Italian in the September of 2015 and a Japanese citizen a month later, both targeted simply because they were foreigners. Certainly, when the Holey Artisan Bakery, a restaurant popular with ex-pats, was stormed in July 2016 and twenty people were hacked to death in a hostage situation, there is little doubt that Jamaat-ul-Mujahideen were behind it, although ISIS claimed responsibility.

As a consequence of these activities throughout our time in Dhaka, there were an increasing number of days on which some or most students would not come to school. As I was teaching Economics to students in Years 12 & 13 this had potentially severe consequences in terms of their grades and university entrance.

We built our own teaching model to overcome the difficulties; there were no obvious templates. By and large, we had motivated students and they could be expected to turn up to online lessons, get on with the tasks required of them and submit work when it was due. In about twenty per cent of the cases, it was evident that no amount of pushing would stir them into action. It is at this point that parents were brought further into the equation to apply further pressure on their unwilling offspring; I guess they were effective in half of the cases of recalcitrance.

However, there were also some students who physically attended the school. At a minimum, these would be the children of teachers, although depending on where they lived and especially if their homes were nearby, others found it relatively easy to get to the school. This created a problem for the teachers, as suddenly each lesson became two lessons: one for those students who are present and one for those at home. Try as we may, the tendency was for us to teach the students in the classroom in the same manner as we were teaching those at home; thus the perceived benefit of being in school began to deteriorate.

The problem was simply a matter of the workload increasing too much for us to cope. We worked together in teams trying to maximise our effectiveness and were fully supported by a grateful management for our efforts. Where additional support was required from the ICT team, it was immediate and focussed. The responsibility lay with the teachers and the teachers stepped up. The whole process was organic, cooperative and teacher-led. It was tough going, but we were successful. In retrospect, it was nothing compared to what hit us in Malawi, where few of the positive elements identified above could be said to have applied.

Bishop Mackenzie International School (BMIS), Lilongwe, Malawi: April - June 2020

Against a background of street violence, protesting forthcoming lockdowns related to Covid-19 and heavily politicised, the government ordered all schools closed. BMIS had already predetermined the date for campus closure, which had given us a little preparation time. On Friday 20th March, two days after my birthday, the campus closed.

There were two main emotions. Firstly, there was one of relief that the hybrid system had come to an end and that we could focus solely on online teaching or distance learning as some prefer to call it. The second was the sad realisation that we were going to be seeing the last of our students. Even though the school announcements held to the line that we could reopen before the end of the school year, the teachers knew that the chances of this were virtually non-existent and many of the students had the same feeling.

Friday 20th March turned out to be a party day at school. I did point out that they were holding it two days too late but to no avail. The Year 13 cohort, who had anyway been due to go on study leave in the lead up to their final examinations, requested that their leaving procession went ahead anyway. This has always been a big event at BMIS and all the students from kindergarten to the oldest kids come out to see them off. Due to the significance of the day, the Year 13's party mood cascaded throughout the school and everyone ended up celebrating what was in effect the closing of the school campus.

I was in tears on several occasions. Some of the kids might have thought we would see each other back in class again, although I knew we would not. For the majority of the students, the day was not terminal, they thought of it at the time as the start of an extended holiday. For myself, this was it. My last day with the kids. Full stop. There may be another three months of teaching to go, but this was it as regards physical presence, this was the substitute send-off for the one I had dreamed of: the final day's assembly, the cheers, a standing ovation from the kids, the short speech while looking the whole school in the eye and trying to hold back the waterworks until after it was done.

It was with a sinking feeling that I returned to my room, only to find around fifteen students had tracked me down. There were more tears and there were hugs, even though social distancing was becoming the norm and elbow bumps were replacing handshakes. On that day, there were no known cases of Covid-19 in Malawi.

When the last student left, I sat in my classroom alone and wept. It was as if the world had ended. I scanned the empty desks, noted the odd bit of litter on the floor, looked at the open laptop screens with registers and lesson plans still open and tried to visualise the laughter, the questions and the eureka moments; they would not come. Some of the wall posters, a few of which had been with me for years, sagged at the corners, begging for early retirement. I was not.

And on Monday 23rd March classes started as per the new normal. I occupied the same seat, in the same classroom, with the same posters and, ironically, the same pieces of litter on the floor. It was on the same timetable, with the same students, undertaking the same work, although they were not physically there.

At the end of the last lesson on the first day of online teaching I dismissed the kids with, "OK, it's time to go home now!" My Year 7s had to think about it for a while before they pissed themselves laughing.

Later I will outline the details as to how I handled the teaching aspects of the situation, however, it is worth identifying the logistics of the administration before that as well as the circumstances within the country.

We had a fortnight before the two-week Easter holiday, then six weeks until the reporting session ended and a further three weeks up until the end of term. It may seem trivial to throw in the reporting deadline, but functionally it is an important date as anything after that is not considered serious work for, or by, the students. If you are thinking that is an enormously long period for no serious work to be done, then I and many of my colleagues would agree. To maximise learning benefit it is essential to engage students for as much of the school year as possible. As soon as they learn that their marks no longer count, the majority simply take their foot off the accelerator, a significant minority step on the brake pedal and others leave the vehicle.

The reason for the three-week dead period once again comes down to the administrative requirements of the management team. This is a process that varies from school to school, although in BMIS they were not only obsessive, they were also long-winded. Not only are the students' reports checked and double-checked, but many are also amended and it is sad to say that the teacher who wrote the report may often not know what went into that final report. Once again, this comes down to a lack of trust between the management and the teachers. Even if they wanted to check the reports in the manner they did, there are so many systems of report writing available that this three-week hiatus could easily be reduced to a single week.

The upshot of the three-week dead period is that each teacher is required to put together a series of lessons, typically ten to twelve hours, when they can entertain the students to the maximum, to ensure engagement in a project the prime purpose of which appears to be to keep the lid on things. In many cases learning takes a back seat, in others it disappears entirely and some teachers seem to get away with showing videos and babysitting classes that become more and more unruly as hour after hour goes by with minimal engagement.

I had used my time wisely in the days before the campus shutting down. Every single one of my students had course material loaded onto their laptops, including those who were already in self-isolation; with their parents having acted as Sherpas. This might seem like an unnecessary action as materials can be accessed online, however that simply indicates a lack of understanding of Malawi's internet provision.

Before I switched my business away from them, a company called Skyband had been my internet provider. Although today they are also providing some fibre optic service, for most of our time here everything has been based on cellphone-style networks. We switched because their service was so poor in the area we live, although others had very few problems with them. Our new provider was Airtel, with TNM for my wife's schoolwork and both are variants on a hot-spotted telephone SIM. Virtually all the teachers and students at the school use similar systems and they have the disadvantage of not only being slow, but they are also extremely expensive. Malawi has the most expensive mobile data in the world[18]. The result of this is that many parents are reluctant to have their children download files of substantial size (video material falls into this category) or to have them engaged in long-winded video calls.

The latter are now an integral and growing part of teaching online and if both the originator of the video call and the partakers are on typical European or American Wi-Fi networks and purchasing systems, there is no particular additional cost. However, when the originator and the partakers are all on pay per gigabyte systems, the total revenue to the data supplier is massive and the cost to all involved in the call is both equal and high.

---

[18] Carmen Ang. '**What Does 1 GB of Mobile Data Cost in Every Country?**' Visual Capitalist. 3/7/2020

By supplying students with resources and installing them on their hard drives, the need for downloading was minimised and the content of the video conferencing calls could be reduced as so much of the information was already available to the students. At least, that is the theory. The problem was that as the need for online teaching exploded, so did the use of online apps, something primarily perpetrated by the teachers and the management of schools. In Malawi this had significant cost implications, one that many teachers, whose data costs were covered, did nothing to ameliorate, leaving the parents with unnecessarily high bills.

I am the first to confess my luck in being able to get material out to all my students before online teaching began in earnest. I was also lucky in only having five teaching groups. I was additionally lucky that my work only covered two-year levels, which meant only two sets of preparation work. I was enormously lucky that all the work required of my two groups was geared around online research. Amazingly that luck continued its streak, in that all year my students compiled, wrote and stored all their work digitally. And to pile on an even larger dose of luck, all my administration was digital.

Well, it has to be thought that I am one lucky bugger or maybe it is just called planning or maybe being future proof.

It is a little unfortunate that some students failed to get their heads around the fact they had stored, usable data. A significant minority could only manage to view and use files if they downloaded them just before use; they were almost completely incapable of using hard drive stored files. The blame for this can be landed entirely at the feet of BMIS because we failed abjectly in giving them proper ongoing training in the use of their laptops.

Having been so concerned about the poor ICT standards exhibited by our students, I had offered on more than one occasion to take an additional lesson with Year 7, added on to our existing Humanities time, so that these issues could be tackled. The management responded that this would be dealt with in a somewhat different manner, although it was not noticeable that they achieved any success and I am still unsure how any programme if it ever existed, was delivered.

One fundamental problem of moving onto online learning was that the management team had almost no idea what had been going on in the classrooms. A classic example of this was that they kept telling students new to the secondary school, which included those coming up from our primary programme, that a laptop or tablet was recommended. Firstly, a tablet was not appropriate and had not been for several years, with the possible exception of those with external keyboards. Secondly, a laptop was essential, a recommendation was simply not enough, although it is accepted that a tiny minority of parents were unable to make this provision because of financial constraints.

The reason the decision-makers did not know what was going on in the classrooms was that they never went into the classrooms. In my four years at the school, I had only three lessons observed by members of the management team. Two were a part of the normal appraisal process and in the second of these the individual concerned told me he had no experience of lesson observation at all. The third followed a request from myself because I felt a small group of students needed additional learning support. That this state of affairs existed was incredible, particularly as I advertised from day one at BMIS that I ran an open-door policy in my lessons, meaning that anyone was welcome to come in at any time.

To be perfectly honest, I had a better idea about what was going on in Languages, Design, Maths, Science, P.E. and English than the management because I visited teachers in their classrooms. Although it has to be confessed that I steered clear of the Arts lessons, not only because of my background as a student in the subject but also because they are generally so messy.

It came as quite a shock therefore that when we commenced online teaching, suddenly the management became obsessed with what was going on in lessons. They set up monitoring programmes from the start, requiring advance details of what was to be taught in each lesson, followed by an even more detailed description of what happened in those lessons. The question left hanging there, high up over their heads and some might have thought a little like a guillotine blade, was that if this information was needed now, why had they made no attempt in my time at the school to elicit such information before?

The answer was simple. The classroom is not a place where parents hang out, but the home is. Lessons delivered into the home were visible to the parents and the one nightmare of the decision-makers had come true; there would be more visibility to the parents of the interactions between the teachers and the students.

I have often encouraged parents to come to my lessons. It is best if they can steer clear of the ones their own children are in, largely because it is so embarrassing for the kid, however, there are always parallel or similar lessons they can observe or even take part in. Usually, they love it. Just occasionally they find they are outsmarted by every kid in the class and embarrassment takes over.

During these scribblings, I have mentioned on several occasions that the management of BMIS was very keen to control teacher-parent contact. The moment we became a distance learning institution all the rules were reiterated. At one point it seemed that even emails between teachers and students were to be vetted by senior staff, although I am sure the sheer impracticality of this meant that it was a stillborn concept.

There may have been a feeling of control at the top, although one has to suspect that even they realised that everything was in free fall, but for the teachers on the chalk front the pressures built up daily, as administrative duties became onerous. Contrast this with the process in Dhaka, which I described as organic, cooperative and teacher-led. Here was centralised, top-down management at its worst.

My workload, notwithstanding my luck, was running at 60-70 hours per week. When the Easter break came, we worked for half of the holiday and slept for the other half. It was during that vacation that some disturbing news began to filter out.

On 6th April 2020, the local paper Nyasa Times featured a story that 60 people were being traced following a Covid-19 outbreak and that they were also tracing students at BMIS because the grandson of one of the carriers attended[19]. In many communities in Malawi, extended families are the norm and it could be expected that the grandchildren and grandparents may live in the same home. There was an announcement from the school, but it had been deliberately low key.

Although the first three cases of Covid-19 in Malawi were only announced on the 2nd April (three people who had travelled back from India) there was another on the 4th, returning from the UK and on the 7th the first death, a lady who had come back to the country from the UK weeks earlier.

The government announced a lockdown a few days later, although it was clear they were no longer in charge of the country. Small-scale traders staged protests across the land, their banners stating that it would be better to contract Covid-19 than to die of hunger. Just before the Easter holiday came to an end, the Malawian courts overthrew the government's lockdown rules which had been due to come into effect on 18th April. It left Malawi in confusing turmoil. Whilst all the schools remained closed, all the other intended restrictions became only advisory and therefore life went on pretty much as usual in the African communities. It was a whole different

---

[19] Wanga Gwede. '**Malawi Puts 60 People Under Surveillance…**'. Nyasa Times. 6/4/2020

ball game amongst the southern Asian, white Malawians and the expats from China, Europe and the Americas.

As many as one in eight of our students' families left the country and around half of the teachers, both groups taking their offspring with them. They left in dribs and drabs to start with, but this soon became a flood. International flights were cancelled from the start of April, although a few charters were arranged to repatriate the escapees. Many people who left, particularly the teachers, ended up not only paying twice for flights but also ended up paying extortionate prices.

By the start of the new term on Monday 20th April, we were not only teaching online but also teaching across different time zones. My most extreme cases were students in Japan, seven hours ahead of Malawi and Houston, USA, seven hours behind us. Although pupils attempted to join the lessons as timetabled this was impossible for many and communication with them extended from the early morning to late at night. Our teaching colleagues were spread a little less extremely, from Sydney eight hours ahead, to the UK just one hour behind. Several students and teachers took their lessons on the continents of Europe, Asia, North America and Australia, although most Africans stayed put.

I guess this is the new definition of an international school.

Our own decision was to stay put. We thought very seriously about the potential difficulties of doing so and gambled on staying healthy. We implemented strict self-isolation, made two of our security staff stay at home on paid leave and banned our cleaner from the house, which left only the gardener working, although both of them continued to live in the staff housing on the property.

Our choices, if you could call them that, were to fly to the USA, where I do not have permission to reside, to the UK, where my wife does not have permission to reside or to go to our home in Mexico, where neither of us (at that point) had permission to reside. In addition, it was becoming clear that the governments of the UK and USA were making a complete mess of controlling the pandemic. There really was no choice.

Following the Easter break, to say the work was hard is a massive understatement. Many of our friends were in self-isolation around the world and many of them had little work to do. Even teachers we knew from elsewhere seemed to be having a comparatively easy time. However, I have not worked that hard and for that many hours over a sustained period since my early thirties. Week after week of high-intensity lessons, geared up by the extremes; the keenest students continually wanting more and the least engaged having to be cajoled into any form of action. When you throw into the mix the additional administrative demands, which escalated logarithmically, you are talking about cardiac territory for someone of my age and background.

To begin with, I had tried to deliver some of my lessons from the BMIS campus, but a school is soul-destroying without kids. On one such day, I came out of my room to stretch out and the headteacher walked past. There were perhaps five people in the whole school. He did not even pass the time of day. No "Hello", no "How's it going?"

Not a word. This incident made me determined not to go onto campus again unless compelled. It was not quite the final wheel coming off, although it was mighty close.

In any teaching job, the work surrounding and connected to a lesson will consume more time than the lesson itself. In our case, with lessons of fifty minutes, it could be estimated that at least two hours should be allowed for that lesson to function. Whilst I have omitted the longer-term planning aspects, the practical issue of teaching each fifty-minute lesson involved:

- Logging details of the lesson the Friday beforehand.

- Setting up the lesson's instructions, files and folders on a digital message, before the lesson.

- Taking a live register, which I did with Google Hangouts, occupying the first 5 minutes of the lesson.

- Engaging in a Google Meet or Google Hangout throughout the lesson with either the whole group, sub-groups, or individuals.

- Fielding queries, both subject-based and tech-based.

- Adapt or add resources throughout the lesson.

- Bring the group together at the end, generally for a round-up on Google Hangouts.

- Enter details of actual lesson content into a centralised log.

- Amend planning for the next lesson or lessons.

Although this does not sound particularly stressful there are several points to consider. In the classroom multi-tasking is second nature to most teachers. The quaint idea that a teacher stands at the front of a class and delivers a knowledge-driven lecture had begun to be unfashionable when I was at school myself. However, the idea persists, particularly in developing countries, occasionally from individual reactionary teachers, but solidly in the minds of many parents.

If a teacher needs preparation time, that is understood, although the absolute quantity of time is rarely appreciated. When a teacher needs time for marking, this is accepted, although the sheer drudgery of it passes the layman by. What has not been taken on board is the impact of the technological revolution on my subject, Humanities.

In almost any other school subject, including for example my recent specialisation of Economics, parameters govern what will be dealt with on the course. There is a limit to the nature of the content. The same applies in Maths, Science, English, Languages, P.E. and only in Design and the Arts is there potentially unlimited scope. An English or Languages teacher questioned by a student about the relationship between the Hadron Collider and the national capital expenditure of the USA would invariably pass this on to a Science teacher or tell the student to find out themselves. A science teacher may explain that the Hadron Collider's greatest accomplishment has been the discovery of the weak bosons W and Z and the Higgs Boson, although would probably leave it at that. The student would not bother asking the Maths, Design, Arts or P.E. teachers, because their focus is so clear to all.

And that leaves the Humanities teacher, who firstly should ensure the student has the skills to find out and it is not simply a question of Googling it, as the information needs interpretation, but also be able to confirm whether the student has found the right answer.

If you do not believe this is how it works, I can cite the example of a question I was asked the other day by a Maths teacher, which was, "Why do some Commonwealth countries have Governor Generals and others do not?" Without wishing to belittle the teacher at all, as she is a friend, I would point out two things. Firstly, it is easy to find the answer. Secondly, by throwing the question over to me, she has probably ensured that the next time that student has a similar question he will not ask a Maths teacher.

As a fourteen-year-old, I asked my Physics teacher about the possibility of a gravitational escape velocity that exceeded the speed of light. This was not something that was dealt with on the Science curriculum of my school in 1972, I just read a huge amount of science fiction and was trying to establish the theory of black holes. The teacher's answer, that such a thing was not possible, demonstrated not only his lack of imagination but also his lack of subject knowledge for a black hole had been identified just the year before, had been named as a concept in 1967, had been defined in the year of my birth, 1958 and was predicted by Einstein's general theory of relativity in 1916. Perhaps the Physics teacher was trying to stop me from coming back with more questions, although I suspect he simply did not know.

The enormous breadth of our subject means that reading around topics that appear in the curriculum is essential; to be an effective Humanities teacher you need to know an enormous amount, although you must also be able to guide students in finding out what you do not know and must then learn. It is wonderful when kids come to you with things you do not know about (one simple example of my own is that of Zheng He, mentioned earlier in this book) and you then feel obliged to not only put yourself onto the same page as the student but also to have read several pages on from where their new skills and knowledge have placed them.

The result of this is that post-lesson work, whilst sometimes extremely interesting, may also be enormously time-consuming. It can also backfire as there are occasions when students come to you with incorrect information and little idea as to how they have come across it; this can use up even more time.

In online lessons, at times I had as many as eight separate Google Hangout chats going at the same time. That is not eight separate kids, that is eight separate conversations, each could have several students on it. It is multi-tasking of a type, although it precludes the multi-tasking required to answer all student queries, this then has to be undertaken outside lesson time.

There is an argument for a balance between synchronous and asynchronous teaching and learning. These are long words that some teachers like and no one else does. In layman's terms, synchronous teaching is where the teacher is present and in online learning, this will necessitate the use of video calls, live chat, or instant messaging.

The kids can ask questions at any time. In asynchronous teaching, materials are made available online and students go through them in their own time; if they have questions they might have to wait for an answer.

What these dramatically overused terms seem to do is to separate lessons into two types. The intent from the BMIS management team was that some lessons could have a teacher in digital attendance (synchronous) and others (asynchronous) would not require this. This is one way of looking at the issue, however, it treats the individuals in the class as an amorphous blob, failing to differentiate between the different needs and speeds of the students.

In a differentiated classroom, which allows for the different abilities, skills and prior learning of each student, asynchronous and synchronous teaching and learning will be going on at the same time and the teacher should be present for all lessons because some students will invariably be in a synchronous phase. Some will require 90% of their time on synchronous learning, others may cope almost entirely by themselves all of the time. It is a matter of knowing your students.

I was hearing horror stories of teachers failing to receive submissions of work. These came my way as a tutor to my Year 9s. I found it hard to believe that of my wonderful group there were complaints about many of them. What were teachers doing? I do understand that it can be more difficult to extract work from students who are working at a distance, although with persistence the problem should be overcome. In the formal work submissions for Years 7 & 9 during the period we were online, I could count the problems and late submissions in my teaching groups on one hand. These comprised some eighty students and even those few problems were resolved promptly.

However, the pace of my Year 7 classes dropped by half. They had so many technical issues and there were so many needy kids it was not possible to move faster. For the handful that could, I was able to accommodate them with interesting additional projects. Whilst we managed to meet the required deadlines, it was tight and one or two individuals were beginning to fall out of the loop. In the final three weeks, I teamed them up with my Year 9s to surprisingly good effect in some cases and zero in others.

The Year 7 work was based upon the rise and decline of settlements. There was a lot about ghost towns, the use of Google Earth and a project focussed on the development of settlement along the Hudson River from the times of New Amsterdam to modern-day New York. In the past it has gone down a storm, during May 2020, it felt just like any other course, trying to get those kids to conceptualise change over a period of time proved difficult when they were not in the room.

On the other hand, my three Year 9 classes were motoring. They had to complete a project based upon religion and present their final product to their parents, who also marked it. This was not an adaptation for distance learning, it had been programmed in for the last three years and was mentioned in chapter seven. The course gave the students a great deal of freedom, they wrote their own parameters to the work, chose their own method of presenting (several picked board games), chose a religion and a major thematic strand within it.

Something that I thought would be an issue was the peer assessment that was supposed to take place. However, my Year 9s were so good they took this in their stride and managed to successfully feedback on each other's presentations entirely online. The biggest problem was persuading the parents to mark the work. In previous years this had been a novelty for the parents, however, in 2020 they were already fed up with having their kids at home and schoolwork scattered across the kitchen table. Asking them to mark their kid's projects probably seemed to them like a teacher's work avoidance. This was a shame as it had gone down so well in previous years.

Again, we hit our deadline, this time with plenty of lessons to spare. I needed a further project to engage the Year 9s, one that would fill five weeks. The skeleton of an idea had already come to me and while I had been in Moshi, we had twice put together books based on ghost stories as an end of year activity. However, as that had been in English lessons and this was Humanities, the idea began to coalesce into creating a reference book and I stole the topic from the final aborted Year 7 programme: Rivers.

In what must be the most impressive burst of activity I have ever seen from students, they managed to produce a near-finished book by the end of the year. Each chapter is based on a different world river and each having between four and six themed double-page spreads. It was magnificent.

The skills those kids acquired in that short period as regards employment responsibilities, workplace structure, writing copy, selecting photographs, determining provenance, citation, page design, proofing, editing, book structure, deadlines, let alone learning about some of the Earth's major waterways, were immense. It is without any doubt the best piece of work I have ever structured at the back end of the year.

The only downside to Rushing Rivers (a name chosen by two of the students who were taking the piss out of the time constraints) was that it was an unfinished masterpiece. The intention had been to bring it to a draft state, issue it to the students as a single PDF document and have a second team, drawn from the original kids, to work on it the following year and to bring it to print. This last intent will be down to my successors in the job and should be run as an after-school service activity. It will be sad if it does not come to fruition, although there is not a great deal I can do about this; it has to be left to the service supervisor and the curriculum coordinator to push it forwards. I am not optimistic.

In three exhausting months the BMIS teachers, on the whole, did a magnificent job and the BMIS management took the credit. The teachers were simply too tired to argue.

When the school broke for the summer holiday on 18th June 2020 there were still fewer than 600 cases of Covid-19 identified in Malawi and only eight deaths.

Thirteen: Crossroads

(Selling Your Soul)

Originally, this chapter was entitled "Don't Look Back in Anger", until I realised that the actual film title was "Look Back in Anger" and I had been thinking of the Oasis song. The song title more accurately sums up the instructions I gave myself after concluding the first twelve chapters. I have been asked the purpose of this book and have to say there is no underlying objective other than to tell the truth about a wonderful career. If there is anger, and I know better than most that there is, it should be applied constructively. However, there was a crossroads and there the devil danced a jig around a bonfire of deception.

Bishop Mackenzie International School (BMIS), Lilongwe, Malawi: June to September 2020

In the last chapter I wrote, "When the last student left, I sat in my classroom alone and wept. It was as if the world had ended." On Friday 19th June I returned to that classroom for the first time in three months. Physically nothing had changed; the litter still lay where it had fallen in March, although a thick layer of dust now covered everything. The room now lacked any soul whatsoever.

Wading through the end of year routines for the last time, I was in full control of my emotions. On this occasion, much of the display material was consigned to the bin, although some of the better pieces were spared, or so I hoped. A series of drawers and cupboards behind my desk became the repository for those items that even mostly digital classrooms still have a use for: glue, scissors, paper, card, felt pens, coloured pencils and so on. Some of my students had told me that mine was one of the better-equipped rooms in the school; it certainly had not been on my arrival four years previously.

The Chinese football shirt and the Bangladeshi, Indian and Pakistani Cricket shirts, which had adorned the walls, went to the cleaner; he would wash them and either circulate them in his family or sell them. At least they would find practical use. I had used the shirts to advertise an international cohesion, I doubt their future would be as esoteric.

The whole process took no more than a couple of hours. Finally, surveying the room, it was clear of everything but chairs and desks and those staples left in the wall where items that were being trashed had been ripped off. All the resources were practically filed and awaited my colleagues' return at the start of the new school year.

All the world is a stage, however, room S8 had been my stage for four years. The data projector suspended from the ceiling took the place of the limes, the whiteboard and posters had been the scenery, the teacher's desks, chair, globe and laptop the props. However, the stage was occupied by an unemployed actor and the students' desks were empty, no one was coming to the finale. The one-off quips no longer shooting like the bullets of an AK47 over the heads of the audience. The short speeches about appropriate behaviour now redundant, the laughs forgotten and those oh so serious questions, now unanswered. The stand-up comedian, now ignored, felt more like the corpse he had played back in 1975.

It had only occasionally been a stand-up, a monologue or a solo performance, because this theatre, truly a theatre of dreams, had been one of interactive performances, when the audience had become participants in the show and the professional actor had to modify his lines and performance for each group. There was no star, but would the cracked actor be remembered…and for what?

In the International School of London Qatar, there is a stapler; it has my name on it. This information came to me because an ex-colleague from Dhaka, who had moved to Qatar, found it and messaged me. At least seven years have gone by since I had used a permanent marker to ensure the stapler would not stray. It is a kind of fame. There are time capsules buried in Suzhou and Guangzhou; one day some class will open them and the teacher will ask if they think those who buried them are still alive. It is not immortality and the contents might come back to haunt me, but it is a kind of fame. Then there are those students who remember you all their lives and even tell their kids about you. I wonder if that gives the odd polish to the philosophers' stone?

However, I suspect that no teacher wants to live forever, because we would be followed everywhere by the actual immortality of bureaucracy and management failure.

There is an archaic ritual at BMIS, called the end of year sign out form. It serves a double purpose, one for those who are leaving both the school and Malawi and the other for those teachers who would be returning for the next school year. As I fell into neither category, parts of the form were inapplicable, to say the least. Various sections have to be signed off and I had already dealt with the librarian, having not only returned all my borrowed books but also donated around sixty of my own for them to add to the school collection. Other required signatures were from the finance officer, the curriculum coordinator, the ICT department and the Head of Secondary, who had to sign to say your room was clear and to later sign again to say all other signatures had been collected.

My room was clear and I called for affirmation. The head turned up looking awkward and quickly agreed my job on the room was done. However, he was not finished and started on an explanation of how things had not gone to plan in the last year, for reasons he was not permitted to tell me. It sounded like an excuse. We were never going to part as buddies and to my mind, too many words had been said, fingers pointed and threats made to make our parting anything other than a relief for me and possibly for him.

However, I certainly do not wish any of my ex-colleagues harm, be they teachers or managers. In fact, I would like to make their lives and those of next year's students as easy as possible. The one thing I knew I had to do was to have my curriculum written up perfectly for the teachers delivering it the following year; not to the school's standards, but to my own, which are far higher. We agreed when I would have this done by and said goodbye.

To complete the work to my satisfaction took ten days of hard work. Not the seventy hours a week that I had been working, although definitely a solid eight hours a day. I handed over my curriculum in as perfect a state as was possible and there were heartfelt thanks from the curriculum coordinator. In some regards, this felt more like the end of my career than did the last day of online teaching or the last day with the kids, months previously. The task was completed before the end of June and it was about the same time we started to receive some strange information.

I should point out at this time that my contract ran up to the end of July and BMIS had agreed to keep our email addresses and logins open until the odd date of 31st October. However, any of the information below, from the 1st July onwards, has been confirmed by sources external to BMIS; there is no breach of confidentiality.

Firstly, we received an email saying that seven members of the administrative department no longer worked at the school. Then came two anonymous emails, the information from which was also published in the local press. From "Concerned People" and "Whistle Blowers" they made a series of damning accusations regarding the management of the school, indicating long and short-term fraud, excessive payments to management, mistreatment of local staff, dodgy recruitment procedures, discrimination against Malawian teachers and outright theft. They also asked for a forensic audit. They very specifically targeted a few individuals, including the departing CEO.

By this stage, it was the new CEO who was having to deal with the fallout. He mentioned to me that he was enjoying BMIS much more than his last school; one can only wonder what was going on there. Certainly, the atmosphere at BMIS was febrile.

A few days later came the official response from the school board of trustees. It said the anonymous emails put the board in a difficult position and then went on to say they would take the allegations seriously, that there was an internal investigation of alleged fraud totalling around US$100,000, several staff members were disciplined or sacked and a full forensic audit was ongoing. In a later email, they claimed that BMIS was, *"...committed to instilling a culture of high moral standards and practising the values that we want our students to have."*

The investigation appears to be ongoing unless something has been discovered that they feel cannot be announced. To my mind instilling a culture of high moral standards should be an ongoing process as well.

While the shit was really hitting the fan and then being sprayed onto the public through newspaper articles, I was trying to resolve my end of year sign off. Having completed my curriculum work the coordinator signed me off immediately and thanked me for the time I had put in. This is how it should be.

It was impossible to get finance to sign me off, even though I had fulfilled the requirements. It appeared everyone who might have signed the form no longer worked at the school. I also struggled to get the ICT department to sign, even though I handed over my staff laptop and Wi-Fi dongle personally. With these two signatures missing the head of secondary would not authorise completion of the process.

This silly form keeps cropping up and it seems awfully petty. However, the threat was that if it remained unsigned you would not receive your outstanding gratuity, which to me was a sum after tax of over US$12,000, covering the two years of my last contract. To be honest, I was concerned about the financial state of the school and its ability to pay, as much as I was about the complete breakdown in their systems.

Eventually, without ever receiving the necessary signatures, I was told on 13th August that payment had been made, although it was a week before this happened and then it was for the wrong amount. One of the main reasons I had to change the dates in this section's header was to allow for the fact that BMIS did not pay in full until 18th September. It was unclear as to whether this was due to gross inefficiency or their having difficulty finding the funds. There was no apology forthcoming when I finally did receive all that was due. I also received information that one member of the teaching staff, who like me had left, had not received her gratuity at all. At the time of writing, I am uncertain as to whether this situation had been resolved.

From March to August, it was clear that many international schools around the world were failing to make payments due to teachers. Obviously, with many being private enterprises they were hamstrung by serious cashflow shortages, although the same situation impacted the trust schools. At BMIS, we had been asked if we would find a reduction in salary acceptable, which is a tough question to answer when your working hours have increased by fifty per cent and you are operating under the most incredible stress.

It was becoming clear that the new school year would commence online and that many staff would not be in the country by that date. To their credit, BMIS appeared to meet all its financial commitments, with the possible exception of that mentioned above but had to shuffle some teachers into unexpected redundancy. They eventually opened the school campus for some students around mid-September and phased in the rest before the end of that month.

There was room for optimism as the new school CEO seemed to be on the ball, although he was only to last twelve months before he quit. The financial scandals need to be resolved and management systems put in place to prevent an occurrence. At least the kids were back at school. However, the implications of Covid-19 will mean that the school will continue to operate with the constant fear of infection and potential partial or whole school closures, just as all schools around the world will.

Bishop Mackenzie International School (BMIS), Lilongwe, Malawi: November 2018

Let us examine the statement made by BMIS, *"...committed to instilling a culture of high moral standards and practising the values that we want our students to have."* Has this been true?

La Carretera de la Muerte winds through these pages from the commencement of the tale until its close. For the devil dances along that road. There are plenty of uneven surfaces, too many roadblocks and numerous forks along the route. However, there is only one crossroads along the way, the place in myth where the few sell their soul to the devil whilst others pass unmasked, unhindered and unscarred.

An event that has so far gone unremarked in these pages was a decision made in the back end of 2018. It was one of those bizarre happenings that could only have occurred at BMIS and involved our Year 11 Humanities groups and their choices for their final subjects for the IB diploma. To this date the subjects on offer had been Economics, Geography and History; this order reflects their historic popularity.

There were two of us teaching Year 11 at that time; a Geography teacher and I teaching Economics. Without our knowledge, the students were taken off by two members of the management team and given the chance for an early choice of subjects. Those choices were Global Politics and Business & Management; there was no mention of the three subjects currently being taught. Not only were we not given this information in advance, but we were also kept in the dark after the event and only found out when some of the students let the cat out of the bag a couple of weeks later.

We learned that our main subjects were being dropped from the syllabus from the students. The perfidious behaviour of our management was to my mind the worst example I have seen of its kind. What is worse is that there were several students who were desperate to take Economics and were not permitted to do so. Does the question have to be asked as to why this happened?

There was no satisfactory explanation from the management team. The only point they made is that some parents had requested a Business course. It did appear as if it was a top-down decision that had been made from somewhere very near the top, which would have meant someone with a Maths background, certainly not someone specialising in our subjects. The only conclusion that I could reach, although it is hardly satisfactory, was that there was a desire to impress the accreditation teams who were due the following year, the subject of Global Politics being the new kid on the block.

Whilst that may go some way to explaining why the choices of subject had been changed, there was no explanation as to why the subject teachers had not been consulted, informed in advance nor advised as to what had occurred in the aftermath. The only conclusion that can be reached as regards these matters is that there was a genuine fear that the arguments against the changes were extremely strong and that those arguments could well be supported by many students. In the aftermath, History, the least popular of the previous choices, was added back in. Supposedly it was due to student demand, but in actuality it was the fact it was taught by one of the management team.

It is impossible to conceive of competent management following these courses of action. The whole process was a sell-out, both teachers and students being traded down the river. When management is prepared to subvert normal practices to this extent it is clear who has taken possession of their souls and it is equally clear who will be scratching the epitaphs on their tombstones.

All Around the World: 2020 and Onwards

There is a bigger issue regarding education as a whole, that being the fact that a significant proportion of students have thrived working from home and probably the same number failed abysmally in the same scenario. It would be hard to put numbers on this, however, my estimate would put these two groups in the top and bottom quintiles. Performances for the students in the three more centred quintiles all appeared to fall off to a smaller or greater degree.

There is something reminiscent about this breakdown of student performance to that in my first two schools in the UK, where we were educating deselected kids. By physically separating the students in lockdown, the strengths of the ablest became more apparent, just as happened in the UK Grammar schools. However, the effect on the weaker students, and those who were reliant on their peers to pull them through, was catastrophic. It will take time to identify just how harmful these events surrounding Covid-19 will be seen in hindsight.

Interestingly, the students born in the period of the financial crisis of 2008 appear to be significantly weaker than those born beforehand. These observations are personal rather than scientific; it would be interesting to see worldwide research undertaken to prove it one way or the other.

What is clear is that the west needs a shake-up of its educational systems. There needs to be a greater engagement of the weaker or most disadvantaged students and there needs to be greater flexibility for the more able students. These two processes, if done independently of each other, will widen the gulf existing between the groups and what is needed is greater engagement. It is also imperative that access to education be available to all equally and to be accessible online when required or preferred.

I am not an education specialist. This sounds somewhat strange coming from a teacher, but that is the limit of what I am, a self-admitted old school teacher who believes there are three important aspects to the job: the teaching and learning of a subject in the classroom, writing curriculum to enable that process and pastoral care for the students.

Hang the Teacher Out to Dry is perhaps a process that has continued for my lifetime and will possibly continue through my retirement and eventual demise. Already we regard ourselves as facilitators rather than teachers, although the old name remains, and we cope with systems of education that cannot be as progressive as required due to the inherent conservatism within our societies.

A crisis was needed to push back on that conservative ideology and Covid-19 is that crisis. Governments seem particularly unaware that students will not follow their orthodoxy. An article from the Guardian[20] demonstrates the inherent innocence of the British government and its desire to control access to information.

"Schools should not under any circumstances use resources produced by organisations that take extreme political stances on matters"... such as "a publicly stated desire to abolish or overthrow democracy, capitalism, or to end free and fair elections"; opposition to freedom of speech; the use of racist, including antisemitic, language; the endorsement of illegal activity; and a failure to condemn illegal activities done in support of their cause."

I am sure that most of us would support most if not all of the elements listed above, but that is not the point. Students will always access information and will be more inclined to do so if it is seen as off-limits. When I taught in Bangladesh, we accessed websites that were trading in illegal arms, organs and slaves; they were truly fascinating and were a real eye-opener for the students. Not one of those students would have come out of the course advocating slavery or a free for all in either the arms or organs industry.

From a personal point of view, I object to being told that the overthrow of capitalism is an extreme political stance. It is a failed system and desperately needs a major overhaul or complete

---

[20] Mattha Busby. '**Schools in England told not to use...**'. The Guardian. 27/9/2020

replacement. It is right that students should know that certain people hold these views. It is far better that students are exposed to different points of view in a controlled system where they can be discussed, than for them to be lured into extremism in the quiet of their own bedroom by anti-vaxers, religious fundamentalists or far right (or left) hate groups. It is as if the teachers are not trusted.

I have taught courses on religion over many of the last twenty years. In the last few years, the students have been free to select their topics for more detailed study. I am an atheist and fundamentally believe that everyone else should be. Have I, as a teacher, ever spent my time trying to convert students or try to coerce them to abandon their beliefs? Of course not. For I am a teacher. Please do not tell me that certain points of view should be banned from lessons. Please do not tell me that I must condemn the storming of the Bastille, as I will be failing *"to condemn illegal activities done in support of their cause."*

Trying to prevent access to materials is nearly always a failure. Allowing elitist groups to prevent the much needed and widespread changes needed in education will simply take the present system closer to its already approaching breaking point. The passage in italics simply highlights the reactionary attitudes that are ensuring a large proportion of our students will be failed by the education systems that are being propped up.

Something new is needed, although I am not the one who can come up with the plan. I am sure it should involve a significant amount of peer-teaching, with the brighter, more able and more willing supporting those who have fewer of those attributes. I am also certain there will be a role for teacher-facilitators but know now that I will not be one. There will certainly be much more cross-curricular learning, but it is equally important that the basic skills taught only in specialist subject areas should not be forgotten.

One focus of this book has been the need for better management in some schools. If we are to have schools at all in the future, this is incredibly important. Identifying management systems and managers' attributes that work, not only in select schools but across the board, is essential. It must become easier to eject poor managers and teachers from schools quickly before they cause lasting damage.

Mark Whitworth: 2020 and Onwards

After finishing my curriculum work for BMIS, I fired off a series of emails to around ten international schools in Africa, indicating my willingness and availability to teach Economics to their students online if their teachers could not. There were a few positive holding letters, even though the start of term was still a long way off in many cases. However, there was a dawning realisation that I did not want this work, in fact, the idea failed to excite me at all. It would have meant some useful pocket money for teaching something I could practically do in my sleep. Not interested.

My conclusion was that however hard I had worked in my career, this had done little to improve school management, made only incremental acts to improve individual schools, had vastly improved curriculum for some students and had made a positive change to the lives of many of my kids. How can these positives be achieved when working at a thousand kilometres distance, in three hours a week, on a fixed curriculum examination course? They cannot.

My career as a teacher was over. I found I did not miss it as I thought I would. John Maynard Keynes said, *"Worldly wisdom teaches that it is better for reputation to fail conventionally than to succeed unconventionally."* It is a delight that I managed to succeed unconventionally and quit before being forced to fail conventionally. It may be the end of my teaching career, but it is certainly the opportunity to succeed or fail in a new career; mine will not be a quiet retirement.

I had never thought of my father as a teacher. Sure, he was involved in education and retired as head of the Science and Technology faculty at Birmingham Polytechnic, although I never imagined him in a classroom. Shortly after my mother died, I had taken my dad for a walk up to Moseley Golf Club in Birmingham, where he was still a member; I believe it was the last time he visited the place, for he was certainly not physically capable of swinging a golf club anymore.

A few older guys walked into the clubhouse and he was greeted with, "Hi Reg, we thought you were dead!" Banter followed and the odd beer. It was when I was standing at the urinal that one of the group approached me. His words still run around my head. "You know, your dad was the best teacher I ever had. The best."

My relationship with my father had never been the easiest. Our outlook on life was and still is, completely at odds. However, I realised that I wanted dad to know that I had students who would have said the same thing about me. I guess it is an appeal for respect or approval.

I had considered including a series of anonymous statements from the students in my final year of teaching to bring this account to a close. However, seeing as they are all still of school age and mostly still attending Bishop Mackenzie International School, it would perhaps not be ethical to elicit their comments or use earlier remarks without the permission of the students, their parents and the school.

Instead, I will conclude with one personal email from an ex-student, an extract from an ex-student's speech at the online Graduation Ceremony, an email from a parent of one of this year's Year 9 students and an email from a colleague. All four have given their explicit permission to include their words and their inclusion here is no indication of their agreement with any of my views.

Nuo Chen joined BMIS at the same time as Andrea and me; at the time she had little English. She graduated from the school as an eighteen-year-old, with a good bilingual diploma, awarded by the IBO, and left Malawi in June 2020. She sent me these thoughts:

Dear Mr. Mark,

I cried so hard when I read your letter, I didn't even cry on graduation day, but your email really touched me! You were the first teacher I met on my first day at BMIS, and I was just scared because it was my first time in the pure English environment. I was afraid I wouldn't understand what you were saying and I was afraid to speak. But both you and Mrs Kidd have been helping and encouraging me throughout the years. Although when I first met you I thought you were a bit mean looking! Ha ha!

You are a wonderful teacher and it was truly an honor to meet you and Mrs Kidd. I'll keep your personal email address and maybe someday in the future you'll get an email from Nuo to ask you to help her with some problems. Please don't say no! I really, really appreciate you and miss you and love you so much. In my heart you and Mrs Kidd are more than just my teachers, although I don't get to talk to you and Mrs Kidd very often at school! (because I'm shy and I am not good at saying some sweet things) but I really like you and Mrs Kidd, and I hope I'll see you and Mrs Kidd in the future. I'll send you which university I will go to by my personal email address, so maybe we'll meet again one day! (so don't forget about me!) Be sure to email me if you and Mrs Kidd are traveling to China in the future!

I hope you and Mrs Kidd are both healthy. Good health is the most important thing! I really love you! Please tell Mrs Kidd I love her sooooo much as well!

Thank you!

Nuo

Doctor Miriam van Goor is mentioned in this book in the chapter entitled "Stayin' Alive". She is the mother of one of the students I taught during my final year.

Dear Mark,

Hope you and your wife are well.

We all knew THE day was going to come. The day which will be your last day of teaching INS at BMIS.

Although we only got to know you in August last year, we have been so impressed by the fantastic INS lessons my daughter received.

She loves the subject and your enthusiasm makes her enthusiasm even more. She has learned a lot regarding citations and referencing, writing and presenting skills.

Thank you very much. We will miss you.

Hope you are going to enjoy some peace and rest (and more time to exercise:).

Stay safe and healthy.

Kind regards,

Miriam.

Ewen Nettleton has been a close colleague for several years. No one can remember when he joined BMIS, he just seemed to slide in through the back gate. He has the massive disadvantage in this life of being Australian and for that reason believes he has a sense of humour.

Hey Mate,

As you sit in your computer chair, in this strange reality that we find ourselves and most likely filled with some nostalgia, I would like to say a massive thank you. You have been a great mate and mentor. You have set a standard that I will try and emulate for the rest of my career. Your process of deep thought into school systems and your critique of them made for many interesting discussions.

There is plenty more to say, but the most important part is THANK YOU.

I have met some Poms in my time but I would have to say, that you are one of the better ones. Perhaps your countrymen will learn to master the games that they created!

Enjoy your final day. I hope it is filled with many warm memories of the relationships that you developed with your students and colleagues.

See you this afternoon for a beer!

Cheers, Ewen Nettleton

Umar Chaudhry joined BMIS as a four-year-old. When I joined the school, he was in my Year 10 and then Year 11 tutor group. Whilst I did not formally teach him in his final two years, I did give some assistance with his Economics. He left the school, as valedictorian, having achieved the highest academic grades in the leaving year group and is now at the University of Nottingham in the UK. This is an extract from his speech as valedictorian.

"Therefore, I take this opportunity to thank all the teachers at BMIS for making us who we are today. I know it sound incredibly cliched to say this, and it has been done year after year after year, but there is no other analogy which better represents a teacher than a candle that gives up its own light to light the way for others. So, on behalf of the class of 2020, we thank all of our teachers for lighting our way and showing us the correct path.

In my fourteen years at this school I have seen the coming and going of numerous staff and teachers and I will always remember some of them for the knowledge and wisdom they have given me and to countless other students. But one name will always stick out. A teacher who went the extra mile to make sure the students felt comfortable and respected. He was also always real with us, not sugar coating our victories and making sure we were never held back by our losses. I came into Year 10 as an arrogant, big-headed kid, who was determined to outwit the next person he saw. But through the guidance of this teacher I learned real raw values of respect and compassion towards others. This person, I am sure you will already have guessed, is Mr. Whitworth. And while he will tell you he did nothing of the sort, it is because of him that I learned there are more important things to life than a set of grades and some books.

His four years in this school have changed me and many, many others, from being arrogant big-headed kids to being less arrogant and less big-headed. No matter how much further down the line we go, I will always remember Mr. Whitworth making me the captain of the volleyball B team, and acting as if it was a promotion from, just how he put it, another regular player on the A team. You know very well sir that I deserved to be in the A team or at least in the teams that won a game!"

In the heat of the moment, I looked up what you were supposed to write in an epilogue and find that much of it is covered in this chapter. Perhaps I am supposed to say what happens next! Who knows which way the wind will blow?

The teacher is dead!
Long live the teacher!

Then Socrates sat down, and "How fine it would be, Agathon," he said, "if wisdom were a sort of thing that could flow out of the one of us who is fuller into him who is emptier, by our mere contact with each other, as water will flow through wool from the fuller cup into the emptier. If such is indeed the case with wisdom, I set a great value on my sitting next to you." – Plato, Symposium

Printed in Great Britain
by Amazon